Planning Matter

Planning Matter

Acting with Things

ROBERT A. BEAUREGARD

The University of Chicago Press   Chicago and London

ROBERT A. BEAUREGARD is professor of urban planning in the Graduate School of Architecture, Planning, and Preservation at Columbia University.

The University of Chicago Press, Chicago 60637
The University of Chicago Press, Ltd., London
© 2015 by The University of Chicago
All rights reserved. Published 2015.
Printed in the United States of America

24 23 22 21 20 19 18 17 16 15   1 2 3 4 5

ISBN-13: 978-0-226-29725-5 (cloth)
ISBN-13: 978-0-226-29739-2 (paper)
ISBN-13: 978-0-226-29742-2 (e-book)
DOI: 10.7208/chicago/9780226297422.001.0001

Library of Congress Cataloging-in-Publication Data

Beauregard, Robert A., author.
    Planning matter : acting with things / Robert A. Beauregard.
        pages ; cm
    Includes bibliographical references and index.
    ISBN 978-0-226-29725-5 (cloth : alk. paper) —
ISBN 978-0-226-29739-2 (pbk. : alk. paper) —
ISBN 978-0-226-29742-2 (ebook)   1. City planning.   2. City
planning—United States.   I. Title.
    HT165.5.B43 2015
    307.1'2160973—dc23
                                                    2015007463

♾ This paper meets the requirements of ANSI/NISO Z39.48-1992
(Permanence of Paper).

Contents

Introduction

Urban planners are concerned with cities and neighborhoods, buildings and parking lots, wind turbines, commuter rail lines, wetlands, and billboards. They work with property maps, desktop computers, consultant reports, and cellular telephones. And yet these elements of planning—these nonhuman things—are mostly absent from the way practice is theorized. Planners have always acknowledged and even privileged the material world; they have not, however, been willing to treat it as more than epiphenomenal. For the most part, the rule of humans is unquestioned.

Early in the twentieth century, with their attention drawn to smoke-belching factories, unsanitary housing, debris-strewn alleys, and traffic-clogged streets, advocates for a nascent profession of city planning launched countless initiatives to reform the industrial city. Within the United States, Chicago emerged as the model for local elites who could no longer tolerate a built environment so undisciplined that it stifled commerce and repelled an emerging middle class (Boyer 1983; Smith 2006). The city's businessmen believed that Chicago's physical fabric had to be totally remade so that people and goods could more easily move about, slums could be removed, and public spaces express the city's cultural and political aspirations. The mandate they gave the architect Daniel Burnham and his firm was to develop a scheme to replace what then existed. The famous 1909 *Plan of Chicago*, a milestone in the City Beautiful Movement of the time, was the result.

Planning then, and for decades afterward, seemed to be

about changing the material world. Yet planners do not themselves demolish slum housing or plant trees along newly designated parkways. They craft plans and technical reports that enable these actions to happen, and by doing so they distance themselves from the world they wish to change and the changes they hope will ensue. Plans first erase what exists in order to propose what has been imagined. Real places and real people are temporarily suspended, set aside, as planners work with technical data and city-making principles to craft an alternative future. As a result, plan makers remove themselves from the materiality of the city. Too messy to engage on its own terms, the physical world has to take a different form before its replacement can be realized.

Despite this ambivalent relationship with the city's materiality, government planners in the 1960s were accused by newly mobilized activists within the profession of being physical determinists: of believing that design could make people's lives better. They were denounced for "assuming that changing people's physical environment [would] somehow take care of the social inequities that warped their lives" (Fainstein 2000, 464). In effect, these government planners were labeled naive materialists who failed to acknowledge the built environment as a consequence and not a cause of human behavior. Critics claimed that the physical city was only a means to an end. To believe otherwise was to strip the city, and planning, of both its people and its politics.

These accusations came mainly from an emerging group of politically left planners swept up in such social movements of the 1960s and 1970s as civil rights, environmentalism, nuclear disarmament, counterculture, antiwar, and women's liberation. At the core of their criticism was the ostensible complicity of government planners in perpetuating racial segregation and oppressing a marginalized and urbanized African American population (Sandercock 1998, 37–42). Aided by these planners, local governments were demolishing low-income neighborhoods, constructing large public housing projects devoid of a sense of community, and using limited-access highways to physically divide people. "Bricks and mortar" were taking precedence over human needs. The city is its people, critics shouted, not its buildings. Planning should be for people, and planners had a moral responsibility to focus on the real ills of American society and directly confront racism and poverty. Naive materialism had to be replaced by a social engagement informed by a Marxist-based, historical materialism.

To resurrect a phrase from those times, government planners were deemed "handmaidens to capitalism." In cities across the United States, left-wing critics impeached municipal planning agencies for displacing the proletariat from putative slums, destroying neighborhoods to build highways for commerce, and approving subdivision schemes that excluded all but white families. These activities mainly served economic interests, and government planners were portrayed as willfully ignorant of the many ways people and cities were harmed so that capitalists could profit. The overriding issue to be addressed was the struggle between capital and labor that enabled capitalists to become rich by exploiting workers. Out of this struggle came class differences, racial segregation, poverty, and enduring unemployment. Planners had to decide which to cast their lot with—capital or labor. In short, planners were insufficiently materialist. Having succumbed to the conceit of physical determinism, they were blind to the real material roots of society's ills—the contradictions of capitalism.

At the same time, government planners were being denounced for hiding their complicity behind an ideological curtain of technocratic and apolitical planning. Believing that the world could be known objectively and that facts, independent of ideology, could guide decision making, they were reproached for posturing as purveyors of technical truths and thus placing themselves outside politics. The ills of the city were presented as objective conditions whose solutions could be found in scientific analysis. To realize the public interest, mainstream planners believed, they had to be apolitical and nonpartisan. To their critics, this argument was wholly bankrupt. Not only naive materialists, these planners were idealists who placed their trust in ideas rather than acknowledging the imperatives of material conditions and the necessity of mobilizing politically to combat the city's problems.

With this book I hope to add a third materialism to this history. Known as the "new" materialism, it avoids the naïveté of physical determinism, retains the critical perspective of Marxist political economy, eschews an idealist position, and goes beyond buildings and streets to encompass nature, technologies, and nonhuman things of all kinds. My goal is to craft an understanding of planning that brings theorists and practitioners closer to the material world they wish to change. As Coole and Frost (2010, 36) so aptly point out, "ideology and power [and planning] operate most effectively when embedded in the material practical horizons and institutions of everyday life."

New materialism encompasses a variety of intellectual projects: speculative realism, posthumanism, object-oriented ontology, critical realism, and actor-network theory. What they have in common is the recognition that humans live in a profoundly material world and that any action they take has to account for their relationships with non-

3

human things. "What characterizes humans," Bruno Latour declares, "is not the emergence of the social, but detours, translations, the enfolding of all courses of action into more and more complicated . . . technological arrangements" (2013, 294). This fundamental idea is the impetus for exploring the nature of human and nonhuman matter, the way humans and nonhumans are entangled, and the implications this has for individual and collective action.

One of the most basic of new materialist assumptions is that the material world is independent of our minds.[1] Materiality is not "a mere pretext for our exercise of mental pleasures" (Jameson 2003, 79). For critical (Sayer 2000) or speculative (Harman 2009) realists, moreover, the world is not exhausted by what we know about it. Instead, our representations of the world are always deficient, not in the sense of being wrong but in falling ever short of completeness. Material reality always exceeds our grasp and exists regardless of what we know about it. Never equivalent to human understanding, the world is beyond any full appreciation and cannot be reduced to its representations. New materialists thus vigorously resist attempts to subordinate the material world to such nonmaterial things as "language, consciousness, subjectivity, agency, mind, soul . . . imagination, emotions, values, meaning" (Coole and Frost 2010, 2). Their objective is to avoid an idealism that, at its extreme, presumes that the material world exists only because the human mind comprehends it.

Just as important is that the new materialists question the "brute thereness" (Coole and Frost 2010, 7) of matter; they reject unequivocal distinctions among humans, other living things, and even nonliving things such as rocks or traffic lights. Nonhuman matter is considered vibrant rather than inert (Bennett 2010), and matter, whether sentient or not, is always deemed active rather than passive. Glaciers move toward the sea, wildebeests migrate and adapt to changing habitats, viruses spread, and insects destroy pine forests. Technologies such as automated investment programs and computerized braking systems act, and are meant to act, independent of human control. That they often escape control, as when nuclear power plants go awry, speaks to their autonomous qualities. Matter has "morphogenetic capacities of its own" (Van der Tuin 2012), and this immanent vitality makes it an active participant in the world. Consequently, to believe that the material world passively awaits human command is simply wrong.

This understanding raises serious philosophical and practical issues

1. For an insightful review of various meanings of materialism, see Lehtonen 2009.

around what we mean by humans and how we distinguish them from nonhumans (Bogost 2012; Sayes 2014). Posthumanists reject the notion that humans have a universal essence and function "as the abstract universal marker of the site of foundational voice, vision and vitality" (Shildrick 1996). Humans are not "the origin of meaning and history" (Badmington 2004, 1345). To bolster this claim, frequent mention is made of how science has thrown this view of humanity into doubt by uncovering the ways animals and genetic material, for example, exhibit characteristics (learning, cooperation) heretofore thought to be confined to humans (Sacks 2014). How dependent humans have become on technologies such as medically implanted pacemakers and cell phones provides additional evidence for the many ways the world is coconstituted by humans and nonhumans. Here we find the cyborg, "a hybrid of machine and organism" (Haraway 1990, 191) that blurs the boundaries between humans and machines as well as between the physical and the nonphysical. "The world [is] made up of hybrid objects, heterogeneous networks, and fluid identities" (Murdoch 2004, 1357) that subvert not just the actual dominance of the human species but its philosophical subjectivity as well.

The new materialist is thus intent on dissolving the divide between culture and nature that Latour (1993) characterizes as one of the defining moments of modernism. He proposes that any separation is wholly illusionary; the world is constituted by hybrid forms in which humans are only one of many actors. Latour thus rejects the Promethean myth that "divine intervention awarded [humans] a privileged position in the cosmos" (Sagasti 2000, 597). When humans act, it is almost always with the nonhuman things of the world, whether tools such as pencils, technologies such as computer software, weather patterns such as tornadoes, or animals such as guard dogs. To the extent that the world is constituted by hybrid forms, the culture/nature divide disappears or exists solely as a human conceit. As a conceit, it is a poor and untrustworthy guide to either explaining the world or acting within it.[2]

The actual workings of the world reveal complex alliances (Braun 2004). Hybrid action removes the barrier between "dull matter and vibrant life" (Bennett 2010, vii). For this reason, new materialists avoid individualism (with its strong commitment to humanism) and any collectivism that is confined to people and their associations. Catego-

---

2. As for human conceit and the deficit of self-reflection, consider this comment by sociologist Barrington Moore Jr. (1973, 14): "Among living things, humans are evidently quite extraordinary for the amount of cruel violence they inflict upon members of their own species."

ries functioning as social facts are also suspect. We cannot explain the world by calling on globalization, neoliberalism, culture, or political will. Rather, if we are going to embrace the notion that humans never act alone but always act in alliances with nonhuman things, we need to focus on the actions that produce and maintain these alliances. New materialists thus shift the emphasis from structure to agency. What matters is how participants keep alliances stable and yet in motion. Most important is that new materialists do not confine political agency to humans. Politics is always a meeting of human intentions and things, never more obvious than when it takes the form of terrorism and war.

To state this more theoretically, for many new materialists (particularly actor-network theorists, as we will see) the constituent form of action is the network or assemblage of heterogeneous actors (Marcus and Saka 2006; McFarlane 2011). Within these forms, humans are given a priori neither dominant performative nor dominant ontological status. Yet, as Bogost (2012, 11) has written, "all things equally exist, yet they do not exist equally." Humans are still acknowledged to have the greater ability to respond rather than simply react to stimuli and to provide direction (even if partial and tentative) to heterogeneous networks (Bogost 2012, 7). Entangled with nonhumans in myriad ways, however, humans are not masters of these assemblages (Braun 2004, 271).

Important to this perspective is that while humans and nonhuman things exist before being assembled, they take on significance only when embedded in networks. Another way to say this is that humans and nonhumans are coconstructivists such that their importance and influence depend on their being placed in relation to each other. For example, although humans become physically weaker—less muscle mass, poorer eyesight, less flexibility—as they age, these human qualities have value only when they are named by others or experienced in certain types of settings and situations. The elderly and women might have a biological fate, but the significance of those biological conditions depends on the social context in which they are perceived (Kruks 2010): "Materiality and sociality are produced together" (Law and Mol 1995, 274).

This way of thinking about the always elusive qualities of humans and nonhumans enables new materialists to avoid both an anthropocentric essentialism that might recommit them to the culture/nature divide (Braun 2004) and an equally unacceptable belief that language creates the world. The world has to be represented and is socially interpreted, yet discourse never exhausts reality, and reality continues to exist even without representation. Consequently, acting is always a matter of both discursive understandings and material engagements.

From a planning theory perspective, the new materialism is an antidote for the antirealist stance that planners embraced in the 1950s and that has, in one form or another, dominated planning theory since the 1980s (Harrison 2014). That stance rejects the "independence of reality for theory or belief about it" (Ruben 1989, 61) such that discursive and analytical formulations rule. The story begins after World War II when planning education—and practice—in the United States turned to the social sciences and away from architecture and civil engineering (Perloff 1957, 8–18). Transportation planning in particular became enamored with statistical modeling techniques to analyze data and develop plans (Black 1990). Abstract representations were used to capture the movement of vehicles, the placement of highways, and the location of parking garages. Through various translations, the world being acted on became less and less concrete. The planning process was imagined as a rational sequence of steps disassociated from the substantive dynamics of the problem being addressed (Banfield 1959). Rational-comprehensive planning was indifferent to whether the plan was for replacing slum housing or siting suburban public schools. The planning process became a universal tool only tenuously connected to the material context in which planners operated.

Process-oriented planning came to define planning theory and dominate how planning was taught. A backlash was inevitable and quick to emerge, but the antirealist perspective survived. In fact, it deepened in the 1980s with the reaction against a Marxist political economy that offered robust critique but little practical guidance. What was needed was a planning theory that could make practice more effective as well as more socially responsible (Innes 1995). The result was a communicative turn that displaced rational analysis with persuasion, communication, and collaboration. Communicative theorists retained the focus on process, however, and critics accused them of paying too little attention to the material world (Fainstein 2000). The specific criticism was—and still is—that a process-oriented planning (or planning theory) is insufficiently attentive to the substantive consequences of planning and, specifically, to issues of social justice. The antirealists were accused of being apolitical and yet suspiciously conservative. The critics wanted to turn the debate back to an earlier materialism, though with fewer Marxist overtones.

Nevertheless, planners are not people who lay hands on the physical world. They are not manual laborers planting sedum on "green" roofs or erecting the prefabricated walls of affordable housing units. They do not make the objects they plan. And yet they use objects such as computers and photographs to plan. Planning is an array of social activities centered on learning about the world, engaging with publics, prescribing actions, and gathering resources. Planners are advisers, mediators, and facilitators, and what they directly produce are reports, models, maps, and meetings, not office building plazas, bikeways, or landfills. Planners shape attention, develop proposals, mediate understandings, persuade, negotiate, and listen. Their activities focus on talk about the material world. At the same time, they do not act alone but act with the tools, technologies, and nonhuman things that ground their deliberations.

Background

My understanding of the new materialism comes mainly from actor-network theory as developed by Bruno Latour, Michel Callon, and John Law, among others, and from science and technology studies.[3] Two articles by Latour—the social theorist, philosopher, and historian of science—have particularly influenced me. The first was his "Why Has Critique Run Out of Steam? From Matters of Fact to Matters of Concern" (Latour 2004a). In it he argued against the antirealist position that all of reality is discursively constructed, a position that supports, for example, deniers of climate change and those who dismiss the health risks of smoking. His response to the antirealists notes how facts become matters of concern when they gather around themselves a variety of human and nonhuman actors such as reports, professional associations, ideas and values, and technologies. So configured, they resist opposing viewpoints. Climate change thus becomes less deniable when the many scientific facts in its favor are adopted by environmental organizations, acknowledged by international bodies, written into coastal-zone plans, experienced through more and more severe storms, and given legal status in carbon trading legislation. Ideas become stronger as they are increasingly entangled in the world. No longer isolated as facts (that is, as ostensibly objective and irrefutable conditions),

---

3. These two literatures overlap to a great extent with Latour and with Michel Callon—who claims to have coined the phrase actor-network theory (Callon 1986), central to both. I also include various authors who address speculative realism and the new materialism. I am not alone in applying actor-network theory and related literatures to planning: see Boelens 2010, Harrison 2014, Rydin 2012, and Rydin 2010.

these matters of concern cannot be easily dismissed. Latour thus offers two ideas for a more materialist planning theory: first, that claims about the world become effective to the extent that they are connected to the material world itself, and second, that facts and values (ostensibly subjective) matter only when they are tied to each other. Matters of concern matter, not facts or values in isolation.

This theoretical perspective encourages us to think of planners not so much as discovering good ideas on their own and then offering them to publics, but rather as crafting good ideas by gathering people, knowledge, and material things. Planning proposals are strengthened—and planning becomes more effective—by being more engaged with a heterogeneous arrangement of actors. Moreover, by dissolving the sharp distinction between facts and values, as Latour does, the inherent normativity of planning is revealed. With facts and values inseparable, planners can leave aside the false dichotomies of objectivity and subjectivity, political and apolitical, and scientific and social. Support for contextual zoning or mixed-income housing, for example, is neither a fact nor a value but a matter of concern. Consequently, these distinctions make sense only insofar as people use them ideologically to position themselves in relation to others. Planning is always and simultaneously value-laden and factual—always political.

The second article was "Where Are the Missing Masses? The Sociology of a Few Mundane Artefacts" (Latour 1992). There Latour used a number of evocative examples to demonstrate the hybrid nature of human action and the relation of this hybridizing to social responsibility. He proposed that nonhuman things, such as door closers and speed bumps, had to be treated as ontologically equivalent to humans. Not only is all matter vibrant, but humans frequently delegate their responsibilities to nonhuman things. These two conditions make the nonhuman material world both theoretically significant and active—not passive—in the face of human intention. The automatic door closer/opener acts for, with, and on humans and, among other consequences, relieves them of the responsibility for politely holding the door for others.[4] It is one of the many technologies and built forms (for example, bollards that keep the sidewalk free of automobiles) with which humans fill the world. To tools such as computer tablets and screwdrivers we can add various representatives of nature such as house cats that keep homes free of mice and the foliage planted to shade buildings.

4. See Latour 1994 on the swapping of properties between humans and nonhumans, particularly as regards delegating human responsibilities to things.

Latour's point is that thinking of the world as populated only by humans leaves most of the world unacknowledged. He thus offers a way out of an intellectual dead end in which, I believe, planners have become trapped. Planning can now be reconnected with the materiality of the world in a way that is theoretically defensible and practically consequential. This is neither a naive materialism nor a historical materialism clinging to the culture/nature divide. Rather, it is a materialism that accepts the inseparability of humans, nature, and technologies.

Actor-network theory coexists quite comfortably with other literatures relevant to planning. In particular, I have drawn on writings that address the formation of publics and the nature of politics as developed by American pragmatists such as John Dewey, arguments regarding social justice as developed by Iris Marion Young, and notions of deliberative democracy that connect what planners do best—shaping attention—with the many publics without which they could not achieve their goals. Less explicitly discussed, but nonetheless a foundation for my thinking, is a critical theory that assumes the existence of a culturally mediated, capitalist political economy whose consequences redound to the benefit of a few, leaving the many struggling, sometimes unsuccessfully, to live well. My perspective is meant to be avowedly (new) materialist, critically realist, morally engaged, politically progressive, and pragmatic.[5]

Although written from a planning theory perspective, this book is not *a* planning theory. My goal is to give meaning to planning, not to explain it. What theory there is, is strategic and designed to rest lightly on the page. I offer a sensibility, not a formal argument. Ideas, as the pragmatists tell us, are "provisional responses to particular unreproducible circumstances" (Menand 2001, xii), and their value lies in their usefulness, not in their theoretical elegance or their compatibility with universal truths.

In presenting city and regional planning, I have tried to respect the diversity of the profession. This has an important implication for the discussion. Over the years, I have defined planning in different ways and avoided the urge to settle on a single one. I am untroubled by allowing the idea to take on different meanings depending on the purposes for which it is being used. No one definition can hold true over time and space. Planning practice includes a range of activities from developing strategic plans to organizing the location of bike-sharing

---

5. I will not attempt to reconcile the differences between actor-network theory and Marxism on the issue of materialism, but see Kirsch and Mitchell 2004.

facilities to working with community groups to achieve food security in low-income neighborhoods. Moreover, planners are highly likely to adapt their approach and their behavior to the circumstances they face. Planners are similar neither in their ideological orientations nor in their activities. As a mongrel profession (Sandercock 2003), planning resists generalization.

At the same time, ways of thinking and acting exist that should be labeled planning while other ways should not. Relying on price signals and the market to distribute housing to households is seldom considered a planning solution. Nor is planning equivalent to making decisions based on political calculations meant to strengthen or weaken the positions of individuals and groups in a struggle for resources. Planners, moreover, are neither spontaneous nor instinctual. One can think like a planner or not, act like a planner or not, devise and follow a plan or not. Planning is not everything, but it is many things.

Because my intent is to present a materialist planning, I have been particularly attentive to its applications. Stylistically, this has meant being generous with empirical examples. A planning theory that eschews examples, remaining at a theoretical or philosophical level, does not deserve the name. It is something else. Consequently, and with only a few exceptions, all the chapters are anchored in one or more extended illustrations. In this way I hope to convince readers why and how this new materialist perspective matters in practice. And while my examples are mainly taken from the United States, from both the present and the past, I hope they resonate with planning (and planners) in other countries as well.[6]

My approach is also unashamedly normative: explicit in its commitment to more democratic practices and institutions, greater equality of conditions and opportunities, and resistance to structural injustices. Planning theory cannot and should not avoid engaging with widely shared norms. Even attempts to describe and explain what planners do force the theorist to take a position on the rightness or wrongness of their actions. What John Law (2009, 155) notes for social theory applies to planning theory as well: "To describe the real is always an ethically charged act." Otherwise, as Flyvbjerg (2001) has convincingly argued, it fails to be practical and thus consequential. People and institutions plan because they want to impose themselves on the world in

---

6. Although planning occurs at various territorial scales—suburbs, small towns, regions, neighborhoods, and urban areas—most of my illustrations are drawn from planning in and for cities.

a very specific fashion and because they believe there are better ways to live. Planning theory has never been merely about explaining practice; it is also about changing it by suggesting what planners should do and how social responsibilities can best be realized. If politics has to do with talking about and acting on the way we wish to live together, then planning is always political. And since it is political, it is also normative.

Overview

Rather than a text that converges on a single formal argument, I have written interlocking essays, each treating an aspect of planning. All of them together hardly exhaust the issues to be discussed, much less treat fully the ones I have chosen. Heterogeneity and contingency characterize the world, and I wanted to reflect this in the text, even if inadequately. Additionally, I hope the essay form encourages readers to be more engaged with the claims I make. Essays allow for a less linear argument, the juxtaposition of different perspectives and types of knowledge, and a more fluid style.

The chapters have a deliberate sequence that moves from interpersonal relations to planning's place in a world of institutions. The first chapter is a statement of the core ideas—the central tendencies—of planning practice as I understand them and is meant to establish the background for subsequent discussions. I then offer various perspectives on the micropolitics of planning, beginning with the functions of talk and action (chapter 2) and then reflecting on how planners always talk and act both with other humans and with nonhuman things (chapter 3), always talk and act in specific places that influence what is said and done (chapter 4), and always confront, as they talk and act, the responsibilities they have to others (chapter 5). At this point the book shifts to applying the new materialist perspective to planning's macropolitics and its engagement with institutions like the state and larger formations such as cities. Chapter 6 explores how principles of practice connect planners to the material world. This general discussion is followed by three chapters that reflect on the limits to planning: one (chapter 7) focused on obduracy and the conflicts intrinsic to planning, a second (chapter 8) that investigates how time paradoxically limits and strengthens practice, and a third (chapter 9) that reflects on the constraints on the promise of planning posed by a capitalist political economy. And whereas the book has been written to intertwine theory and practice, I conclude with two chapters that address concerns associated more with planning theory, one having to do with its worldliness and the other with modernity.

Finally, and despite my earlier disavowal of any single definition of planning, a particular notion has guided my thinking: planning means collectively imagining how we can live well with others and then acting together to realize those aspirations. I hope the book conveys the potential for this phenomenon we call planning—by taking on a material presence—to contribute to that more democratic, more just, and more tolerant world.

ONE

Ontographies

What does it mean to think and act as a planner? This is a daunting question, and any answer is going to leave much unsaid. Not only are its key terms—think, act—problematic, but planning (in both theory and practice) appears to us in various manifestations. One of the most common approaches to the question, and the one I have selected, is to juxtapose what lies within the fuzzy boundaries of planning with what lies beyond them. This is most often done by contrasting planning with its purported adversaries—the usual suspects being markets, particularly capitalist markets, and interest group politics. My foil, by contrast, is a particular way of representing the world. Before proceeding with further explanation, though, I need you to read slowly through these four lists:

transportation planner, negotiation skills, curb cut, GIS, plaza, air quality, mitigation fees, EPA, neighborhood activists, business incubator, variance, traffic lights, Executive Order 12898, density, property rights, Metropolitan Planning Organization (MPO), illegal conversion, work-live space, public trash bins, wind turbines, court decision, tattoo parlor, microunit, empty nesters, eminent domain, block face, zoning officer, budget shortfall, group home, website, land seizure, arts district

flood zone, AICP code, nonprofit group, infrastructure, Census data, sidewalk cafés, construction loan, retail, Powerpoint presentation, woodland stream, business retention, growth boundary, automobile drivers streets, 3D modeling, single-family house, stormwater runoff, building codes, soil contaminants, TOD, topographic map, trucks, housing tax credits, storeowners' association, public hearing, signage, administrative expenses, light standards, retaining wall, neighborhood surveys, movie theater, impact fee, visioning, calm streets

planning director, hazard mitigation, pedestrians, historic district, zoning ordinance, coastal zone management, certification, impact fee, car sharing, green buildings, AICP examination, endangered species, vacant lot, marina, planting, scale model, noxious facilities, eviction notice, interest rates, slum, access ramp, developers, staff directory, scenic views, street glare, trips, light rail stop, grants, air rights, BID, townhouses, cell phone tower, parking space, lease, trash, square footage, soccer stadium, residential conversion, Livable Communities Act (1995), retention pond, site survey, plan amendment, shopping mall, license fee, land use lawyer, payroll, redevelopment authority, value capture, disaster plan, city council, cars, abandoned factory, New Urbanism, speed bumps, riverfront parks

Each of these clusters is an ontography. The items are randomly arranged, and there is no obvious logic to the sequence. The intent is to embrace the arbitrariness inherent in lists and to subvert any complacency about the orderliness of everyday life and the elegance of our understandings. In a pure ontography, the items would also have nothing in common. These lists, however, are impure; all the items are drawn from the world of planning.[1]

Ontographies challenge planners—both practitioners and theorists—to think differently about how they engage the world. Every item in these lists is either a process, a law, a tool, an object, or a place that comes into play as planners go about regulating the built and natural environments and improving the conditions under which people live. Such items also frequently appear in the writings of planning theorists as they strive to explain and advise on planning practice. Planners, however, would never display them in such disorderly fashion.

The qualities of ontographies are incompatible with those that, since the early twentieth century, have defined the planning ideal and its many means of practice. As one illustration, consider how planners' embrace of orderliness, rationality, and predictability is antithetical to the onto-

---

1. I collected the items for these ontographies by reading through the annual conference program of the American Planning Association for 2013 and issues of the professional journal *Planning* for 2012 and the first half of 2013 and writing down the various items I encountered. From that master list, I created the four ontographies with the intent of maximizing variety and minimizing obvious affiliations between adjacent items.

graphic commitment to arbitrariness. In short, the values represented by ontographies constitute a world radically different from that of planning.

In this first chapter, my goal is a reading of the core qualities of planning from an ontographic perspective. Because the perspective is so alien, it provides a stark contrast with planning's central tendencies. It is a way of thinking that almost all planners would reject. By comparing planning to an antithesis, planning's qualities are accentuated and clarified. My specific focus is planning thought that I present not as settled dogma but as a cluster of dispositions that enable us to distinguish planners and planning from other types of actors and actions. Implicit in this is that a planning cast of mind is only one way to imagine the world. This should challenge planners to think of themselves less as experts applying a fixed methodology to produce a definitive answer and more as technically informed citizens engaged in a collective and open-ended endeavor.

Ontographies

I first became aware of the existence of ontographies (although not under that label) in doing research on the history of urban decline in the United States (Beauregard 2003). Across the twentieth century, lists of urban problems have been commonplace in both popular and scholarly writings about the condition of cities. When commenting on the dire conditions in the slums of Philadelphia, say, observers are likely to put forward an inventory: high unemployment, juvenile delinquency, entrenched poverty, racial discrimination, substandard housing, rapacious slumlords, fatherless families, poor schools, unscrupulous storeowners. One purpose of such lists is to convey the breadth of urban decline—its multiplicity—and the difficulties any policymaker or community group faces in trying to ameliorate it.[2] Decline is not one thing but many things, and implicit in these lists is a conviction that reversing decline means acknowledging the interconnectedness of conditions and the need to act comprehensively. Because they reminded me of incantations, I thought of them as litanies. They differ from litanies and pure ontographies, however, in implying that such conditions are so intertwined as to make decline even more intractable. Consequently urban decline is considered obdurate, even if the sequence of the items

2. Such lists also represent places in terms of measurable conditions susceptible to government policies and reinvestment.

in the list is arbitrary. The arbitrariness, however, is mitigated by suggesting what the items have in common—they are all qualities of specific places. In this way, one of the standards for a workable list is met.[3]

Years later, I encountered lists in Bruno Latour's (2005b) writings on actor-network theory. Actor-network theory proposes that humans do not act alone in the world but act in conjunction with tools such as felt-tip markers, technologies such as geographical information software and zoning regulations, nonliving things (for example, bicycle racks), and even living nonhuman things such as sedge grasses, storm surges, and deer populations. These things, including humans, enable Latour to convey what he calls the heterogeneity of the world and to remind us how far human actions require not just nonhuman allies but nonhuman entanglements.[4]

As an example, consider Latour's *We Have Never Been Modern* (1993, 2). He begins this well-known book by commenting on what he has found in the daily newspaper:

On page eleven, there is a slag heap in northern France, a symbol of the exploitation of workers, that has been classified as an ecological preserve because of the rare flora it has been fostering! On page twelve, the Pope, French bishops, Monsanto, the Fallopian tubes, and Texas fundamentalists gather in a strange cohort around a single contraceptive. On page fourteen, the number of lines on high-definition television bring[s] together Mr. Delors, Thomson, the EEC, commissions on standardization, the Japanese . . . , and television film producers.

Note how Latour's list extends beyond human subjects to include nonhumans, thereby introducing us to the variety of things that make up matters of concern: the consequences of mining, birth control, and the manufacturing of televisions. Another example comes from his research into the politics of science that expected to find "citizens, assemblies of 'mini-kings,' ideologies, deliberations, votes, elections; the traditional *sites* of political events" but instead found "[a] vaccine, an incandescent lamp, an equation, a pollution standard, a building, a blood screening procedure: those were the new *means* through which politics

3. During this time I was also influenced by Italo Calvino's *Invisible Cities* (1974), in which Marco Polo describes to Kublai Khan a seemingly endless list of cities he has visited, with each subsequent city unlike the one before. Polo begins one tale thus: "Of all the changes of language a traveler in distant lands must face, none equals that which awaits him in the city of Hypatia, because the change regards not words but things" (47).

4. For a particularly good application of the notion of heterogeneity, see McCann 2008 on the world of policy mobilities.

was being carried out" (Latour 2007a, 812–813; emphases in original). For Latour, any controversy—or planning event—contains a differentiated array of actors that gives the controversy its political salience.

Latour, however, never allows his lists to become pure ontographies. They have a heterogeneous quality—note the inclusion of a blood screening procedure and an incandescent lamp in the category of political things—with each item part of a single category with a particular purpose—"science" in this instance. Or, as regards Fallopian tubes and the pope, they are entangled with a contraceptive device, women's bodies, and nonprocreative sexual intercourse. These lists constitute domains that Latour calls networks or assemblages that represent the constituent forms of the material world. Latour (2010a) thus views scholarship and social practices as compositional activities; that is, they put things together to enable intellectual positions and material conditions to become stable and endure.[5]

One of the purest of ontographies comes from a famous essay—"The Analytical Language of John Wilkins"—written in 1942 by the Argentine poet and short-story writer Jorge Luis Borges (1964, 101–105). In discussing an attempt in the seventeenth century by John Wilkins, a principal of one of Oxford's colleges, to develop a universal language, Borges mentions a list ostensibly discovered by a Dr. Franz Kuhn in a Chinese encyclopedia titled *Celestial Empire of Benevolent Knowledge*— all of which, given his attraction to labyrinths and magical realism, might be a Borgesian fabrication. The list is of animals and reads as follows (103):

Belonging to the Emperor
Embalmed
Tame
Suckling pigs
Sirens
Fabulous
Stray dogs
Included in the present classification
Frenzied
Innumerable
Drawn with very fine camel-hair brush
Et cetera

---

5. Latour's lists are closer to bricolage than to ontographies. A bricolage is "a (loosely coupled but relatively coherent) set of information resources and tools" (Bowker and Star 2000, 82).

Having just broken the water pitcher
That from a long way off look like flies

    This list seems wholly arbitrary, lacking any sense of coherence or boundedness. While all the characterizations are meant to apply to animals—we can imagine a cat knocking over a water pitcher or rabbits being innumerable—the list does not serve a single purpose. That is, neither does it depict the essential qualities of animals, nor are the items (such as "fabulous" and "frenzied") necessarily confined to them. Consequently, the list allows readers to imagine nonanimals (for example, "innumerable" pebbles on a beach) that conform to the classification scheme. Moreover, Borges has inserted a most disconcerting item: "Included in the present classification." On first reading this seems redundant, needless to mention, yet it also seems perfectly appropriate for an ontography; that is, for a list meant to be capacious. Here we begin to sense what a pure ontography might be. And by listing flies, brushes, dogs, and the emperor, Borges also offers us a glimpse into Latour's heterogeneity. His intent seems to be to subvert the list as "a practical tool for organizing work" (Bowker and Star 2000, 137).

    Although Ian Bogost (2012, 35–59) does not mention Borges's list in the discussion of ontography in his *Alien Phenomenology*, he does draw examples from the writings of Latour, Roland Barthes's autobiography ("*I don't like*: white Pomeranians, women in slacks, geraniums, strawberries, the harpsichord, Miro") (41), and a wonderful song by the Brazilian composer Antônio Carlos Jobim titled "Águas de Março" in which the lyrics depict the things seen and heard in Rio de Janeiro: "It's a sliver of glass; It is life, it's the sun; It is night, it is death; It's a trap, it's a gun" (43), continuing in this fashion over the rhythms and harmonies of a bossa nova.

    For Bogost, an ontography is a list that allows each item to be imagined in its specificity and repleteness; that is, to be perceived as having an integrity that would be stifled in a more structured setting. Opposed to minimalism, an ontography embraces the plenitude, the density, and "the jarring staccato of real being" (40). In an earthy metaphor, Bogost likens an ontography to a landfill, in contrast to a Japanese garden (59). The intent is "the abandonment of anthropocentric narrative coherence in favor of worldly detail" (41), thereby decentering humans in order to reveal the "countless things" that litter the material world and the infinite couplings possible among them. Bogost proposes an ontology of multiplicity and contingency. Along with Latour, Barthes, and Jobim, he wants us to look at the world without the lens of classificatory presumptions; he wants us to see it anew.[6]

While all this seems only tenuously connected to planning and, in many ways, antithetical to how planners think and act, the otherness of ontographies strikes me as useful for reflecting on planning's central tendencies. In our relations with others, the differences matter the most. This truism also applies to thinking about what we are doing when we plan; that is, the differences between planning and not planning. To explain this, I first need to expand on what I understand to be the core qualities of ontographies: heterogeneity, symmetry, repleteness, and contingency.

Ontographic Qualities

First, heterogeneity. Ontographies encourage their readers to embrace a world that comprises a diversity of things whose similarities are obvious because, and only because, they are socially constituted through the making of categories and classifications. In this latter form they are useful and enable work to be done (Bowker and Star 2000). From this premise emerge two important claims. One is that humans are not alone in the universe. The other is that humans cannot undertake purposeful action without the participation of nonhumans. The former challenges the notion that action is a matter of humans deciding what to do and then manipulating and shaping the world around them. From an ontographic and actor-network perspective, there is not a world "in-here" made up solely of humans and a world "out-there" made up of nonhumans passively awaiting human instruction (Lieto and Beauregard 2013). Heterogeneity is taken to mean not just that the world consists of different kinds of things, but that all things participate in making that world. Humans do not act alone.[7] This is often characterized as the symmetry between humans and nonhumans, with each potentially influential in any assemblage of actors. Positing a

6. Of course this is impossible. We cannot wholly escape previously adopted categories; at best we can recognize, critique, and modify them. On this point, see Lakoff 1987 on objectivist categorization versus prototype theory that views categorization schemes as involving human experience and imagination as well as technical assessments. Between objectivist categories and ontographies lie the lists of actor-network theory.

7. For a good example of how poststructuralists use the concept of heterogeneity to destabilize our understandings of capitalism, class, and gender relations, see Gibson-Graham (1996) 2006. She (they) does not address the culture/nature divide, however.

nonhierarchical or flat ontology, actor-network theorists refuse to privilege humans over nonhumans, thereby undermining the very basis of
humanism (Latour 1987, 145–176).

Moreover, it is not just humans who use tools (for example, an
earthmoving machine to shape the landscape) or engage with animals
(for example, when they attempt to control the population of deer in
an area by introducing coyotes). Actor-network theorists additionally
argue that nonhuman things are also active agents with tool-using and
collaborative capacities. The deer react to how they are being culled by
changing their daily paths, the cell phone reminds you of an upcom-
ing appointment so as to maintain good relations with your client, and
the speed bump relieves you of the moral calculation of how much
to slow down while driving in a residential zone (Latour 1992). Nonhuman things are not passive; they create effects with and irrespective
of humans. Without their participation, moreover, we could hardly
manage.

Rather than an asymmetrical world where humans dominate, the
argument is that nonhumans are ontologically equivalent to humans,
the second quality of ontographies. Both have the capacity "to act as
quasi agents or forces with trajectories, propensities, or tendencies of
their own" (Bennett 2010, viii). More important, both influence relationships among actors, thereby having effects that must be acknowledged. Adopting symmetry is a way of recognizing that nonhumans
are as consequential in making the world as humans. When humans
and nonhumans act together, whether in concert or in conflict, they
have to be given equal standing in any interpretation of their actions
and the consequences they produce.

In addition, piercing the barrier between culture and nature makes
a statement about morality. Our moral obligations are expanded such
that humans share individual and collective responsibilities with the
animals, plants, and things that surround them (Nussbaum 2006, 325–
407; Young 2011). These responsibilities, moreover, extend beyond
family and nation as human constructs to those others with whom we
share the planet. Action and morality are thus cast as inseparable.

Underlying heterogeneity and symmetry is the slippery activity
of classification. When we classify, we create useful distinctions that
enable us to achieve particular objectives; for example, minimizing
the negative externalities from land uses by distinguishing between
industrial and residential properties or creating medical records that
list causes of death and thereby provide knowledge that contributes

to improving public health (Bowker and Star 2000).[8] Differentiating one thing from another, however, runs the risk of creating a boundary that does not exist in reality, thereby distorting our view of the world (Zerubavel 1991). For example, consider such fuzzy distinctions as political and social, skilled and unskilled, or formal and informal—or, more mundanely, the contours on topographical maps. In addition, certain things—cyborgs, for example (Hacking 1998)—challenge what seem like settled categories. Even more daunting is the difficulty of stating what is human about humans. Do humans, but not animals, negotiate their intentions? Are humans sensitive to what is said about them, conforming to the categories (for example, underachiever) in which they are placed, while rocks and amoebas are immune to this recursive effect (Hacking 1999, 31–32)? Do humans, but not nonhumans, conceive of their projects before implementing them? Do they plan?

To return to ontographies, if Bogost's claim is that they enable the items on the list to be understood as specific and full (replete), this assumes that the reader or listener understands these things as distinct from each other. Would a skeptical reader, for example, accept Latour's implicit distinction between the pope and French bishops? That reader might point to the hierarchical nature of the Catholic Church and thus to the possibility that in practice these are not two separate interests, two separate items. As with all qualities of ontographies, repleteness is neither automatic nor uncontested. One observer's specificity is another observer's chaotic concept (Sayer 1982). Modernism might be a single thing to one social theorist but to another a variety of different conditions and dynamics specific to historical periods and cultures (Chakrabarty 2000). Heterogeneity and symmetry depend, in the last instance, on how one thinks about repleteness, while repleteness brings us back to the difference between ontographies and performative classifications.

Finally there is contingency, the fourth quality. Behind the random sequence of ontographies is the idea that the things that compose it can be casually added and subtracted and thus combined in a multitude of ways. A suckling pig, for example, might or might not be tame or embalmed. Numerous combinations are possible, but predicting them before engaging with a clearly defined setting would be pedantic, an exercise in formalism. And while not anything is likely

8. Among the causes of death listed in a seventeenth-century table of casualties for England were "executed, drowned, leprosie, poisoned, rickets, shot, swine-pox, and 'suddenly,'" with the major cause of death between 1636 and 1659 being "consumption and cough" (Bowker and Star 2000, 22–23).

in a particular historical time and place, ontographies remind us that these sureties enable life to happen even though other conditions are always possible. To this extent, ontographies have a critical foundation, one that does not simply accept the world as it is but asks how it might be or might have been otherwise. An ontographer is not a determinist or a naive positivist, but more like a critical theorist who recognizes the possibilities of a contingent world (Calhoun 1995). Unlike the critical theorist, however, the ontographer is not interested in stipulating the hidden forces that operate behind our experiences. For her, the empirical world and the actions carried out within it are the only reality.

The Qualities of Planning

The qualities that define planning are antithetical to those associated with ontographies. Ontographies are disorderly and intuitive, while planning is systematic and self-conscious. For example, plans, maps ("system[s] of notation . . . that place things in relation to each other" [Kurgan 2013, 16]), and the planning process itself are meant as an antidote to an ontographic view of the world. Planners shun heterogeneity, repleteness, and contingency as these notions are understood by their ontographic counterparts, and they are only beginning to recognize the symmetry of the material world. In contrast, we mean something specific by planning, and what we mean is central to how planning is taught, how planners think of themselves, and how they are perceived by those outside the profession. Yet no consensus exists as to the specific attributes that make planning distinct. Its attributes are dispositions, central tendencies, rather than historically and culturally fixed qualities. They are also not unique. Planning's commitment to social reform is shared by the professions of social work and public health, while its desire to imagine the city in its entirety—to be comprehensive—is something to which urban designers also aspire. Nevertheless, certain qualities appear frequently enough to differentiate what it means to plan from what it means to act spontaneously, allow the market to decide, or turn over all public matters to political calculation.

Consider Leonie Sandercock's (2003, 31–33) claim that there is a "heroic model of planning" and that it rests on six "pillars": rationality, comprehensiveness, science, the future, the public interest, and value neutrality. For her, what defines mainstream planning is a reliance on institutional modes of rationality to make public decisions; a quest to achieve all-encompassing and integrative understandings and plans; a belief that science trumps experience in explaining the world; a commitment to thinking about and anticipating the future and the future consequences of present actions; a presumption that the state can be progressive and reformist and deflect economic influences; and trust that people share interests that can be identified and whose fulfillment will benefit society as a whole. She rightly notes that for decades these pillars have been criticized within the profession. The world of planning is too diverse for consensus. Although more technically inclined planners, clinging to instrumental rationality, might argue for a value neutrality that respects the strictures of science and avoids the biases of political entanglements, others might point out that the facts that matter can hardly be separated from values (Lindblom 1959). And still others put forward a planning that is consciously and explicitly engaged in ethical judgments (Campbell 2006). No single quality and no combination of them receives universal acclaim or rises to the status of inviolability.

That said, five qualities of planning strike me as particularly important: its essential humanism; a belief that the world is knowable as well as amenable to purposive change; a vision of orderliness; a commitment to the public good; and an assumption that analysis can produce valuable advice that is convincing to both decision makers and publics. Broad, encompassing qualities, each has a core idea around which peripheral ideas (for example, the importance of government regulations) can be arranged. The whole leads to an unstable assemblage that is suggestive rather than preemptive. In short, these qualities constitute a way of thinking about and acting on the world that distinguishes planners from other kinds of actors, but not unequivocally.[9]

First, planners are essentially humanists; they approach the world from a perspective that privileges humans over nonliving things and other forms of life.[10] The things that matter in enabling plans to be realized are land use lawyers, pedestrians, planning directors, storeowner associations, automobile drivers, zoning officers, transportation planners, and neighborhood activists. Nature is placed in a subordinate position and exists mainly as a resource to support human life and as a world that humans act on. Karl Marx's ([1867] 1967, 177) notion of

9. This characterization of planning, I believe, applies not just to the United States but to many other countries as well; see Friedmann 2005, Urban 2012, and Ward 2002.

10. This definition of humanism is tailored to my argument and thus is limited in its reach. On whether the world is socially constituted or (without humans) wholly natural, see Latour 2003a.

labor nicely reflects this argument: "Labour is, in the first place, a process by which . . . man . . . opposes himself to Nature as one of her own forces . . . in order to appropriate nature's production in a form adapted to his own wants." Planning thus rests on the proposition that two spheres exist, one of humans and the other of worlds external to them; that is, an in-here and an out-there. The task of planners is to direct and mobilize humans and their various organizations to intervene in the world out-there in order, for example, to build seawalls to protect cities from storm surges and encourage travelers to shift from automobiles to mass transit to lessen carbon emissions and protect the ozone layer. To be a humanist is to believe that culture is distinct from nature and that the object of planning is a world out-there that is subordinate to human intentions.

This privileging of humans is mediated by planners' interest in cities and regions, places where humans, nature, and technologies are intertwined and about which planners claim expertise. The relationship poses a dilemma for planners by raising the question whether planning is meant to serve people (for example, improving their quality of life, enabling them to live together in a more just world) or whether planners must focus instead on making cities and regions function efficiently and equitably, with people secondary to these objectives. From planning's inception in the reformist response to rapid urbanization and industrialization in the late nineteenth century, planners have had an interest in issues of poverty, public health, and education. At the same time, they have been concerned with the management of land use, low-income housing, and infrastructure. Consequently, within planning there exists another humanist divide between those planners, once known as social planners, who focus on the immediate needs of people and those who focus on the built environment (Beauregard 2008).

Implicit to this humanism is the belief that planners can control the world out-there. Justified by superior insights into nature conferred by science, mobilized by technologies like air quality monitoring, and supported by the powers and resources of governments and corporations, planners are able to undertake purposive interventions meant to produce specific and predetermined consequences: a growth boundary, housing tax credits, calm streets, scenic views. Only humans are able to plan before they act and then act in ways that impose their intentions on animals, plants, sand dunes, and stormwater. The reverse is not true; animals, plants, sand dunes, and stormwater do not have collective concerns that include humans. They encounter humans and react to them, but they do not set out to control and change the human world. By contrast, humans incessantly—sometimes inadvertently and often unsuccessfully—work to bring the natural world into conformity with their aspirations.

Second, the actions of planners are rooted in the belief that knowledge enables them to control and manipulate the world. Wildavsky (1973, 131) states it bluntly: "The first requisite of [national] planning is causal knowledge." To know the world is to be able to influence it. Intentional action requires scientific or technical understanding.[11] This belief is based on a deeper assumption that reality is more rather than less structured and that this coherence can be discovered through collecting and analyzing evidence and interpreting the findings. Planning is scientific; it searches for the causal forces that result in blighted business districts, traffic congestion, and urban population loss. By uncovering the causes of public problems, planners can then identify points of intervention to reduce the harmful and amplify the beneficial consequences of these forces. Planners reject indeterminacy; their plans rely on a causal understanding of the realities being planned.

Planners do not live in a radically contingent world. They assume that the world is predictable and thus that they can expect the intended consequences of their actions to be realized. In fact, they argue that their analyses of and insights into conditions and trends enables them to reduce the uncertainty associated with action (Benveniste 1977). One plans because one wants to achieve specific ends while minimizing undesirable consequences: illegal conversions, stormwater runoff, street glare. What planners offer is a way to act that is purposive—that promises to produce the desired results. Such thinking implies that we have choices. If no alternative ways of acting are available yet we still must act, there is no need to plan. We simply do what we have to do. But planners imagine themselves in neither a radically contingent world nor a radically determinative one where choices are absent. Choices, they believe, exist and can be rationally assessed. This is what scientific analysis offers—the ability to make rational decisions that emerge from systematic ways of thinking. In this way planners hope to make the world more coherent and thus more understandable and predictable. This enables them to be effective.

Periodically, and in certain places but not others, the forces that underlie urban and regional development go awry. One is then left with housing markets that are unaffordable for the people who wish to live

11. Herein lies the tension, embodied in the expert, between planners and democracy (Healey 1993, 234). For a very insightful reflection on this issue, see Turner 2001.

there, population growth that outstrips infrastructure provision, and aquifers that need protection. From planning's contemporary origins in the late nineteenth and early twentieth centuries, planners have endeavored to bring coherence to the city, whether by making it more aesthetically pleasing (the goal of the City Beautiful Movement in the United States), more efficient for commerce (the City Functional Movement), or more just (the just city argument of the early twenty-first century) (Fainstein 2010; Scott 1969; Spain 2001). The intent in all instances has been to think of the city holistically—comprehensively is the word commonly used—and to organize it to produce specific consequences. From the city's inception, planners have been committed to making it function better. In this sense they consider themselves reformers (Hancock 1967).

Out of this flows planners' commitment to orderliness, what Boyer (1983) characterizes as the need to discipline the city. Consider a few items from this chapter's ontographies: traffic lights, flood zone, building codes, property rights, scenic views, certification, retaining wall. Each of these things contributes to the orderly functioning of cities and regions—to a functioning that follows a planning logic. This is the third quality of planning. If planners were to adopt a single motto, my choice would be "a place for everything and everything in its place."[12] This captures not only the quest for order and the belief that coordination is always preferable to individual volition, but also the inherently spatial nature of city and regional planning (Beauregard 1990; Ward 2002). The focus on where things are placed is what distinguishes planning from policy analysis and public administration on the professional side and from sociology (but not geography), political science, and most of mainstream economics on the social science side. Planning questions are not only about how to act in an organized fashion to achieve specified ends but almost always about the spatial distribution of things, from vacant lots, highway access ramps, and historic districts to group homes and noxious facilities. The objects of planning are often conditions and things that are absent or out of place. What planners do best is to develop and propose spatial arrangements that are more efficient, more aesthetically pleasing, or more just. Space matters to planners, and what matters about space is its orderliness.[13]

12. This homily has various forms and is associated with the uplifting sensibilities of the (European) Victorian era of the nineteenth century.
13. One can trace this concern with order to the proposals for utopian communities in the nineteenth century in response to rapid industrialization, population growth, and urbanization (Benevolo [1963] 1971).

Fourth, planners see this quest for order as serving the public good. The public good is what benefits everyone in the city. It is in everyone's interest, planners argue, that the city function efficiently so that commerce and people can move about without wasting time and businesses can be productive. Or, from a different perspective, a just city serves everyone since all people are susceptible to ill luck that might leave them in need of (public) assistance. More broadly, making cities and regions better—riverfront parks, light rail stops, disaster plans, business retention, improved air quality—is itself a public good. This is one of the responsibilities of local governments. As political scientist Otis Graham (1976, xii) wrote about planning at the federal level, "Planning assumes that modern industrial society requires public intervention to achieve national goals; assumes that such intervention must touch all fundamental social developments; must be goal-oriented, and effectively coordinated at the center; must be anticipatory rather than characterized by ad hoc solutions and timing dictated by crisis." Through their involvement with the state, planners do their civic and professional duty.[14]

What has stifled planners in their quest to serve the public good is the difficulty of knowing exactly what it is (Altshuler 1965, 299–332; Meyerson and Banfield 1955). Before it can be addressed, it has to be identified. Here is where planners often fall back on their place within the government, arguing that democratically elected officials are the source of the public good. These officials set the goals that planners pursue. The clash between the interests of mayors and aldermen and those of various publics, however, has led some planners to engage with residents in public forums to determine the public good independent of government policy (Innes and Booher 2004). An additional complexity emerges when planners enter into these participatory frameworks yet hold to the belief that their expertise gives them special access to the needs of neighborhoods, cities, and regions. In one scenario, planners defer to elected officials and governments because without their support they would not be able to plan for the public. In another scenario, expert assessment of the public good trumps what elected officials and citizens say it is. And in a third scenario, planners gather knowledge from citizens and integrate it with their own ideas; that is, they jointly produce knowledge (Corburn 2003). Dedicated to serving the public,

14. Characterizing government planners in this way leaves their legal obligation to elected officials unattended, complicating (and often compromising) their pursuit of the public good.

beholden to elected officials, aspiring to be democratic, and committed to science in the form of their expertise, planners are conflicted.

A further difficulty arises with the notion of "public." In a socially diverse society like the United States, it is difficult to defend the position that a single public exists. Rather, planners are faced with multiple publics. In contemporary planning they are called stakeholders; that is, people and groups—neighborhood activists, automobile drivers, real estate developers—with a direct interest in an issue.[15] For any given issue, a set of concerned individuals and groups is said to exist, and the concerns of these people must be taken into account. Latour (2007a) argues that without issues, politics disappears, and that without people coming together to form publics, issues evaporate as well. Here he draws on John Dewey's ([1927] 1954) argument that democratic politics gives rise to multiple publics. This understanding challenges the notion, inherent to planning expertise, that for cities and regions to prosper, they must be efficient, sustainable, just, or all three. For planners, the conditions that constitute the public good are independent of public assessments; they are intrinsic to places. Planners' specialized knowledge once again rises to the surface. If these places have organic needs, planners are the experts who can identify them.

This quest for the public good is a significant part of planners' commitment to reform and thus to their moral purpose (Krueckeberg 1983). Planning has always been a reformist profession, and to varying degrees this has meant more than simply making cities and regions work better. The historical roots of planning, whether in the United States, England, or Germany, reach back to a period of rapid industrialization and urbanization and the horrid conditions this created for wage laborers and their families (Hall 2002, 14–47; Steffens [1902] 1957). On the one hand, planners were concerned with issues like public health that impinged on all who lived in the city. On the other hand, they were appalled by the living conditions of the lower class. These conditions could potentially harm the whole city and everyone in it. A yellow fever outbreak could not easily be confined to the poor and their neighborhoods. In addition, there was the fear that the poor and the oppressed would revolt. Throughout their history, then, planners have been inclined to help those who have fewer choices (Krumholz 1982). For many, this is where their social responsibility lies. And while local

15. See Callon, Lascoumes, and Barthe 2011 for a critique of this way of identifying relevant publics.

government planners are often accused of solely serving the local government and its bias toward corporations and developers, this moral purpose has not been wholly stifled.

Last, planners attempt to achieve their various objectives by giving advice to those with power and influence. "The job of the planner" Altshuler has written (1965, 1), "is to propose courses of action." As empiricists, planners base their advice on the analysis of evidence: geographical information systems (GIS), scale models, Census data, and neighborhood surveys. An inclination to empiricism means they need time to do their analyses. In fact, this period of reflection, this pause, is one of planning's defining qualities. Planners are prudent people who, faced with a choice or a need to act, want to carefully consider their options. To plan is to imagine, before acting, what one might do and what consequences might ensue. Consequently, planners make a conscious effort to slow the pace of events and to counsel caution. Others might respond instinctually or adopt an ideologically preferred solution. Planners are meant to do neither. Their preferred course is to consider the alternatives by analyzing the evidence and weighing the findings against their experiences and their understanding of how cities and regions are suppose to function. To plan is to reflect upon and imagine what might happen in different scenarios.[16]

For this reason, and because planning has historical roots in the utopian formulations of the nineteenth century, planners are engaged in "a forward-looking activity" (Friedmann 1987, 1). Planners "attempt to shape the future" (Brooks 2002, 9) so that it conforms to human intention. Control over and predictability of the future are central to planning's identity. The present already exists, and the past can only be rewritten, not materially changed. Only the future holds the possibility of reform. And while planners are now less likely than early in the twentieth century to attempt to imagine the city twenty-five years in the future and set guidelines to ensure that their vision comes about, they still systematically consider the consequences of public actions before taking those actions. Counseling caution, planners want us to act in the present in ways that do not limit the choices and quality of life of those who will follow.

16. Benveniste (1977, 5) writes: "The modern Prince, if he is wise . . . [and] since his policies can have unforeseen consequences" hires planners to reflect on those consequences and give him advice. There is a Chinese saying often attributed to Deng Xiaoping during the post-Mao liberalization era in China: "We will cross the river by feeling the stones under our feet, one by one." This is not planning.

Planning Is Not Ontographic

control, value neutrality, space, consequences, reflection, analysis, social reform, orderliness, humanism, expertise, alternatives, public interest, rationality, advice giving, imagined futures, predictability, choices, holism, rigor

The sequence above is not a pure ontography. A yet unorganized list, all its items are associated with the act of planning. And even though the list is not meant to be comprehensive—another defining quality of planning—and critics might reject one item or another, implicit is that alternative ways of acting are possible. Thus, while planners can more or less be distinguished from nonplanners, they can also be distinguished from each other. At the same time, it should be obvious that planning is far removed from the values that inform ontographies. The commitment to knowability, analytical rigor, orderliness, rationality, holism, and control sits uncomfortably with the embrace of repleteness, heterogeneity, contingency, and symmetry. An ontographic planner would be an oxymoron.

Consider the commitment that ontography has to the specificity and repleteness of individual things, whether ideas or plants. Each thing is assumed to have an integrity that has to be grasped and admired. Such an impulse encourages us to explore the uniqueness of what it means to be a zoning officer or a curb cut (Bogost 2012). In doing so, we are being asked to forget any relationship the zoning officer has with the zoning map and the Zoning Board of Appeals; that is, to ignore the relationships that humans and things have with other humans and things. Instead, the objective is to consider each item in isolation. If we are to truly understand a curb cut—its materiality and form—we must focus solely on its "thisness" and not put it into a relationship with anything else.

A pure ontographic position is antithetical to planning. Planning is a social practice; it is about relationships and connections. It is in the world. A zoning decision cannot occur without the zoning officer's interacting with members of the zoning board, the director of the city planning department, and the property owner inquiring about putting an addition on her house. Planning is inherently and necessarily a social endeavor ranging from the micropolitics of interpersonal relationships, one-on-one deliberations, and committee meetings to the macropolitics of managing the advice of planning in relation to citizen groups, government agencies, funding cycles, and elected officials. No single thing can be isolated. Things are connected, and this connectedness is what planners claim to understand and believe they can manipulate. Furthermore, connectedness contributes to their belief in and commitment to the public good.

Making connections, however, requires a prior understanding of disconnectedness. Before we connect, we first need to distinguish. Consequently, the planning worldview is filled with categories. Take as an example planning's core function, the regulation of land use. It proceeds in terms of land use types (residential, heavy industry, open space) that are then arranged in zones (medium-density residential, light commercial) that classify the spaces of the city in terms of their uses. Open space is divided into wetlands, forests, meadows, and rivers. Planners take the world as it is initially experienced and reimagine it in terms of categories that enable them to develop plans and regulations that frame subsequent interventions.

After breaking the city down into its activities, conditions, and places, planners then put it back together. Current thinking regarding the downtowns of US cities, for example, calls for

density, work-live space, sidewalk cafes, green buildings, arts districts, car sharing, townhouses, riverfront parks, calm streets, empty nesters.

The task for the planner is to organize these elements into a coherent whole and to do so in a specific city under existing economic, political, and demographic conditions.

In effect, planners aspire to a holism that requires a prior negation—an analytical deconstruction—without which, planners believe, understanding would be impossible. This disposition is reinforced by the placement of the planning function within the state. Governments desire control that will enable them to tax individuals, businesses, and property and to deliver services. This works best when they "see like a state" (Scott 1998); that is, through standardization, categorization, and large-scale data collection that monitors citizens, noncitizens, business activity, and property. Being part of the state solidifies planners' analytic impulse and makes it unlikely that they will stray from their fascination with being systematic, orderly, and rational.

This partially explains planning's avoidance of contingency and arbitrariness. Planning is nearly impossible in a contingent world where events happen randomly and consequences are unpredictable. Under these conditions, planners cannot choose rationally among alternative courses of action. With all consequences equally unknowable, all alternatives are equally unattractive. One does not need planning in such a world. In actuality, of course, planners are faced with uncertainty, ignorance, and contingency. Consequently, they struggle with how to adapt their procedures to conditions that often resist them.

Planners strive to reduce uncertainty through various technologies (for example, population projections, zoning code enforcement) and by aligning themselves with those who have the power and influence to coerce the world to behave a specific way. For this reason, they enter alliances with elected officials, government legislation, and business interests. Planners might lament the intrusion of politics, but they cannot escape it. They have to adapt to the politics that exist or act politically (Altshuler 1965). Consider a purist who sees politics as subverting understanding and undermining the reasonableness of planning advice. What she wants is a world in which the planning director approves a zoning ordinance that regulates vacant lots, the city council agrees, and developers, businesses, and households respond by investing in these properties, thereby curbing deterioration and producing a livable neighborhood. What she wants is a world alien to ontographers.

As a final comparison, consider the way ontographies implicitly challenge planning's humanism. Rather than envisioning a heterogeneous world where humans, technologies, and nature share responsibility and engage in collective action, planners take the stance that humans are privileged and act on the nonhuman (and human) world mainly for human benefit. Planning has a center, and it is occupied by men and women. In contrast, an ontographic perspective gives equal ontological status to nonhumans and thereby decenters collective action. Action always entails alliances, and alliances always require acting with migratory birds, levees, and government agencies. Even more important, an ontographic perspective treats nonhumans as potentially as influential as humans (Latour 1992, 1993). Planners are not so ready to concur. For them it is transportation planners, Metropolitan Planning Organizations, and automobile drivers on one side of the practice equation and cars, trucks, curb cuts, streets, traffic lights, air pollution, and parking spaces on the other.

In brief, a plannerly way of thinking exists. What I have described is a set of qualities that most planners would, in general, accept as distinguishing what they do from how nonplanners act, thereby separating them from other professionals such as architects and lawyers. Which of these are essential qualities and which are not is another matter. Nevertheless, if planning is to have any public meaning, it can neither be anything nor be everything (Wildavsky 1973). Insiders, of course, have a collective sense of what planning is and what planners do. They also disagree among themselves. Without an enforceable consensus, deviations from "best" practices are never severely punished. And while planning is neither ontographic nor singular, the ways to do planning are many, but not unbounded.

The absence of definitional integrity has implications for the practice of planning as well as for planning theory. In practice, much of what planners do seemingly could be done by others: policy analysts can do the analysis, urban designers can craft comprehensive visions of the physical city, geographers can investigate spatial distributions, consulting firms can forecast the future, architects can "animate" streets, and economists and business consultants can advise on infrastructure investments and ways to foster innovation and job growth (Perloff 1957, 32–34). Faced with the ever looming possibility that they are dispensable, planners have argued that their unique contribution is the ability to synthesize the knowledge of various experts around holistic understandings of the city (Beauregard 1990). Here is the vaunted claim to be "generalists with a specialty" (Perloff 1957, 35). More successful has been planners' adoption of land use and zoning regulations as their primary domain in the management of cities and regions. Land use lawyers might claim equivalent expertise—and greater prestige— but only planners work for "the public" on land use matters. In this way, planners have been able to partly overcome the status of being a minor profession, less influential and less in control than lawyers and doctors (Glaser 1974).

For planning theorists, the fuzziness of planning has been both a gift and a handicap. With planning an indeterminate, theoretical object, the field is open for writing many planning theories, from those that focus on process to those that focus on urban form (Allmendiger 2002; Yiftachel 1989). The result is a body of literature that is mainly characterized by its fragmentation. Every so often a particular perspective (for example, Marxist political economy in the 1970s and 1980s or communicative action in the 2000s) gains ascendance, but hovering nearby are others exploring the utility of Lacanian psychology, reasserting rationality at theory's core, or importing actor-network theory.

Yet planning is crisply articulated when inserted into ideological debates about the relative merits of markets, planning, and politics in public decision making (Lindblom 1977). In such public controversies, planning is viewed as having an integrity it seems to lack within the profession, or at least within academia. Planning is never so precisely defined as when it is being vilified and treated with contempt. For conservatives and neoliberals who celebrate markets as the best way to allocate private and public goods, planning is clearly the market's enemy. Planning substitutes the decisions of experts gathered in oppressive institutions for the free choices of individuals who best know their own preferences. Free to choose, any rational person will choose markets so they will be free to choose again.[17] Planning is also well defined when counterposed to democratic politics. The question is, Do we want to be ruled by experts, or should the people decide either through collective forums or through their democratically elected representatives? These are much different forms of governance.[18]

Ideological debates, however, serve mainly as deep background to the everyday planning that occurs in localities throughout the world. Every so often such debates erupt to challenge planners—often around the "taking" of property rights—but they are seldom part of planners' quotidian deliberations (Frick 2013). While such ideological disputes confer on planning a clearly defined identity, planners are averse to such rabid politics, finding them unwelcome. This is not to deny the democratic importance of public debates. In responding to them, however, planners need to present themselves less as truth-carrying experts and more as technically informed and active citizens. Such debates also suggest that planning might best be defined by what it is not:

spontaneous, present-oriented, intuitive, impetuous, self-serving, ad hoc, indifferent to place, irresponsible, individualistic, aspatial, disorderly, opportunistic, smug.

17. This is a reference to a book and ten-part television series by the famous conservative economist Milton Friedman. The book is *Free to Choose* (1980).
18. Wildavsky (1973, 132) muddles this distinction by declaring that "Planning is politics." This is not the same as saying that planning is political.

TWO

Talk, Action, and Consequences

In 1965 Alan Altshuler, then associate professor in political science at the Massachusetts Institute of Technology, began his seminal study of city planning in the United States by affirming that "the job of the city planner is to propose courses of action, not to execute them" (Altshuler 1965, 1). For many planners at that time, and likely today as well, this was a discomforting observation. Throughout its existence, the planning profession has been haunted by the fraught relation between plans and the consequences meant to follow. Believing themselves to be purveyors of good ideas, planners have become disgruntled by the mutations their advice undergoes as it is filtered through land use lawyers, architects, and financial analysts; the criticisms (sometimes helpful, sometimes not) mounted by individual citizens, business interests, and community groups; the accommodations required to gain approval from elected officials; and the unintended outcomes that ensue when their plans, now modified, are implemented. And for large projects, making matters worse, an indeterminable time often elapses between conception and completion.

Planners want to leave an imprint. They want their efforts to produce more compatible land uses, housing markets affordable for low-income families, floodplains devoid of development, diminished use of automobiles, and energy-efficient buildings. What planners intend when they plan are the consequences they deem beneficial. When these consequences are not forthcoming, planning seems incomplete, and they become frustrated (Beauregard 1980, 313–314). What good is a plan, practitioners and theorists ask, if it does not change the world? Planners' responsibility thus extends beyond crafting advice; they have to influence the actions required for plans to be accepted by publics, adopted and funded by government, and implemented by developers, public agencies, and households. From this perspective, planners fail when they are satisfied solely with good intentions (Baum 1980, 294). Altshuler implied the opposite—that planners are successful when they develop good plans and advice, regardless of what happens thereafter.

Judith Innes summarizes the dissent from Altshuler's position. She claims that "planners [are] actors in the world rather than observers or neutral experts" (Innes 1995, 184) and thereby implies, along with Dalton (1989), a responsibility not just for giving good advice but also for ensuring that the advice is taken and the intended consequences are realized. Yet this tells us very little about the actions that are peculiar to planning and thus about the troubled relationship between intentions and consequences. It is not obvious, given the thrust of planning thought, that planners are equipped to close, or even wish to close, the gap between planning and implementation (that is, carrying out or effectuating intentions). We expect planners to act, but what exactly do we expect them to do? Does the commitment to planning oblige planners to ensure that the consequences proposed are the consequences that result?

When planners practice their craft, prominent in what they do is talk.[1] This talk ranges across topics, but what makes it planning talk is more than offering reasons for what has been proposed. Intentions and consequences are fundamental to planning discourse. In this chapter we will explore the relation among talk, action, and consequences as prelude to considering in detail the activities involved in implementation as well as implementation's problematic place in planners' worldview. In addressing these issues, I draw on a number of case studies of practice, beginning with two insightful texts—by political scientist Alan Altshuler and planning theorist Bent Flyvbjerg—that reveal the daily activities of planners. I then discuss implementation, grounding the discussion in a case study from policy scientists Jeffrey Pressman

---

1. The commonly used word for the interrelated and routine activities in which professionals engage is "practice" (Beauregard 1980). Planners, lawyers, and doctors practice; carpenters, bus drivers, and store clerks work. See Reckwitz 2002 on the relation of practice to things and the body and how far practice is "more complex than 'knowing that'" (253).

and Aaron Wildavsky along with consideration of various instances when planners have become implementers. The overarching issue is whether planners can escape the pull of intentionality for the unknown rewards of consequences.[2]

What Planners Do

In *The City Planning Process* (1965), Altshuler presents four case studies of city planning, each involving the staff of the city planning department of either Minneapolis or St. Paul, Minnesota. The cases bear on the location of an inner-city freeway, development of a land-use plan, the siting of a hospital, and preparation of a plan for a central business district. Altshuler's primary concern was to understand the politics of planning. To satisfy it, he documented what the planners said and did as they carried out their responsibilities.[3]

Many of their activities revolved around a basic premise—that knowledge is the basis for action. Altshuler (1965, 55) writes the following about C. David Loeks, the planner involved in selecting the path of an intercity freeway in St. Paul: "He chose to study as much as resources permitted and to confine his recommendations to matters on which he had highly persuasive evidence." Loeks and his colleagues collected and analyzed data and then discussed the findings among themselves to develop a sense of the city and the issues facing it. For the St. Paul land-use plan, they made population estimates "to determine the future land-population ratios for each major category of land use" (Altshuler 1965, 105). This knowledge led to internal discussions about the recommendations to be conveyed to elected officials. It also became part of plans and reports that were shared with other agency personnel, various governing bodies, and community groups. Rodney Engelen, the lead planner for the Central Minneapolis plan, spent much of his time writing memorandums to a small group of business

2. Throughout this chapter I write mainly of planners who are employed by the government, where the great majority of US planners work (two-thirds in 2006). The rest are employed as private consultants (often working with clients to negotiate government regulations) or by nonprofit organizations (which often receive government funding) (Dalton 2007). For a planning theory text that focuses on a different category of planners, see Sandercock 2003.

3. Admittedly, these case studies are over fifty years old, and the practice of planning has changed. Altshuler also wrote about only two cities. However, contemporary descriptions of planners match quite closely, in overall form if not detail, what these planners were doing. Planners still make maps, even if GIS is now the preferred technology rather than pen and vellum. They still speak of blight, traffic congestion, and subdivision plans. And in defense of generality, St. Paul and Minneapolis were hardly outliers in how planning was being done.

and community leaders concerning the goals of the plan and how to present it to the public (Altshuler 1965, 242–246).

Planners devoted considerable effort to discussing their proposals with others inside and outside the planning department. They acted not as isolated individuals but as actors situated in organizational and social networks. Of particular importance were relations with the city's operating agencies such as public works and urban renewal. This social dimension of planning became most obvious when they scheduled and attended meetings, spoke in citizen forums, and presented their ideas to planning commissions and city councils. In these settings, they shared information, argued their case, parried criticisms, listened to suggestions, and refined their thinking. All of this involved being with and talking with others: listening, speaking, and deliberating. Reports were often the basis for this talk. For example, the planning staff assigned to the Central Minneapolis plan produced a "discussion draft" of its goals and solicited comments by sending four hundred copies to political and civic leaders and community organizations (Altshuler 1965, 236). The planners reviewed the comments and subsequently modified their recommendations, redrew the maps, redrafted the plans, and transmitted the revised documents to interested parties.

Often it became necessary for the planners to venture outside the office to attend meetings and visit sites. Carl Dale, the planner heading St. Paul's new land-use plan, "drove up and down every street in St. Paul, to get the 'feel' of each street and neighborhood, to note extraordinary features not shown on base maps, and to discover changes that had occurred since the maps had been drawn" (Altshuler 1965, 96).[4] Planning took place not only in the planning offices but also in a variety of places from neighborhood sidewalks to the conference rooms of civic organizations. By being in the world, engaging with the community, planners hoped to learn all they could and then to convince others of the soundness and sincerity of their proposals.

The planners stayed informed by reading technical documents, talking with planners from other cities, attending professional meetings, and maintaining their professional networks. The more senior planners' days were taken up with managing the department, hiring staff, and keeping track of the budget as well as meeting with their counterparts in other city departments and with elected officials and commu-

4. In the early 2000s, the director of city planning for New York City spent "endless hours walking the city's neighborhoods to learn their quirks" (Agovino 2009, 26) so as to be better prepared to undertake rezonings and establish design guidelines for developers.

nity groups. All their activities were meant to ensure that recommendations and plans had public support and would be adopted by the mayor and the city council either in the form of new laws and regulations or as projects that would be funded and implemented. Thinking strategically, Altshuler (1965, 196) noted, the planners in Minneapolis aimed every proposal "at a specific audience of potential allies . . . [with] . . . each audience . . . chosen largely for its capacity to bring proposals to fruition, without antagonizing too many other potential audiences." Their goal was to influence the actions that shaped the physical form of the city and the forces that governed its development.

Consider a second illustration of what planners do. This one is drawn from Flyvbjerg's (1998) case study of an initiative by the city government of Aalborg, Denmark, to relocate a bus terminal and redesign traffic patterns in the city's downtown. The planners in Aalborg behaved much like those in St. Paul and Minneapolis thirty years earlier.[5] Documenting current conditions (doing research), gathering information from secondary sources, and analyzing and assessing data constituted the basis of all their subsequent activities. For the Aalborg planners, a twenty-six-page memorandum analyzing seven possible locations for the bus terminal was the core of their proposal (Flyvbjerg 1998, 20). In attempting to persuade government departments to support their ideas and elected officials to give their approval, they constantly referred to good planning principles and to the facts on the ground as they understood them. In commenting on the need to convince one alderman that he should support the project, the chief of planning said: "If we are to get something done about which he is not convinced already, a strong documentation will be necessary. If it is something which we know he supports, then we in fact do not need to have very much documentation" (Flyvbjerg 1998, 33). Writing memorandums and reports, preparing plans, and explaining these documents to possible allies, while defending them against critics, filled much of their workday. To do this, they had to talk among themselves and with others, focusing on what should be done to ensure that their advice was adopted.

Task forces of various experts were formed, telephone calls placed, committee meetings organized and attended, and public presentations made. The planners persuaded, negotiated, deliberated, decided, and

5. The institutional setting in Denmark is not that of the United States, but the daily activities of planners do not differ significantly, although Danish planners (and planners in Western Europe generally) seem more engaged in physical planning and project design than planners in the United States.

explained. They strove to cooperate and shunned confrontations that would harm them politically, though these were often unavoidable. As one planner noted, "It is awfully regrettable, I think, but you know, it's all political. [Constructing a square] produces a few more votes than some bike paths. The alderman himself admitted this when I asked why" (Flyvbjerg 1998, 197). They also responded to criticism with letters to newspapers and spoke with their critics, while striving not to become emotionally involved. They answered requests and applied for approvals from various agencies. Much of what they did consisted of thinking with others; all their actions—attending meetings, making presentations—were opportunities to explain and persuade.

The Aalborg planners recognized that their position in the deliberations was constrained by their being staff to the elected and appointed officials and not part of an operating agency. As the chief of city planning commented, "We have no capital construction budget. And it is a thesis I have that he who controls the capital construction budget has the power. . . . City planning will always be dependent on sectoral planning, and sectoral planning is the planning which controls the budget. . . . It is sector planning which determines when things are implemented, not us. . . . We have only persuasion, only argument and persuasion, as a weapon" (Flyvbjerg 1998, 40).[6] Planners' frustrations also surfaced when politics derailed their efforts: "It is unsatisfactory to participate in a task for 2–3 years with an infinite number of meetings, studies, memoranda and reports, and afterwards experience that a relatively undocumented polemic in the press and pressure from, among others, the Chamber of Industry and Commerce . . . leads to a puncturing of a plan which has been approved by a nearly unanimous City Council" (Flyvbjerg 1998, 133).

These brief illustrations demonstrate that much of planning practice is about talk (Healey 1992; Hoch 1996).[7] Planners talk about ideas; about relationships with other agencies, elected officials, citizens, and interest groups; and about and with things such as reports, maps, newspapers, and budget documents. Planners also manipulate things when they produce written documents in hard copy, print out GIS maps, post drawings on walls, make telephone calls, record data, and develop

6. By sectoral planning, he is referring to agencies that deliver services. A planner in the United States made a similar comment within the context of a community-based planning study (Needleman and Needleman 1974, 246): "But when the planner doesn't have federal money, he must depend on other city departments. He's at their mercy."

7. Planners also think, silently and aloud. The act of contemplation—how one does it, when, with what aids—is a topic generally ignored in planning theory.

visual presentations. And they move about in space when they travel to attend committee meetings, public hearings, and citizen forums. Most important, talk is a way of linking knowledge to action. It is not all talk, but talk is mainly what planners do.

Intentions, Knowledge, Action

Is not talk, though, somehow distinct from actions that achieve real, material consequences? My sense is that most people believe talk and action are not the same. Consider an anecdote involving US President Barak Obama in 2011 (Coll 2013, 20). In commenting on the US government's concurrence in the deployment of NATO fighter jets to protect civilians in a war-torn Libya, Obama remarked, "When the entire international community almost unanimously says that there is a potential humanitarian crisis about to take place, we can't simply stand by with empty words. We have to take some sort of action." This distinction takes a more prosaic form: "Don't just talk, do something!"[8] Talk simply does not seem like action. One can persuade, but others, it seems, have to act so that the plans and advice become real. When they do not, planning is somehow incomplete. Widely acknowledged, moreover, is how talk and action diverge. As Fuller (2000, 7) comments, "To be sure, the loose and often reconstructed (perhaps even fabricated) character of what we say in relation to what we do is a common feature of everyday life."

Talk, of course, is action. Latour (2005b, 71) defines an actor as *"any thing* that does modify a state of affairs by making a difference," that is, by changing the relations among actors. Action is any behavior that has effects—that produces consequences for oneself or others and thus engenders a response. By this definition, talk qualifies as action.[9] It weaves together various forces (Latour 2005b, 74) to establish new juxtapositions of actors and thereby to modify perceptions, motivations, and constraints. Thus, while talk is not the physical removal of a building addition that is in violation of the zoning, the actual signing of documents that commit bond financing to a light rail transit project, or marching in front of a beloved building slated for demolition, it (like action) changes the world in some way.

8. Zizek (2009, 11) deems this "one of the most stupid things one can say, even measured by the low standards of common sense."

9. This would also make teaching a kind of action, thereby casting a different light on the aspersion that "those who can't do, teach."

Networks of actors are often, but not always, different after planners have spoken. Speaking shapes attention, shifts perceptions, inclines people to reassert or modify their positions, and reveals new possibilities for acting together with other humans and nonhuman things (Forester 1989, 137–162). When a St. Paul planner met with a member of the Site Committee of the Ancker Hospital Commission to voice his reservations about certain sites being considered and to propose that a particular site be selected, the committee member took the proposal to the committee and argued in its favor (Altshuler 1965, 144–188). The planner's reasoning became part of the deliberations. Similarly, when the planners in Aalborg suppressed a report critiquing the position of the Social Democrats regarding downtown development (when they decided not to talk further about it), they did so to maintain good political relations. Knowing that they would have to work with the Social Democrats in the future and that releasing the report might cause animosity, they acted with discretion (Flyvbjerg 1998, 170–171). Additional talk would have been injurious.

Talk and action are intertwined. Action not accompanied by talk, as the philosopher Hannah Arendt (1958, 178) has written, "would not only lose its revelatory character, but, and by the same token, it would lose its subject." In order to do things with others, we need to communicate with them. Talk is what conveys the reasons for acting. We can act alone and impulsively, but acting collectively with other humans almost always requires sharing knowledge and experience along with intentions and a sense of the consequences one hopes to realize. Acting together also creates additional knowledge and leads to more talk.

What planners talk about, then, is saturated with the knowledge they have gathered and then analyzed, the planning ideas they learned in school and gathered from experience, and assessments of the political and socioeconomic feasibility of their proposals. In short, to perform effectively, planners need knowledge. This relationship between knowledge and action, however, raises two issues. The first is whether knowledge does or does not precede action. The second is how knowledge is actually connected to action's consequences. Many decades ago, Friedmann and Hudson (1974, 2) wrote that the core activity of planning is the "linkage between knowledge and organized action." That linkage is not solely a theoretical matter; it has practical consequences as well. But what are they?

One way to think through this issue is to ask whether knowledge precedes action or action precedes knowledge. The question is not meant as a riddle: it is a serious inquiry related to how planners learn about the world, maintain objectivity, and act democratically.[10] If knowledge precedes action, this justifies planners' withdrawing into their offices to gather and analyze data and develop recommendations before creating task forces, setting up meetings, releasing reports, and speaking to public audiences. Planners retreat to a world in-here to do their knowledge work and travel out-there only to search for validation and support. In this way they become detached from the politicized realm of daily life. Subsequent engagement with the city's residents is circumscribed, since the planners have settled their assumptions and formulated their recommendations, even if tentatively. No matter how open to modification, these assumptions and recommendations, because they have been talked about and agreed on within the planning world, will resist substantive change. This particular interpersonal theory of action, as Schon (1982, 360–361) describes it, attempts to achieve the task as it has been defined, unilaterally control that task, and ensure that the planner's advice is adopted.

What about a different relationship—that action precedes knowledge? This does not mean acting impulsively, without forethought. Rather, it points to the need to engage the world in order to learn about it. As Sayer (1992, 13) has written, "Knowledge is primarily gained through activity both in attempting to change our environment (through labor or work) and through interaction with other people, using shared resources, in particular a common language." Relying solely on theories—always severely limited in their predictive power— is ill-advised. For example, in Aalborg the Chamber of Industry and Commerce opposed a proposal to close an intersection along a major shopping street based on the argument that it would lessen traffic and reduce the number of shoppers, thereby lowering retail spending (Flyvbjerg 1998, 197–199). The intersection was closed and traffic volume decreased, but shopping was undiminished. Action yielded understandings that, until then, had only been predicted. Planners can draw on theory and experience, but there is no substitute for actually acting in the world.[11] To confine gathering knowledge to reading reports, collecting data, and speaking with others seems an unnecessary constraint. Moreover, if planners assume they can act only when they have sufficient knowledge, including knowledge of the consequences,

10. By objectivity I mean reflection on one's actions and their consequences, not disengagement—the opposite of an individualized subjectivity.

11. This description closely follows American pragmatism (Hoch 1984) and is also related to the insights of Lindblom's (1959) "muddling through," and the experimental methodologist Donald Campbell's call for an experimenting society (Dunn 1998).

they fall victim to what Lindblom (1959) labeled one of the debilitating qualities of the rational model—the paralysis of not knowing. To comprehend the consequences of action with any certainty, the planner has to act.

The second issue has to do with how knowledge is connected to action and to consequences. The linkage between knowledge and action is neither obvious nor direct. When considered in terms of the relation of intention to consequences, the claim is much too schematic. How does knowledge become intention? How is intention translated into the actions that produce desired consequences? It would be more accurate to state that the purpose of planning is to turn knowledge into shared intentions, shared intentions into collective actions, and collective actions into desired consequences.[12]

Of course, no single path exists from knowledge to intentions to actions and then to consequences. For a start, not all knowledge is of equal value, so we have to determine the specific knowledge that actually matters. Often, though, we know what matters only after we have engaged with the world we wish to change. In addition, knowing the world is not the same as knowing what to do about what one knows. A specific intention does not automatically follow from studying, defining, and describing a condition of concern. It reveals little about what might actually be done. Take as an example a community development corporation with an antigentrification policy designed to minimize the influx of residents with higher incomes than those living in the neighborhood, block involuntary displacement, and forestall rising property taxes. It could lobby the city council for rent controls, speak before the planning board when developers submit their proposals for new residential buildings in the neighborhood, picket construction sites, or attempt to fill empty lots with affordable housing. What it chooses to do will depend on the resources it commands, its organizational mission, community support, the development dynamics in the neighborhood, and support or opposition from elected officials. Knowledge is the basis for action, but not a sole guide. Deriving what ought to be done from what is poses a variety of difficulties, not least negotiating ideological predispositions for certain types of action over others.[13] The relation

12. The scheme is completed, in policy analytic terms, with an assessment of the consequences so as to generate more knowledge. I have stated it in linear (nonrecursive) form only for rhetorical purposes.

13. The is/ought conundrum is usually associated with the philosopher David Hume (Pigden 2011). My position is that moral choices can be reasonably argued with and justified, in part, by empirical evidence.

between an undesirable condition and an appropriate response has to be crafted out of more than technical knowledge.

Intentions are antecedents to action; this is what is meant by policy, "a broad statement of goals and objectives" (Pressman and Wildavsky 1973, xx). Consider that city planning agencies intend to enforce zoning regulations. This is government policy, and as with all policies, slippage often occurs between intention and realization. The agency might lack the staff to monitor zoning infractions, lack the enforcement capacity to remove infractions and punish offenders, or be overruled by the planning commission. In short, planners can intend to act but not produce the consequences they had promised. The former director of city planning for New Orleans, Louisiana, pointed to this discontinuity when she wrote that "each and every good intention [that] a plan includes requires a local government to take specific action to bring the intention about" (Ford 2010, 93). The decision to act is influenced by factors beyond the deliberations of planners. Action does not flow automatically from good intentions.

If planners, then, wish to reject Altshuler's description of them as solely advice givers, they need to have ways of turning intentions into actions (Alexander 2001). This is where consequences become important. Ideally, planners should opt to do what best achieves the desired consequences; that is, follow the rules of instrumental rationality. Theory will be of some use, maybe. If fines are levied on architects who violate zoning regulations, then increasing the cost to architects and the developers who employ them should cause both to adhere to the regulations. The experiences of other planning agencies are helpful as well: How have they managed to minimize zoning violations? The planner might also engage in talk, meeting with architects and developers to discuss how they view the regulations and how best to achieve conformance. By moving back and forth between possible actions and likely consequences, the planners can devise regulations more attuned to the actors and conditions at hand.

From this perspective, all action is distributed action. As Latour (1999, 288) has written, "Action is not what people do, but is instead the '*fait faire*,' the making-do accomplished along with others." He means two things by this. First, when the planner acts, she interacts not only with other humans but also with nonhuman things. Action is heterogeneous, always occurring with tools and objects. The planner from the community development corporation goes to a city council meeting armed with pages of research findings, photographs of high-income apartment buildings, and residents who can attest to displace-

TALK, ACTION, AND CONSEQUENCES

ment. She does not go alone but brings along both human and nonhuman allies. Planning and its politics are object oriented (Latour 2005a); they are all about things.

Second, Latour has something equally profound in mind—action is networked (Bennett 2010, 20–38; Healey 1993, 238). Actors engender responses that reverberate throughout the networks in which they are situated. These responses are themselves actions, with the thick intricacy of these collective endeavors blurring easy identification of the sources of initiatives. Intentionality thus becomes a frail guide to understanding. Subjectivity is not simply extended to things; the subject/object distinction is itself dissolved (Khong 2003; Latour 1999, 197). Action is a property of alliances and networks, not of individual actors.

In this sense actions are overtaken by their consequences. They are "not reducible to the motives, goals, and intents of those who carry them out" (Disch 1994, xi). The community development corporation's antigentrification policy might lead to a local councilman using it to advance his own interests, while property owners and some residents might speak against a policy the corporation believes was designed to improve the neighborhood. The corporation's efforts are overrun by events. Action is never mastery; we are never in full control (Latour 2005b, 43–46). Rather, action is always boundless and a surprise, producing consequences we neither anticipated nor intended. It is "the spontaneous beginning of something new, because its results fall into a predetermined net of relationships, invariably dragging the agent with them, who seems to forfeit his freedom, the very moment he makes use of it" (Arendt 1958, 234).

Knowledge, then, does not automatically lead to action. More likely, a planner intends to act, develops the knowledge that justifies that intention and then searches for and crafts actions to realize it. At other times she is attracted to a solution and looks for a matching problem, or a new actor or novel condition appears and a discarded solution or an old problem becomes relevant again. This is different from saying that the purpose of planning is to connect knowledge to action. The path between the two is circuitous and incalculable.[14]

Before taking up how planners might move beyond intention to consequences, I want to reflect briefly on how planners expect planners to act. What qualities of action are most valued? I think there are four: intentionality, reflexivity, accountability, and responsibility (Gid-

14. Kingdon (2003) captures this in his argument concerning how policy ideas, policy communities, and policy problems become aligned.

dens 1982, 30–32; 1984, 5–16). To be a planner, a person must act intentionally, reflect on and learn from her actions, be accountable to others, and recognize her responsibilities to publics.[15] These qualities apply to talk and to nonverbal actions such as forming a task force or releasing a report to the public. They are also quite general and thus not confined to planners. What matters is how planners fuse these qualities into an identity.

Before they act, then, we expect planners to have a sense of what they hope to accomplish; that is, to act purposively and thus in relation to goals. This indicates both thoughtfulness and seriousness. Though good intentions are never an acceptable substitute for desirable consequences, they nonetheless carry weight. And while intentions can also be controversial, as when a viable neighborhood is demolished to build a sports stadium, intentional action is preferred to impulsiveness. Second, we expect planners to have thought about what they are about to say and do, the responses likely to be engendered, and how this knowledge might modify their ideas and enable them to do better. Such reflection is highly valued. Not only does it reinforce intentionality, it also implies a commitment to learning and improvement (reform), two qualities central to planning practice.

Third, we expect planners to give reasons for their actions. Giving reasons allows their intentions to be questioned and their actions made accountable (Tilly 2006). The statement "we did this because" shows respect for others. Moreover, it contributes to democratic deliberations by signaling that others matter. Planners should be willing to explain their recommendations and thought processes and expose them to public criticism. Then nonplanners can join in the discussion of whether those recommendations and the reasons behind them are acceptable. Last, we expect planners to act in responsible ways, giving due consideration to their place in the world and to the necessary and constant repair and strengthening of the moral fabric that enables us to live well with others. Planners must take responsibility for their actions and act responsibly as regards the world's injustices.

All of this said, we are not much beyond Altshuler's characterization of planners as those who propose so that others can act. I have merely pointed out that planners are constantly acting, in part because they are constantly talking. Moreover, their talk—and not speaking out

15. Although too unequivocal, Zizek (2008, 83) makes a similar observation: "Human acts are rationally intentional and accountable in terms of the belief and desires of the agent." My list of qualities, moreover, assumes fixed subjectivities, whereas the subjectivity of planners is likely to change as they act—in fact, to be defined by their actions.

when it seems counterproductive—has consequences. In short, I have brought action into planning but have not addressed the frustration planners feel because their plans and advice are often unrealized. This requires a different discussion, one that begins with the issue of implementation and considers whether planning practice can and should be extended beyond what is done to whether it is done at all.

From Intentions to Consequences

What does it mean to make something happen? What tasks are involved? If we can understand the activities associated with implementation, then we can consider whether this is what planners ought to do.

An outstanding text on the topic is Pressman and Wildavsky's (1973) aptly titled *Implementation*.[16] The authors present a rich case study of a federal government initiative that was overseen by the Economic Development Administration (EDA) of the time. The goal was to generate jobs through public works projects at the Port of Oakland in California. Pressman and Wildavsky focus on the actions that occur after an issue has been identified, goals have been set, a plan has been produced and adopted, and funding has been committed. These are the initial conditions, they write, that enable actions to be taken so that intended consequences can be achieved.

This segmentation of proposal from execution echoes Altshuler's claim and conforms closely to how planners view their activities. Planners develop plans and proposals and then advocate for them before various individuals and groups. More specifically, they identify conditions requiring action, formulate goals, and specify the broad actions (for example, increase in building code enforcement, height restrictions on high-rise apartment buildings) to achieve those goals and produce the desired consequences. Once that is done, they appear before neighborhood groups, planning commissions, and city councils to present their proposals and listen to comments. All the while, planners work to convince their audiences of the soundness of their ideas, hoping to persuade the governing body to adopt their proposal and dedicate funding for its implementation. And although advocacy and persuasion—political activities—were considered outside the scope of planning when the rational-comprehensive model was ascendant,

16. For a good overview of the multiple dimensions of implementation, see Van Meter and Van Horn 1975.

they are now recognized as crucial to planning's realization. Following successful policy adoption and program funding are the tasks of implementation.

One of the implementation stories told by Pressman and Wildavsky involved the construction of a new marine terminal. To begin, the EDA hired a consultant to negotiate with the Port about providing bay fill for the terminal site. Then, because the EDA disbursed funds only after a project was completed, the Port staff worked with banks to obtain interim financing. For various reasons, the original site was deemed undesirable, and the Port and EDA had to agree to relocate the terminal. Architectural and engineering contracts had to be written by the Port's lawyers, firms hired, and preliminary plans produced and accepted. Other regulatory agencies had to be consulted and approvals obtained. The US Navy, for example, was concerned with how the terminal would affect flight paths to its nearby airfield, and it had to certify the project. Contracts were let for dredging and fill, and the work was done and monitored. Contractors were hired to construct the building, and the construction was overseen by Port staff. On completion of the terminal, grants had to be drawn down from the EDA, permanent loan financing arranged, personnel hired, and management procedures put in place for the terminal's operation.

This schematic depiction of events emphasizes the major decision points for moving from a proposal for a new marine terminal to its realization. The most eventful activities were securing commitments from actors to do certain things (for example, sign a contract, give an approval) at specific times. A bank had to agree to provide interim financing so the Port could request contractors to bid on the project; the Navy had to endorse the site so construction could begin; the dredging company had to finish so the terminal could open; and, throughout the process, the EDA had to approve changes expeditiously so the project could stay on schedule. At each of these decision points, agreement had to be reached among various actors. Project commitments, however, frequently deteriorate over time. Consider a few possibilities. The bank agrees to provide interim financing, but then the Port fails to develop a detailed cost estimate or secure EDA grants quickly enough for the bank to maintain its previous agreement. Poor weather delays the contractor providing the bay fill, and this prevents the terminal contractor from starting the next stage of the project. In response, the terminal contractor shifts machinery and workers to another job.

Pressman and Wildavsky thus define implementation in terms of this complexity of joint action, the tendency for commitments to erode, and the many ways for delay to breed further delay. All threaten the completion of the project. Implementation requires that agreements be made and that actions occur in a timely manner. When this does not happen, and because any project entails an array of interconnected actions, implementation slows so that agreements unravel and have to be renegotiated.

I am less concerned with the argument about the difficulties of realizing a complex project than with the actions required for commitments to be obtained, nurtured, and realized.[17] If planners wish to contribute to fulfilling the plans and proposals they have crafted, they must be involved in effecting agreements, coordinating commitments, and assessing progress. These actions, however, do not look that much different from the actions required to create the plans and proposals. Applying for regulatory approvals, mediating contracts, monitoring performance, developing budgets, and submitting grant requests might involve specific technical knowledge (for example, of bore-resistant pilings) that planners lack, but what is mostly being done is talk. Implementation requires meetings, discussions, presentations, negotiations, gathering and analyzing data, listening, and persuasion—all of which planners are trained to do. It also requires forethought and technical knowledge. Even planners working outside the government and intent on being engaged and having an impact find themselves mainly doing analysis, attending meetings, and commenting publicly, even if they also walk in picket lines, post flyers around the neighborhood, and clean up the trash on an empty lot. One such planner (Hartman 2002, 20) wrote: "We met with community group clients, prepared professional critiques of official plans, drew up alternative plans with the community . . . [and then] publicized the issues, and testified at public hearings."

Because the core tasks of implementation are similar to those for making plans, planners find it relatively easy to work in nontraditional settings, neither government planning agencies nor private consulting firms. Employed by community development organizations, economic development corporations, police or fire departments, housing or transportation agencies, or recreation departments, they conduct research and craft proposals and engage in actions to implement them. When the New York City Department of Transportation undertook the

---

17. Implicit here is that planners are not going to operate the dredging crane, bolt steel beams to steel columns, or write the contract language for interim financing. This is not what they are trained to do, and it is best done by others.

development of a bike sharing program in 2008, it needed to assess its feasibility, obtain city council and mayoral approval, put together a budget, assign staff, identify sites, work with local communities to have the sites approved, write and publish a request for proposals to solicit bike vendors, review the proposals of different vendors, select the vendor, identify a private sponsor, monitor the placement of bike stations, publicize the program, manage the "balancing" of bikes across stations and neighborhoods, and gather data on usage. All of these are implementation tasks, tasks that realize a proposal, and all are easily done—and many were done—by planners.

Even planning departments have become involved in implementation, although the examples are few.[18] In the 1960s Edmund Bacon, then director of the Philadelphia City Planning Commission, attempted to extend his influence beyond simply proposing redevelopment projects; he also wanted to design them and be involved in their implementation (Garvin 2002; G. Heller 2013). For the Penn Center office development across from City Hall, he proposed a below-grade retail concourse open to the sky and stipulated the orientation of the office towers, while for the Society Hill redevelopment project he designed a series of public greenways to weave through the centers of blocks and among the low-rise townhouses. In the late 1960s, the San Francisco Department of City Planning took on the management of a citywide program of recreation, open space, and beautification. In doing so, it limited its activities to seeking funding and overseeing the program and thus avoided becoming "involved in detailed designs of projects, in letting contracts, in construction, or in operating any facility" (Jacobs 1978, 94). More recently, Frieden and Sagalyn (1989) have described the turn to deal making in redevelopment planning, noting that large projects are constantly being modified and that planners are engaged in negotiating with real estate developers as projects are implemented. Commitments regarding design, subsidies, and public benefits need unflagging attention, and this blurs the boundary between proposal and execution.

In effect, no barriers of skill or knowledge impede planners from becoming more involved in implementation. Why is it, then, that planning agencies in the United States have been reluctant to do so and that government planners remain frustrated by their seeming inability

18. In the United Kingdom and Western Europe, government planning agencies have traditionally had more responsibility for project planning than have those in the United States, often stemming from their control over land and development permits (Verhage 2003).

to bring their plans to fruition? Two factors deserve mention. One is institutional and the other concerns the planner's self-image. First, at least within the United States, planning has been mainly considered as a staff function within government and as a consultancy outside government (Perloff 1957, 6–7, 28–32). Its purpose is to advise decision makers, who then direct their agents to act. This leads to the division of responsibilities among planners, who give expert advice to a decision maker, who then instructs his implementers, "who sometimes succeed and sometimes fail to bring about the policies the experts help elaborate" (Benveniste 1977, 7), to carry out the necessary tasks. This tripartite distinction is manifested institutionally by making planning agencies advice-giving entities rather than operating entities that manage programs. Planners in city planning agencies do not implement or administer: they propose. The same cannot be said for planners employed by housing agencies or sanitation departments. And even though city governments have become more entrepreneurial in the United States and more involved in development projects, they have assigned these responsibilities to economic development authorities or urban redevelopment agencies and not to city planning departments.

Second, planners (but not all) are reluctant to take up program implementation because it hinders their ability to range across the issues facing the city. Planners imagine their contribution as offering a holistic perspective on the city, as being comprehensive.[19] The city, not any of its functions, is their primary concern. If they are engaged in program operations, such as waterfront management or bike sharing, this possibility is suppressed. Moreover, establishing and managing programs is time consuming and detracts from the effort required to plan. Ceding the latter seems to deny a significant part of the planner's identity. By taking responsibility for the consequences of the actions they have proposed, planners give up responsibility for the whole city and become just another government agency with a limited agenda.

Progressive Possibilities

Planners face a dilemma. To become involved in implementation is to weaken the ability to make broad proposals about the city and its

19. A substantial percentage of planners employed outside governments and planning consultancies are advocacy planners. Having rejected any responsibility for the whole city, they have instead committed to the needs of a specific community (for example, the South Bronx) or a single issue (for example, urban farming).

development. Yet if planners eschew execution of their plans, they risk frustration and public criticism when implementation is incomplete, faulty, or nonexistent. When implementation fails—when a new zoning regulation, for example, does not halt excessive development—planners seem ineffectual and even inconsequential. That much of this is self-criticism does not make it any less serious an issue. How might we think about this choice that is no longer simply between talk and action but between formulating proposals and realizing them?

We can gain some understanding of this issue by turning to critical social theory and the progressive and radical planning associated with it (Calhoun 1995; Lefebvre 1968, 25–58). Critical social theory can be usefully contrasted with logical positivism. Whereas logical positivists believe that the human experience of the world is a truthful rendition of it, critical theorists argue that what we experience is not all that exists. To understand what is happening, we have to "go behind" the reality we experience and discover the logics that lie below the surface and are hidden from us (Baert 2005, 110).[20] This is not a claim about deception and propaganda or about flawed human perception, but rather a claim that what is does not have to be. A disjuncture exists between the actual and the possible (Brenner 2009, 203). The world could have been, and can be, different. To accept what we experience as inevitable is to embrace a conservatism that refuses to question what has happened. In contrast, a critical theorist tries to understand why certain outcomes occurred given that so many others were possible. The implications for planners should be obvious.

Most progressive theories of planning are critical theories. They call for a material world radically different from the one we have (Fainstein 2010; Friedmann 1987, 389–412; Kraushaar 1988; Marcuse 2009). Reform—that is, incremental change—they argue, leaves intact the logics and structures that perpetuate social ills. Hence these social ills have to be continually ameliorated. Poverty, unemployment, food insecurity, environmental degradation, and residential segregation persist because mainstream planners address the world as it is presented to them. They fail to confront the logics and structures that are deeply embedded in our daily lives. These structural injustices create and perpetuate problems that have to be solved again and again. If any significant change is to occur, planners have to be more critical.

For progressive planners this means embracing progressive values

20. In discussing practice, Mao Tse-tung (1965, 6) wrote that "perception only solves the problem of phenomena; theory alone can solve the problem of essence."

and supporting grassroots political action. Their primary focus is on inequalities and injustices, and their political commitment is to helping the people who suffer from them. And while at first glance this seems no different from a reform-oriented planning, it diverges by rejecting any planning that privileges economic growth and relies on the trickling down of benefits to those in need. Such planning, progressive planners maintain, is designed to serve real estate developers, investors, financial institutions, and corporations first (or primarily), before attending to those with fewer resources, fewer choices, and lessened prospects. Being progressive means making a political commitment to planning for justice. The city's planners should be judged not in terms of whether they make the city more livable (often code for "desirable to the middle class") or more attractive to investors, but whether they make it more just. This often compels progressive planners to reject government employment and private consultancies and instead work for community-based organizations and advocacy groups whose mission and ideology they share.

Strong on specifying what moral positions should be taken, radical and progressive planning theories are weak on specifying the actions that will be required. Flyvbjerg (2001, 167), for example, calls for a phronetic planning whose purpose is "to contribute to society's practical rationality in elucidating where we are, where we want to go, and what is desirable." Marcuse (2009, 194) stipulates the tasks of a radical planning as to expose, to propose, and to politicize, with the last aimed at "supporting organizing around the proposals by informing action." Friedmann (1987, 389) agrees. He urges radical planners to interpret structural problems critically, chart forward-looking perspectives, elaborate images of preferred outcomes, and suggest strategy.

Progressive planners, then, are just as prone as mainstream planners to focus on the proposal side of the proposal/execution divide. Their concern is with what we should value politically, assuming that if the values are right, then the appropriate actions to realize them will be obvious. In practice, the dilemma is resolved by those who work for organizations that engage in direct action by operating homeless shelters or lobbying state and local governments for rent controls to slow gentrification. On the theory side, the solutions are either to point to protest movements as the place where progressive and radical planning can thrive or to call for planning that empowers marginalized communities. This means more than building constituencies for progressive planning. It also means building political coalitions and progressive networks that can pressure governments to act democratically, resist unwanted incursions, and foster collective action. I suspect, though, that progressive planners are just as frustrated with the lack of consequences as mainstream planners. They also seem as reluctant as mainstream planners to shift planning away from its core activities.

This reluctance suggests an insight that we should honor—proposing progressive possibilities for what we should do is as important as realizing what is already feasible (if not more important). The world needs more talk about how to act in just and democratic ways. Talk should be used to create progressive possibilities and "to undermine those in power with patient ideologio-critical work" (Zizek 2009, 7). City and regional planners—knowledgeable about the workings of regions, cities, and neighborhoods—are one source of ideas. If what is done is simply what seems obvious and appropriate, then planners risk becoming like the logical positivists; that is, behaving as if what is has to be. A primary function of planners should be to generate proposals for how to make the city more just, and then to attract public support by advocating for them. In this way, planners will not only be using their knowledge and skills but tapping into the field's now-defunct utopian tradition as well.

What planners do best is to think about the city and how it can be improved. What they have to do better is to engage—transparently and democratically—with publics.[21] Criticism, distortion of their ideas, and rejection will follow, but they are reasons for neither withdrawal nor frustration. In addition, engaging with publics is not simply a matter of seeking out people who are dissatisfied. People are encumbered with social relations, tools and technology, nature, and ideas. They do not come to meetings alone. Consequently, planners have to plan not only with people but with people in networks of humans and nonhuman things. Publics are always heterogeneous. Such are the intricacies of taking public action in democratic societies. To flee from this to the world of implementation would be to abandon the very idea of planning.

---

21. Unmentioned here, but not trivial, are the institutional limitations that government planners, consultants, and community-based advocates have to overcome to do what I suggest.

THREE

Planning with Things

The world of planning is filled with office buildings and stop signs, cell phone towers and housing estates, sewers, train stations and airports, hydroelectric dams, and plazas. This is obvious and would hardly come as a surprise to any practicing planner. Most planners spend their days thinking and talking about the things—buildings, structures, landforms, and infrastructures—that give the city its physical presence.

Planning's history is replete with examples testifying to the importance of such objects. Outdoor privies spurred housing reformers in the late nineteenth century. Skyscrapers and the spread of garment factories a few decades later motivated citizens in New York City to call for zoning regulations. Bombs and rubble led to reconstruction efforts in numerous European cities after World War II, and suburban shopping malls in the United States induced planners in the 1960s and 1970s to worry about the visual clutter of commercial strips. In these and numerous other instances, planners acted in response to problems inseparable from the material world. As solutions were devised, new things were added: playgrounds, greenbelts, office plazas, bike lanes, and retention ponds, to name just a few.

This talk and this history have been ignored by most planning theorists.[1] They spin their theoretical webs without snaring the physical objects that make planning both

1. My criticism is directed at the academic planning theories that emerged in the 1950s and thereafter, not with the theory-in-use deployed by planners before that time. Using my argument to understand the planners of that earlier period would mean addressing Murdoch's (2006, 132) claim that "early in its

necessary and useful. The things planned, the tools deployed, and the settings where practice occurs are of little theoretical interest. Rather, planning theorists privilege human actors. Their objective is to explain how planners might change the world and, because planning is inherently prescriptive, change it for the better. But for theorists then to ignore much of that world seems irresponsible. By omitting materiality from their theories (by treating it as contextual or epiphenomenal and thus causally irrelevant), planning theorists neglect the important role things play in giving presence to and mediating the social interactions without which planning itself could not exist. Consequently, the practices they propose, whether they center on negotiation, analysis, or community organizing, omit far too many actors.[2]

My goal in this chapter is to rectify this shortcoming by exploring how nonhuman things matter in planning practice. In doing so, I focus on planning deliberations where talk is the medium through which accommodations are made, what Forester (1999, x) has labeled the micropolitics of practice. We will appraise a typical planning event in which a group of planners and a developer and his consultants negotiate the composition of a proposed apartment complex. Central to their deliberations were nonhuman things whose presence or absence affected the content of deliberations, each participant's perception of the others' commitments, and their common understanding of the project. Without such substantive talk, commitment, and shared perspectives, acting together is nearly impossible. In such situations, planning deliberations are at best unproductive and at worst an impediment to future collaboration.

A Lost World

In the practice realm imagined by almost all planning theorists, humans are the only meaningful actors. Businesses, organizations, social groups, and government agencies contend with and contribute to industrial decentralization, predatory lending, blight, sprawl, and traffic congestion. Practitioners engage these actors to create sustainable environments, walkable cities, congestion-free roadways, and affordable

development planning *successfully incorporated* [my emphasis] physical entities," a claim about which I have doubts.

2. My casting the problem in terms of a "missing" material world comes from Latour 1992. For a discussion of the "missing masses" in urban theory, see Beauregard 2011; in geography, see Murdoch 1998.

housing. Consequently, the purpose of theory is to understand how planners act alone and with other individuals and their organizations to do so. For these theorists, only humans matter.[3]

Yet things are not wholly absent from the writings of planning theorists. Theorists situate planners in actual settings, comment on the things being planned, and reflect on planning's consequences. In explaining the intricacies of persuasive argumentation, for example, Throgmorton (2000) sets his readers first in Iowa City, Iowa, then in citizen forums and the chambers of the city council. There we hear about a water treatment plant, a neighborhood creek, a forty-one-unit housing project, and business firms. To convey to his readers what planners do, Hoch (1996) locates real people in specific places and surrounds them with things. His story of Jorge Cruz begins with Cruz relating why he quit his previous position, a tale that pivots on a meeting in the city manager's office, construction documents, and a poorly built city hall. Cruz's subsequent job entails holding discussions in the mayor's chambers, making presentations to residents in community halls, and referring to apartment buildings, parking spaces, and streets. Planning takes place in "real time and space," Forester (2009, 29) tells us. Acknowledging this, many planning theorists set practice in a material world.

Things and places also enter planning theories when theorists focus on planning's consequences. For just city and right to the city theorists (see Fainstein 2010 and Marcuse 2009, respectively), these consequences include social housing, public transit, inclusive public spaces, mixed land uses, and unpolluted rivers (Fainstein 1997) along with transit-oriented development, compact cities, and racially integrated and income-integrated neighborhoods. These are the desired outcomes of progressive state interventions and populist social movements, and they constitute the "just city," a place where equity, diversity, and democracy reign. And while these three qualities are not physical things, they can be realized, these theorists argue, only through affordable housing, mixed land uses, public transit, and other physical objects and conditions. In short, along with other planning theorists, they use things and places to give a sense of reality to their reflections on practice and connect to a world they find unjust and intolerable.[4]

Recognized by planning theorists, the material world is then rel-

---

3. For the most part, planning theorists also disregard gods and spirits along with the sacred rituals and places that are a part of being human, though see Sandercock 2007.

4. For additional examples of how things and places are implicated in planning practice, see John Forester's *The Deliberative Practitioner* (1999).

egated to being merely context for or consequence of social action. Spaces and things passively await manipulation. In rational model approaches to practice, that world is relevant only because it is the object of planning expertise (Black 1990). Planners know how housing markets work, how to enliven spaces with activities, and where light rail lines will be most effective, but whether the object of planning is affordable housing, a downtown plaza, wetlands, or an industrial park has little theoretical significance for how analysis is done or plans are produced. Communicative action theorists are equally blind to things and places. They focus on how people come together to negotiate understandings, with planners often serving as mediators of specific planning events (Forester 2009; Innes and Booher 2004). The emphasis is on shared experiences, honest communication, respectful listening, and the search for mutually beneficial actions. People might speak of dangerous intersections or shadow-casting office buildings, but the mention of things has no interpretive or explanatory weight. Marxist political economists (Fainstein and Fainstein 1979) and the just city and right to the city theorists treat things and places as the outcomes of the actions of capitalists and planners, the consequences of just or unjust relationships, but not as objects to be theorized. For planning theorists generally, the material world has minimal theoretical value.[5]

Within planning theory, then, humans are given theoretical significance and nonhumans are denied it. Nonhuman things from a city to a light rail line are passive, material objects to be molded through regulations, negotiations, informal agreements, and incentives or, in the case of just city theorists, macropolitics. Only humans are actors, and consequently only humans have earned interpretive status.

A Planning Event

To redress this blind spot in planning theory, I interpret a typical planning event that illustrates the role of nonhuman things in planning practice.[6] The specific example I have selected focuses on the micropolitics of planning and comes from the writings of John Forester, a ma-

---

5. Consider also that the things of the world have moral value. The nineteenth-century English author John Ruskin wrote that "we should want [our buildings] to speak to us '. . . about the kinds of life that would most appropriately unfold within and around them'" (quoted in Lurie 2007, 20).

6. Dalton's (2007) documentation of contemporary planning practice in the United States attests to the typicality of this event.

jor planning theorist and a collector of planning stories. The event is a project review negotiation between a team of local planners and a developer who is proposing to build 180 units of middle-income housing in an unnamed US city. The developer has brought his architect and real estate lawyer to a meeting in the offices of the city's planning department.

Consider this edited excerpt from the transcript (Forester 1996, 244):

Chris (the architect): We have three buildings here, at five, eight, and twelve stories, set back [he explains as he points to the pictorials and a site plan], with an oasis here. . . . These buildings allow entrance from Broad Street and let us put the parking below the buildings. . . . To allow the 180 units, we have the twelve-story tower, which allowed us to maximize the greenery around it. The twelve stories then becomes an issue, so we've done some photo studies. [He shows a view of the proposed project from the major intersection at the corner of the site.]

Tim (planner): Is that taken from Broad Street?

Jan (planner): No, from Commons Avenue.

Barbara (planner): Is this the Burger King? [pointing]

Chris (architect): No, here [pointing].

Barbara (planner): I see—so the playground is over here [pointing over the plans]?

Chris (architect): Yes [Showing the approach to the project on the model]. We tried to get a picture from here [pointing] too.

The transcript goes on in a similar vein with the developer and his architect presenting the proposed scheme, the planners commenting, and the participants jointly exploring various ways of achieving an acceptable site plan. The planners are explicit that their interest is in making the street a desirable pedestrian space that conveys an "urban" rather than a "suburban" feel. Their attitude is prescriptive, underpinned (we might imagine) by a sense of what a good city should be. No resolution is achieved, however, and at the end of the meeting Tim, the lead planner, encourages the developer's team to pursue additional alternative site designs and massing studies.

Forester presents this event in terms that reflect his interest in planning as a series of practical assessments made in fluid social settings. He is concerned with how planners' judgments are anticipatory (that is, look toward the future) and how talk is used to shape attention, formulate arguments, and negotiate as well as to build workable relationships. The planners are simultaneously searching for a resolution and learning what actions are feasible. Moreover, "their talk is not just 'mere talk,'" Forester (1996, 249) writes, "but action for which they are responsible."

What Forester mentions but does not discuss are the nonhuman things without which this planning event would not have happened. Because the material world is considered epiphenomenal—subject solely to the actions of humans—things are not theorized as part of how planners behave. But what if we developed an alternative interpretation, paying closer attention to how things mediate the interactions between the developer's team and the planners? What could we learn about planning practice by giving nonhuman things theoretical status?

Consider the three planning tools mentioned in the excerpt from Forester's transcript: a site plan, a three-dimensional model, and photographs.[7] These things became, to a degree, the reality that was being discussed. Without these things in the meeting room, the discussion would not have occurred. Another discussion, likely with a different outcome, would have taken its place. Moreover, a different relationship would have been established between the planners and the developer's team. Things focus deliberations, and what was said loses meaning if we ignore the objects in the room.

Without the site plan, the planners would have been unable to visualize and thus fully understand the relation of the buildings to the street, the "suburban" feel of the proposed site, or how the site's access points would connect to the surrounding roads. Without the three-dimensional model, discussions of height, massing, and the spatial relation among the three residential buildings would have lacked clarity. For example, when the planner Barbara asked about the site's relation to the adjacent playground and the Burger King, her concerns would have been less obvious to others. By asking, she questioned the representational value of the model and the site plan. Did they really capture what was actually there? The site, a thing no longer obvious, was now being contested through its representations. Barbara was giving voice to the fact that site plans and models embody compromises among planners, civil engineers, architects, developers, zoning regulations, and building codes. To this extent, they are less a prediction of the actual project as it will be built than a temporary stopping point

---

7. The site plan, model, and photographs are simultaneously things and representations of things. Of note, Healey (1992, 18) briefly discusses the function of images in planning deliberations, although she dematerializes them into metaphors.

in a stream of decisions (Yaneva 2005). So understood, they open up numerous possibilities for negotiation.

In the absence of these objects, the discussion would have proceeded with greater uncertainty. Talk would have been highly speculative, with each participant unsure of the references made by others. For the planners, subtracting these two things from the meeting would have diminished the usefulness of their professional terminology and undermined their expertise. Terms like setback, visual buffer, plaza, density, and parcel are more compelling and more serviceable when accompanied by material representations. The things reinforce the words. At the same time, of course, talk about things gives them definition and meaning and makes them more real. The more the model is discussed, the more it—and not the building itself—seems to be the object of the planning event.[8]

From the developer's perspective, the site plan and model are crucial for conveying commitment. They represent costs incurred that signal his intent to bring the project to completion. They are also a measure of the friction involved in making changes to the proposal. Throughout the transcript, Don, the developer, refers to banks and to financing for the project. He notes that changes at this stage would be difficult and would jeopardize agreements he has worked hard to obtain. Delay breeds delay (Pressman and Wildavsky 1973, 87–124), and to go back to his investors and renegotiate the contracts would threaten prior arrangements and thus the project itself. Implementation would be at risk. The developer signals this to the planners with the site plan and the model, things that represent what he is proposing as well as the costs he has incurred. These alliances between people and things substantiate his commitment. At the same time, they silently reinforce his resistance to any major changes in what he is proposing to do. The planners implicitly recognize this. Without these things, the developer's interest in the project would be less convincing.

The photographs join the site plan and the three-dimensional model to facilitate the discussion, but they also do something even more important. Photographs allow the "place" to be brought into the conference room by adding a level of realism to the other two objects. A photograph contains details that a site plan or scale model often

---

8. Latour (2010b, 136n55) quotes Marc Auge on this point: "Telling needs matter at once to represent itself, to speak itself, and to actualize itself; and matter needs talking to become an object of thought."

lacks and provides glimpses of off-site conditions that they often exclude. Even though each person might interpret the photographs differently, they now share the same visualization. Without the photographs, the detailed discussion that each participant expected would have been less easy and less likely. The planners, of course, could, and probably did, visit the site, but this is not the same as viewing these representations in the presence of the developer and the architect in a conference room.

Of course, an alternative to the photographs would have been to schedule the meeting on site; that is, in a different place. This has two consequences from the planners' perspective. First, it could weaken their technical comments by confronting codified planning ideas with the site's particularities. Planning knowledge is formulated so as to apply to multiple instances and to allow routine (that is, bureaucratic) rather than discretionary decisions to be made. Like state knowledge (Scott 1998, 53–83), it is simplified and standardized, and the role of the planner is to interpret standardized knowledge in specific situations. Doing so, however, is fraught with uncertainties.

Adjusting technical knowledge to an actual place and an actual project is always a matter of judgment; it is discretionary. Awareness of that discretion by nonplanners calls planning knowledge into question and slackens planners' arguments. At some point in the review process, site specifics have to be addressed, but they are best addressed later in the deliberations so that planners can first establish the legitimacy of their technical position. For planners, it is useful to begin with a model and a site plan, both standardized in form and stripped of the bothersome particularities of the actual site.

Holding the meeting on site has a second consequence; it moves the negotiations outside the planning department's offices. Being in the planning conference room conveys the formality of the occasion and the pivotal role the municipality plays in the development. It reminds the developer that his project depends on permissions from the government. The site, on the other hand, is the developer's venue and confers legitimacy on him and his experts; the planners' office is where planning authority reigns. As Forester (2009, 32) comments, "Deliberate encounters require *safe spaces.*" In this event, the safe space for the planners was their conference room.

In this event things are also objects being planned.[9] The objects are

9. I am using things and objects as synonyms. Not everyone does (Brown 2001), with things being objects that have become entangled in human and nonhuman relations.

the apartment buildings, parking garages, plazas, parking lots, street walls, driveways, and turnarounds. What might happen if these things were transformed or even eliminated?

At one point during the meeting, when Don, the developer, was becoming frustrated with the suggestion that more work was needed on the site plan and concerned about his financial commitments, he commented: *"I have limited time; I'll lose the project and you'll lose 180 units* [of housing]" (Forester 1996, 246). This captures well, even if elliptically, the central theme of the relationship between him and the planners. Don makes money by building housing, while the planners' goals are to serve an expanding population and improve the city's property tax base. These goals can be met only when housing is built in the correct—that is, planned—way. Things—180 housing units—are the glue that holds the relationship together. If the 180 units are subtracted, this planning event disappears. Without the 180 units, there is no meeting and no material consequence that makes planning talk relevant.

When Don made the threat, he "broke the frame" of the conference room; he strayed from the civility and formality of the setting. The conference room is a professional venue where offensive language, threats, and frivolous talk are inappropriate. Here the expectation is that planners will behave like planners, developers like developers, and architects like architects. In a confined space, moreover, confrontation is often muted. While Don's threat was serious, it also has to be discounted. Because conference rooms suggest norms of behavior, when there is conflict there, people often leave to relieve the social pressure. Don did not do this and thus diminished the force of his threat. Don did signal that he was emotionally committed to the project, an observation that Forester (1999, 201–220) uses to note the importance of passions in planning deliberations. Planning talk is not only about technical matters, and technical matters are not solely technical. Intuitions and emotions have an important role in what is said and decided (Flyvbjerg 2001, 9–24; Sandercock 1998, 207–217).

Moreover, the planners know that Don is unlikely to walk away from a project on which he has, as he states more than once, obtained financing, hired an architect and a lawyer, and paid for photographs, a site plan, and a three-dimensional model. The developer is already too connected to the "world" of this project to withdraw easily. Doing so would unravel alliances in which he has made a significant investment and anger or alienate his many partners, from banks to consultants.

Before making his threat, Don mentioned that he had tried to buy two adjacent parcels, which would have enabled him to develop the site more in conformance with the planning guidelines. If he had made this purchase and directed his architect accordingly, the whole meeting would have been different in tone and intent. The thing—the site—would have been more appropriate for the program and more easily made to conform to zoning regulations. The planners would also have had less leverage over the project and less of a basis for negotiating. The balance of influence within the meeting would have shifted from the planners to the developer.

As a final example of the meaningfulness of things in these deliberations, toward the end of the meeting Walt, one of the planners, comments (Forester 1996, 245): "*Well, this is complicated. We'd like to see more options; I can see twenty-five footprints* [of the buildings] *that might work here. We want to see more ideas.*" Walt wants more site plans and models—more things. He also wants more options and believes that expanding the number of things will provide them. In complex situations where no one knows in advance the solution with which they will be comfortable, more options are highly valued. Additional options hold out the promise of revealing a missed opportunity and a heretofore unrecognized solution.

More options, though, will cost the developer time and money, threaten his financial arrangements by delaying the project, and cause him to reconsider his commitment. Asking for more options is also a not so subtle rejection of the current site plan and thus of the developer's idea and the architect's work. The request risks weakening trust between the two parties. "*We have concerns, but this site plan is a good start and we can work with it*" would have allowed the developer and the architect to feel that they had made progress and to sense a solution. Negotiations could then continue amicably. The point is that the consequences of statements are inseparable from the things to which they refer.

Lessons for Practice

This example testifies to the importance of things—and of places or settings, another kind of thing—to planners' deliberations. Things are participants of a sort, and they carry with them information, arguments, and commitments that shape talk and action. They empower and they disempower, as when a photograph enables planners to comment on site externalities, when a bank's commitment letter makes planners more aggressive in asking for concessions, or—to shift the setting—when archaeologists discover antiquities on a planned tourist site (Forester 1999, 68). In the absence of things, there is silence. And as things are modified—for example, the site expanded when new land is purchased—the deliberations are transformed.

Places are also things, and where an event happens has import for what happens and the consequences that result. They are not simply background to the foreground of planning talk. The city council chamber, the office of the developer, the conference room of the planning agency, and the school auditorium where public meetings are held all embody different norms as to what can be said and done, how it can be said and done, and whose interests are considered most important. Settings thus mediate talk. They also mediate things. Hypothetically, Don could have taken his Real Estate Board "Developer of the Year" award off his office wall and brought it to the meeting in the planning agency's conference room, but it would have lost its meaning the moment it arrived, not because the Real Estate Board is unimportant but because the plaque was "out of place."

From this, we can draw lessons for planning practice. The first has to do with the tools that planners, developers, and architects use to enact their roles. What objects should be brought to a meeting?[10] What qualities should these objects have? Should they be more or less detailed, more evocative (such as photographs) or more open to interpretation (such as a diagram)? In what places should meetings be held? The answers to these questions will depend on the relationship between the planners and those with whom they are negotiating as well as the stage of the discussions. Stronger relationships and later stages can tolerate more substance and detail. In fact, any relationship becomes more defined as more things—humans and nonhumans—and more substance and detail are entered into it (Forester 2009, 183–184; Latour 1987). Commitment solidifies through the connections people establish with each other and with the things that define the situation. This is what it means to form the alliances without which planners would be ineffective.

Second, the quality of planning deliberations is a function of the things entered into them. A planning discussion without physical representations of what is being planned—without visual images, a copy of the report, a zoning map–is going to be abstract and general. Without objects to point to and collectively peruse, the conversation loses

10. See Healey's (1992) discussion of the different types of knowledge that experienced planners bring to public deliberations.

specificity. Planning talk is about things that can be only partially represented with the spoken word. Words need help. Triangulating among talk, things, and mutual understandings is what makes planning deliberations fruitful. If communications are to be appropriately substantive, physical objects need to be present. Ed Bacon, the widely praised planner of postwar Philadelphia, is an exemplar in this regard. As Heller (2013, 2) has written, "He loved the three-dimensional element of models but also relied on drawings, diagrams showing complex movement systems, photo montages, slide shows, and compelling public presentations with dynamic visuals. He believed that telling people something was not enough."

Such objects also "make present the possibilities that are not there yet."[11] They bring the future into the room as well as into the discussions. This is central to what it means to plan—to imagine the future and find ways to achieve it. Scale models, drawings, plans, and montages do not just "stand in" for a reality, they extend the present of the meeting forward. By doing so, they give temporal breadth to proceedings, allowing planners to fulfill their responsibility to the future.

Third, changes in the objects being planned transform relationships among the actors. Planning negotiations are about the material world. As the material world evolves, the actions that make sense need to be recalibrated. Much planning deliberation, in fact, is about the malleability of that world and, specifically, about using that malleability to enable private gains while capturing public benefits (Hommels 2008, 21–37). Hoch (1992, 209–210), for example, tells two stories: one of a planner faced with a building foundation that was prematurely put in place in violation of the city's zoning code and the other about a planner engaged in adjusting a building's setback. To be effective, these planners had to engage with the social and material malleability of things. The pertinent regulations did not exist separately from the physical facts. Consequently, planners had to figure out how to incorporate the malleability (or conversely the obduracy) of these things into their deliberations. That building foundation exists, even if it is illegal on paper, and cannot effortlessly be made to disappear.

Schon (1982) relates a telling instance involving a planner and a developer jointly negotiating the site coverage, number of apartment units, size of a landscaped area, and amount of parking to be provided in order to develop a plan that could be approved by the Zoning

11. Thanks to Turo-Kimmo Lehtonen for encouraging me to make this point. The quotation is from our correspondence.

Board of Appeals. In this case, planning was nothing but manipulating things. Here is the planner discussing a point of contention that linked parking spaces to the size of apartments and, by extension, to the number of occupants: "The parking requirements are slightly different than they used to be. In an apartment house, you have to have one parking space for each efficiency [apartment], one and a half for each two-bedroom, two for each three or four bedroom. I'm not sure exactly how much parking you have provided here now" (356). As a general rule, malleability expands options and enables more relationships to form; obduracy reduces flexibility and constricts relationships. Moreover, the joint reshaping of things reflects the level of trust in a relationship as well as the confidence participants have in each other and in their evolving positions.

As a final lesson, planners need to heed the way things affect the authority of those participating in the deliberations. Things can enhance credibility and indicate knowledge. Bringing reports to the meeting, even if they are just placed discreetly on the conference table, displaying diplomas or awards on office walls, and sitting behind an impressive desk are all signs of authority. The picture of the planning director standing next to the mayor is a thing that signifies and is meant to be read. And although a flawed handout can diminish credibility, this possibility does not negate the potential authority of things and thus their usefulness to planners.

Worldly Action

The discussion above is meant to situate planning in the material world, stripping that world of the epiphenomenal status it has in planning thought. Practitioners—and the theorists who write about practice—need to acknowledge that while cities are places of human interaction, their material form is more than just an object of planning; it is also, in a sense, a subject. Infrastructures, birdlife, landforms, and regulatory technologies give presence to cities, and they also join with humans in alliances. This is more than a matter of knowledge; it is also a matter of action. Simply to imagine a new waterfront park, more units of affordable housing, or the just city leaves the act of planning unfulfilled. The purpose of planning is to realize these conditions, not simply to propose them. For this reason, public (collective) action is at the center of planning practice—not the planning process, not analytical procedures, not communicative encounters, and not ideological positions.

Collective action, then, entails embedding planning in specific, historically conditioned places by recognizing the many entanglements it has with the things that constitute those places. For this to happen, theorists and practitioners must acknowledge the influence things have on practice and to what extent things are not just topics of conversations but actual participants in the deliberations that sit at the core of planning. Theory must probe deeply into how talk, action, and things are mutually constitutive. That said, and within planning practice, action cannot occur without deliberation. Planning action is always relational: it is always a matter of working with others. Talk is how planners learn about the world, share knowledge, exert authority, organize attention, and establish commitments. For these reasons, "what gets done depends heavily on what gets said" (Forester 1989, 23). Talk is particularly important if planners are to act intentionally and be made accountable.

Thus a theory of action attends to the inherently prescriptive nature of planning. This includes not just the morality that infuses public deliberation—its inclusiveness, openness to different types of knowledge, presumption of mutual respect, and sensitivity to emotions—but also the morality embodied in the actions and consequences being deliberated. Talk about marginalizing others or taking from those with few resources to enhance those with many is as morally unacceptable as a discussion of housing policy that ignores housing's affordability and thus its accessibility to those with limited finances.

Planning talk, moreover, is almost always about some thing. It is talk about shopping malls, traffic diverters, green markets, and storm barriers and often is accompanied by maps and documents. Without talk, planners would stop acting, and "without things, [planners] would stop talking" (Daston 2004, 9). Things affect how deliberations unfold, and they do so through their social connections, political connotations, and emotional resonances (Winner 1980; Joerges 1999). They embody social relations, even substitute for them, and appear to us encased in meanings that demand interpretation. To this extent, the politics of planning is a "thing-politics" in which the material world contributes directly to calculations of power and the distribution of resources and opportunities (Latour 2005a). By relaxing the distinctions among things (including actors), a new materialist perspective positions things as "a crucial part of the performance of subjects" (Thrift 1996, 41).[12]

12. This approach to politics rejects the position that for people to become political subjects they must disengage "from the socio-material conditions of their everyday lives" (Marres and Lezaun 2011, 497).

To be more precise, things enter planning either as objects being planned or as objects being used to plan. In the first category we find parking garages, exit ramps, school buildings, retail malls, wetlands, housing units, and bus stops. Zoning officials take responsibility for the height and bulk of buildings, transportation planners for the spacing of buses, environmental planners for soil quality, housing planners for dwelling units, and economic development planners for new office buildings. In each instance, the purpose of planning is to modify, regulate, or bring into existence a thing and the relationships in which it is entangled. In the second category we find maps, telephones, conference room tables, pens, three-dimensional models, GIS software, planning documents, and presentation screens. Add to this list the shelves where planning reports go to die, never to be implemented, at least according to a cliché heard often in US planning circles. For planners to be planners, they need the tools of their profession. As Callon (2002, 214) notes, "The agent who [acts] is not the human being, but the human being equipped with tools."

What constitutes a thing, within planning and without, is of course neither obvious nor a matter of consensus (Jubien 2001). Not all places and things are relevant to planning and, of those, not all their qualities are pertinent to the task. Things—soil erosion, traffic congestion, an illegal billboard—need to be observed, named, and brought into planning discourse. Doing so makes certain qualities (for example, size, location) the subject of measurement and deliberation, leaving other qualities (for example, color) irrelevant. These discriminations are central to the ways planners categorize the world, not only determining what is or is not a planning problem—that is, what is a matter of concern—but also filtering out those aspects of things that are incompatible with the technical understandings and scientific tools planners have at their disposal.[13]

Furthermore, attention needs to be paid to how one thing (for example, a landfill) differs from another (for example, an illegal dump), the functions they serve, and how things came to be (Bibby and Shepherd 2000, 583–584). The last is particularly important given the constant change experienced by places and things. An ever-present slippage exists between our representations of things and their current and past state, a problem particularly apparent in historic preservation, where proponents contend with buildings in physical and symbolic motion (Tait

---

13. This is essentially Latour's (2004b) argument that distinguishes objects (matters of fact) from things around which have been gathered various actors and intentions (matters of concern).

and While 2009). Buildings, and things more generally, are "contested gathering[s] of many conflicting" claims (Latour and Yaneva 2008, 86; see also Latour 1994), and those claims are constantly changing.

Places are also things. They are material objects invested with physical qualities, history, and social meanings. When action occurs, it occurs somewhere, with the setting both preceding the action and reproduced by it. Consequently, buildings and cities, two of many kinds of planning places, inevitably contribute to "the meaning of speech that unfolds within them" (Mitchell 2005, 4); it matters where something happens. A planner strolling along the canals of Amsterdam is just a tourist, but in her office at city hall, she is an authority. As Gieryn (2006, 21) reminds us, "Place is normative: certain behavior patterns and dispositions are expected from people in part because of where they happen to be." Similarly, a thing out of place—a zoning map as wall decoration in the municipal cafeteria—no longer resonates with the meanings it had in its "proper" place (for example, in the conference room of the planning commission). The reverse is also relevant. A conference room without a long, narrow table, chairs ranged around it, a projection screen on the wall, and an easel with a flip chart in the corner is just a room.

Most important for a theory that embeds action in the material world is the possibility that things enter into planning as actors having influence, not just as passive objects. At issue is the ontological status of nonhumans. Can they be—are they—more than mere things? Latour (2005b, 63–78) offers a compelling way to think about this. He claims that things are actors to the extent that they transform relationships among the people and things with which they are connected. The emphasis is on effects rather than intentions, motivations, or other qualities of individual actors. The essence of an actor is much less significant than the consequences its actions produce (Latour 1999, 308). Consider the soil at a former manufacturing site "resisting" remediation, directional signs "diverting" traffic patterns, and a defective levee "destroying" a neighborhood. This insight also points to how social responsibilities are delegated among people and things as, for example, when our civic duty to provide housing for the less fortunate is shared with homeless shelters.

Of course, this does not mean that nonhuman things have the qualities—intentionality, reflectivity, accountability—we associate with human actors.[14] Latour and other actor-network theorists narrowly

---

14. We can also dispense with animism, the belief that nonhuman things have souls. What we cannot cast aside is how things animate relationships.

define the symmetry between humans and nonhumans in terms of responsiveness and delegation of responsibilities. Collins (2010, 145), however, rejects symmetry altogether, arguing that nonhumans lack the means to participate in deliberations leading to collective action: "Non-humans are not doing any interpreting and they cannot contribute to the consensus because they don't have the language to do it." Less dismissively, Sayes (2014) reflects on what it means to presume that nonhumans have agency. He offers four possibilities: nonhumans as the durable materials that stabilize human networks; nonhumans as mediators among humans; nonhumans as visible actors in moral and political associations; and nonhumans as gathering with humans in associations that act. The third possibility, because it seems to grant collective intentionality and reflectivity to nonhumans, is the most questionable and the one Collins rejects. And yet even the most basic of Sayes's types of nonhuman agency implies that nonhuman things have theoretical value.

In extending agency to nonhumans, actor-network theory points to two related qualities of actors and action. One is that actors are hybrids created out of relationships: "Something actually *becomes* an object [or an actor] only in the context of action and use" (Bowker and Star 2000, 298). Humans always act with tools, nature, and other humans and appear as actors only when deeply engaged with the material world. The second quality is the distributed nature of agency. Agency is always shared among humans and nonhumans and the places they create. It is always connected and situated; it is networked (Latour 2005b, 41). These two qualities are central to how we think about and practice planning; that is, not in isolation but in various combinations with others and always cooperatively. No individual, whether mayor, developer, or capitalist, is solely responsible. What matters are coalitions of heterogeneous actors, the very basis for a democratic planning.

As problematic is the moral status of nonhuman things, particularly as regards their responsibility for their actions, an issue that brings us to shared motivations and intentions. We do not, for example, condemn wolves for leaving behind a pack member too weak to hunt. If a wolf were a human, however, we would take a very different position. Our moral assessments of nonhumans diverge significantly from the way we gauge human behavior. Bennett (2007, 134) captures the difference with her claim that nonhuman things are agents "inside and along-side intention-forming, morality-(dis)obeying, language-using, reflexivity-wielding, culture-making human beings." Such differences, however, do not negate the insight of actor-network theory that actors

73

are always hybrids and agency is always distributed. This can be true regardless of the moral status of the different actors. Moreover, it does not preclude the possibility that humans share responsibility with non-human things such as speed bumps, homeless shelters, and tornado warning systems.

A more bothersome distinction involves the ability of nonhumans to initiate and guide collective action (Fuller 2000, 20) and, specifically, a democratic planning that strives for full and equal participation. The collective imagining that is central to planning is limited by nonhumans' inability to carry out elaborate deliberations with humans. Communication, as it is understood within contemporary planning, is impossible. Nonhuman things cannot give reasons or explain their positions. And when publics are formed out of humans and non-humans, it is difficult to characterize the nonhumans' participation as consensual. The riverbank, even though it can resist, has little say about whether it becomes part of an ecological restoration meant to mitigate flooding. Thus, while we can consider nonhumans as actors within networks—having effects—we need to avoid an anthropomorphism that imputes motives and intentions to them. What counts is how human actors acknowledge the actions of nonhumans (Callon 1986, n. 24). This means that while nonhumans can initiate collective action in the narrow sense of acting in such a way that humans feel the need to respond, they do not initiate action in a collective and intentional fashion compatible with planning. When the river overflows its banks, various government and community organizations and insurance companies mobilize to address those harmed and the damage done, and a few of them work with the river to do so. The river, however, did not deliberately flood.

Things, then, play a central role in the relationships that planners establish among themselves and with others (Harman 2009, 19–20). For planners to act with authority and certainty, they must create alliances, and to create alliances they must gather people and objects to them. Humans become influential by enrolling other people and non-humans in their projects (Callon and Latour 1981; Latour 1988). Take, for example, a planner working in a planning agency of a medium-sized city and lacking an office that provides for private conversations, a conference table on which to pore over maps, access to the government's databases and communication system, a vehicle to take planning commissioners to view the site conditions for a proposed hotel, and friendly relations with clerical personnel. This planner has no alliances. As a result, she has little or no authority and no influence. Only when she has gathered these things and people around her, then stabilized these relationships, will she be able to plan effectively.

The stability of alliances, though, is always problematic. Trust must be maintained, relationships nurtured, and commitments constantly reaffirmed. No future can be pursued without durable networks. Energy must be expended to reproduce alliances and replace relations that have irretrievably decayed. If, for example, a storm destroys much of the city, the way the planning department relates to other government agencies will have to change, the substance of planning deliberations refocused, and the usual role of the department reevaluated. Existing relationships will be destabilized, and the planners' current influence will be eroded (or enhanced). Or consider what likely happened when computers replaced drafting tables in planning agencies and the embedded software of mapping was substituted for manual manipulation of paper. The mapping process became less visible and less transparent. The locus of knowledge and authority shifted inside a machine and to the technicians who read and interpret the code. This widened the gap between the knowledge of the technical staff and that of their non-technical supervisors. Moreover, it reduced the supervisors' ability to "know" how maps were created, thus conferring greater autonomy and power on the technical staff. New alliances were formed.

Things and places matter in how we relate to others. When they change, our relationships are altered. Consequently, a planning theory that omits most of the world—that omits nonhuman things (including the settings in which planning happens)—misrepresents planning practice while severely limiting planners' ability to act effectively and with influence.[15] I cannot accept that nonhumans are simply epiphenomenal and that things thus have no theoretical significance. I can only conclude, then, that a theory of planning practice has to theorize about the things that populate the world and the places where action occurs. The practical relevance of things is not the end of the discussion.

15. The institutional constraints on planning have not been addressed in this chapter. For one approach, see Bourdieu's (2005, 89–147) discussion of the housing market in France.

FOUR

Neglected Places of Practice

One cannot read far in the planning literature without encountering writings about place. We learn about redevelopment sites, neighborhoods threatened by gentrification, wetlands in need of protection, public squares awash with political protesters, regional shopping malls drawing customers from town centers, office parks proliferating across the suburbs, and more. Because planning is mainly about "the interconnection of people and places, activities and territories" (Healey 2005, 5), the prevalence of such stories is not surprising. Yet little has been written about the ways places enter into planning practice and matter theoretically.[1] When places are addressed, attention is mainly directed at those that have been planned or whose planning is under way. Less often considered are the places where planning practice occurs and the influence these places have on how planning decisions are made.

Reflect for the moment on three stories about the places encountered in the planning literature. The first, by Robert Hrelja (2011), involves a large shopping area called Marieberg on the outskirts of the Swedish town of Örebro. There, a commitment by planners to sustainable mobility, meaning both less sprawl and decreased automobile traffic, was undermined by short-term and seemingly insignificant decisions that sacrificed environmentalism for economic development and competitiveness. In present-

1. The exceptions include Graham and Healey 1999; Lapintie 2007; Smith 2007; and Stephenson 2010.

ing the case, Hrelja mentions town planners, representatives of Öre-bro's Office of Business Development, Steen och Strom (a shopping center operator), municipal commissioners, and local political parties. The second story is from Susan Fainstein (1997), who argues that Amsterdam can serve as a model of an egalitarian and just city. Affordable housing, inclusive public spaces, widely accessible mass transit, and income-integrated neighborhoods are its essential elements, and they emerge from a planning that eschews pro-growth policies and, by extension, subservience to capitalism. The third story is the John Forester (1996) practice case discussed in chapter 3: a planning event in which municipal planners in the United States negotiated with a developer, his architect, and his lawyer regarding the construction of multifamily housing. They met in the planning department's conference room and there discussed various aspects of the site: density, parking, open space, and sidewalks.

Each of these planning stories highlights a particular understanding of place. Hrelja's piece represents probably the most common approach; it focuses on the place being planned. He emphasizes the technical qualities of the place: accessibility by car and by public transit, the mix of retail and commercial uses, changing property values, and the regional competitiveness of Marieberg's retailing. That is, Hrelja describes the place in terms that target it for intervention; that is, as a site. Those involved in the planning process are acknowledged, but we have no sense of where planning decisions were being made.[2]

By contrast, Fainstein's story focuses on the context of planning. Context consists of the sociopolitical, cultural, and economic conditions—in this instance, the Dutch welfare state—that shape the planning process. That, in fact, is her point; planning can be just only when society's institutions are just. As with Hrelja's story, planners are acknowledged, but the places where they act are not. The place of interest for Fainstein is Amsterdam, the city that symbolizes the Dutch context.[3] Last, there is Forester. His story occurs in a conference room of a planning agency. Here is a place of practice, with the site represented in absentia by drawings, a model, photographs, and (of course) the developer and his consultants. Forester, though, is concerned with the

---

2. For similar treatments of place see Beauregard 2005a and Gualini and Majoor 2007, among many such depictions.

3. Fainstein is also interested in the nation, but she treats it as a space rather than a place, a distinction I discuss below.

deliberations that occurred, not with the role this practice place—the meeting room—had in mediating them.

These stories represent three different ways planning theorists think about places: as sites (that is, places being planned); as context; and as settings for practice. When the focus is on sites and context, planning (for the most part) emanates from nowhere. Planning decisions and actions are described, and frequently the planners themselves are identified, but they exist in a shadowy and unspecified realm. The planners in these stories are spatially untethered. Planning stories of the third kind are more likely to tell us where planning occurred—locating it—but often only in passing; that is, treating practice places as a descriptive fact rather than as a consequential practical or theoretical issue. And while the site being planned often figures centrally in planning deliberations, we are not asked to imagine the other places (for example, the developer's office, the zoning board meeting room, the local bank) where planning occurs.

If one believes that where something happens—its setting—is important for how it happens and for its consequences and also believes that planning theory should be about planning practice, then theorists need to acknowledge these places. Not only is planning spatially situated, with consequences for what planners do and what decisions are made, it is also distributed across multiple places networked around the planning event. A practice-based theory positions planners in settings that become practice places as a result of the actions of planners. It embodies the materiality of practice. This is one reason the distinctions among site, place, and context matter. A planning theory that ignores these distinctions and fails to theorize planning spatially is at best incomplete and at worst unhelpful.

In this chapter I argue for incorporating the places of practice in any theory of action concerned with the micropolitics of planning. Where planning happens affects what is deliberated, who is involved, and the publicity afforded those deliberations. To state it bluntly, planning's ability to be democratic depends as much on the array of places across which it is distributed as on the range of "voices" that are allowed to be heard. As illustration, I will delve into the places involved in a single planning event, the attempt by the Bluestem Solid Waste Agency of Linn County, Iowa, to site a new landfill.[4] At the end, we return to site, place, and context.

---

4. The following is a summary of a case written by Michael Berkshire (2003), who was the regional solid waste planning coordinator for Bluestem during this time.

Siting a Landfill

In the mid-1990s, the board of directors of the Bluestem Solid Waste Agency learned that Linn County's landfills were about to reach capacity. It directed the staff to investigate alternative technologies for managing the rising volume of solid waste.

This simple description points to the networked places important for understanding this planning event. First are the existing landfill sites. Second, and implicit, are the places where waste is being generated. Third are the offices at Bluestem where the planners and other analysts tracked solid waste disposal and made a technical determination that existing sites would soon reach capacity. Fourth are the rooms of Bluestem where these calculations were discussed and a decision was made to mount a new planning initiative. From its inception, planning for additional capacity was spread across multiple places. We might think of these interconnected places as an assemblage.

The planning team began by inviting citizens with an interest in waste disposal to join a focus group that would formulate an integrated solid waste management plan. At the conclusion of its deliberations, the focus group would make recommendations to the Bluestem board. A series of meetings was held, we can assume in Bluestem's conference rooms. During this time the staff worked in its offices to provide information and analyses. After concluding its assessment, the focus group met with the board and proposed that Bluestem expand its recycling and composting efforts, build a facility to manage household hazardous waste, and open a new landfill. Existing sites for recycling and composting would be upgraded, a hazardous waste disposal facility would be built, and a new site would be established for handling the disposal of nonhazardous and nonrecyclable materials. In effect, more places would be added to Bluestem's portfolio, thereby expanding its operations and dispersing them more widely across the county.

The Bluestem staff then turned to developing a strategic plan for identifying the new landfill site. At this stage a decision was made to make the planning process as public as possible—that is, to involve all the stakeholders and aim for, if not consensus, a broadly shared understanding of the appropriateness of the selected site. The planners rejected a site-and-defend approach in which they, as experts, would select the best site for a landfill, commit to it, and then defend it against all opposition in as few public meetings as possible. Such an approach reduces the number of places involved, ostensibly making the process more manageable, and concentrates planning within the agency. But it also dampens democracy.

The strategic plan focused on obtaining public input as well as on identifying outside experts to consult on technical matters. The public process began by meeting with "affected parties," including government agencies. Most likely these meetings took place in the Bluestem offices. This was followed by the creation of a citizens' advisory committee of about twenty people. The committee met for five to six months, with the early meetings devoted to informing its members of the work of the focus group and the later meetings to developing site-selection criteria. The committee was discouraged from revisiting decisions about alternative technologies made at the earlier stages of the process and from questioning the need—already documented—for a new landfill.

At this point the planning deliberations occupied four places simultaneously: the room(s) where the advisory committee met, the offices of the Bluestem staff where information was gathered and studies were done, the business addresses of the consultancies, and the hypothetical sites in the county—haunting the deliberations but not yet identified—where the landfill might be located. This last set of places involved not just multiple possible sites but the relation between these sites and other places. The committee considered the land uses on adjacent sites, proximity to the "weighted center" of waste generation in Linn County, nearness to rivers and streams, and road access. It addressed various qualities of the sites as well: existing uses, drainage capacity, soil quality, agricultural potential, depth to bedrock, and (later) the owners' willingness to sell at a reasonable price. During this time the Bluestem staff also met with the county director of planning and zoning in Cedar Rapids to craft an "exclusive use" zoning ordinance for the new landfill. This added a fifth place—the county planning department's offices—to the assemblage.

In the end, and with the assistance of the staff, the advisory committee identified thirteen potential sites, all privately owned. The property owners were notified, and a public meeting was announced and held in a large auditorium. It attracted nearly four hundred people and turned into what one Bluestem participant called "the meeting from hell": "There were tears, grandstanding, cheering, clapping, and many horrible accusations about Bluestem staff" (Berkshire 2003, 172). It was an informational meeting, and the planners were not allowed to respond: "We had to just sit there and listen" (Berkshire 2003, 172). This large public meeting was followed by a series of open houses held in various venues around the county. There, the staff set up information booths that presented the rationales behind the selection of sites and specific information about each one. The booths had representatives either from Bluestem or from one of the consultants. Each open house attracted between four hundred and five hundred people.[5]

During this time, the county planning director was working on the zoning ordinance. Much to the chagrin of the Bluestem planners, he proposed incorporating language that prohibited any place from being used as a landfill if the land had a Corn Suitability Rating (CSR) that indicated it was high-quality farmland. All thirteen potential sites had land with ratings that eliminated them from further consideration. At one of its meetings, the county board of supervisors adopted the ordinance and effectively negated the work of Bluestem's advisory committee.

The planners then met with the Bluestem board. The board recommended that they narrow the search to two or three sites and postpone addressing the new ordinance (which some of the planners considered illegal). When the planners went back to the advisory committee, however, it refused to proceed, believing the county board of supervisors would reject any site with a high CSR. The advisory committee suggested instead that new criteria be developed and, furthermore, stated emphatically that it would deal only with "willing sellers." The Bluestem staff subsequently began talking with property owners who were inclined to sell. This drew representatives from real estate offices, law firms, and banks into the process along with their places of business. After a year or so, Bluestem found a property owner (named Hennessey) who was interested in selling his land, and detailed negotiations began. The parties could not agree on terms, though, and the negotiations stalled. Consequently, Bluestem considered a public taking of the site through eminent domain.[6] In addition, the property was partially within the boundaries of the city of Cedar Rapids, and the Bluestem planners had to negotiate with the city planners there and hold public meetings with the Cedar Rapids Planning Commission.

The single site became the subject of negotiations around a sale price and the object of hydrological and environmental studies, thereby mobilizing additional actors and places where elements of the planning process were being assembled. The studies were necessary, since

---

5. On raucous public meetings, see Frick 2013.

6. At this time the state legislature in Des Moines was debating changes in the existing condemnation (i.e., taking) law. This added another place to the process and increased the pressure on the Bluestem planners to act quickly.

the landfill needed an operating permit from the state Department of Natural Resources (DNR). The planners began that application process.

Then three places far from Linn County, Iowa—Washington, DC, Altoona, Pennsylvania, and New York City—entered into the planning event. Bud Schuster, a Pennsylvania congressman, was successful in passing a bill in Washington that would stop a new regional landfill in his district from accepting waste from New York City. The law prohibited landfills within a certain distance of an airport—as was the proposed regional landfill in Altoona. Bluestem's preferred site also violated the restriction. A delegation was sent to the Federal Aviation Administration (FAA) offices in Washington to discuss the law and to determine if it applied to the Eastern Iowa Airport near the proposed Bluestem site. The likelihood was that the FAA would prohibit the Linn County landfill.

In response, the Bluestem board suspended its efforts at eminent domain. A short time later the FAA ruled that the Bluestem landfill site would be allowed. But because other permit work had been suspended, the planners were now, in late summer of 2000, in violation of the DNR's permitting timeline. Moreover, the DNR would not issue a temporary permit to allow purchase of the property, even though a settlement had been reached with the property owner. Given the situation, the Bluestem board suspended planning for a new landfill. As Berkshire concluded (2003, 180), "There were just too many 'ifs,' way too many things out flapping in the wind, for them [sic] to spend any more money to develop a landfill on the Hennessey property." Despite having undertaken what Berkshire (2003, 180) proclaimed "the most extensive solid waste planning process that had ever been conducted in the State of Iowa," the process was terminated before it could achieve its objective.

Places and Practice

Read from the perspective of the micropolitics of planning, this case illustrates two aspects of practice places that deserve our attention. The first is their multiplicity; the second is their influence on what is said, who participates, and whether what happens there becomes public. Both aspects speak directly to concerns—deliberation, negotiation, and collaboration (Forester 2009; Innes and Booher 2004)—that occupy practitioners and theorists and to the goal of democratic and just planning. The array of places within a planning event has consequences for whose voices are heard and poses strategic considerations regarding how planners might engage diverse publics. Insofar as specific places signal expectations about behavior, the array of places also influences what is said and, depending on their openness, affects what becomes known beyond their bounds.

First, this relatively simple planning event involved many diverse places. There was only one lead agency, the problem was clearly defined, and the solution was known, yet planning was still distributed across numerous places: the offices of the Bluestem planners, county and city planning departments, the lawyers, state and federal agencies, and consultants; the room used for the focus group, advisory committee, and public meetings; and the many sites being considered, publicly debated, and privately negotiated. These places were located across Linn County and in the Iowa state capital, Washington, DC, New York City, and Altoona, Pennsylvania. Different activities occurred in each practice place, with certain places more important than others.

Note also how the planning event oscillated between relatively private places where access was controlled and relatively public places where almost anyone could participate.[7] The process began in the privacy of the Bluestem boardroom and its offices and also outside those offices, in public, as the disposal of solid waste pushed against the geographical boundaries and geological qualities of the county's landfills and the limits of recycling and diversion. With the decision to make planning for the landfill a public event, the deliberations traveled to more open arenas, beginning with the places where the focus group and advisory committee met and the general public was convened. The deliberations subsequently oscillated between private analysis and public engagement, and places appropriate to these activities. Each successive widening of public involvement returned the planners to a more private place where data could be analyzed, public presentations put together, experiences discussed, and strategy debated. The planners moved through places of varying transparency in order to enable the process to go forward as well as to assess and reassess their understandings and modify their positions.

All the places were connected through the actions of the planners and the various other actors engaged with the location decision. The diminishing capacity of the existing landfills became organization-

7. Winkler (2011, 260–261) points to such differences with her typology of closed spaces, invited spaces, and claimed spaces. Clearly, the public/private distinction is a crude one. I use it simply as a way to enter the discussion.

ally and politically meaningful only when the planners, in their offices, translated their data and observations into technical calculations and findings. In doing so, they merged the physical environment with newly formed representations to trigger this planning event. As a second example, a decision in the Bluestem boardroom required a recommendation from an advisory committee that was being informed by analyses developed in the offices of consultants. Places were networked and "bled" into each other, with their edges porous as decisions and activities undertaken in one traveled to another. Yet they were not equal in their contributions to the deliberations. The appraisal office where the market value of a proposed site was estimated was less central to the mobilization of ideas and influence than the Bluestem conference room. The latter was more connected to the flow of actions and decisions and, for that reason, a dominant node in this assemblage of places.[8]

The temporal sequence by which places were added, moreover, was hardly linear. The event did not move from the small places of expert and policy deliberations to the large places of public announcement and engagement and then back to Bluestem's boardroom where a final decision was made. Planning deliberations moved about, oscillating among different places, and occurred in multiple places at the same time. Not only was the process spatially and temporally disjointed, but the planners had only partial control over it. The planners had to negotiate among different stakeholders and various places—sometimes simultaneously—with each negotiation revealing different opportunities and constraints.

The second aspect of place critical to practice has to do with how places (much like nonhuman things) influence what is said, who participates, and whether the goings-on in that place are revealed to the larger public. Our understanding of what a place is shapes what actions occur there. Consequently, the content, meaning, and value of talk depend on where it happens. Laboratories and government offices are unlike street corners and athletic clubs. The "contexts for communication" are different in each (Mitchell 2005, 3). The substance of what planners say and how they say it are not the same when walking a potential landfill site as when facing a skeptical audience in a school auditorium. Of course planners have some discretion over where to speak and when. As Meyrowitz (1985, 41) reminds us, "By selectively

---

8. As Callon (2001, 65) has written, "The more a place is connected to other places . . . the greater its capacity for mobilization" of influence.

exposing ourselves to events and other people, we control the flow of our actions and emotions" as well as the flow of the talk, actions, and emotions of others.[9]

This connection between place and talk has been acknowledged in the planning literature by both postmodernists and feminists. Postmodernists urged attention to the spaces where the voices of the marginalized and oppressed are squelched and then to interstitial spaces where they can speak freely (Bhabha 1994; Sandercock 1995). The feminists concurred, noting, for example, how Progressive Era women reformers were kept out of corporate boardrooms and city council chambers where men made the "big" decisions about the city. Women had to find other places where they could speak and act (Spain 2001). The spatial segregation of women has always been a way to control their conversations, limit their access to male spheres, and diminish their status (Spain 1992). In short, "people behave differently in different social 'situations' depending on *where* one is" (Meyrowitz 1985, viii; emphasis in original). Our actions and words might not be determined by the places where they occur, but they are nonetheless influenced by them.[10]

In their offices, the Bluestem planners debated alternative approaches to public engagement, commented on the costs and benefits of each, and spoke openly about the implications of public involvement for their control over the process, its outcomes, and the agency's political standing. There they could express themselves freely and hypothetically. Many of their conversations would have been inappropriate at a large public meeting where citizens expect clarity and certainty from experts. Larger venues are better suited to conveying information and offering opportunities for dissent rather than engaging the public in discussions of priorities and consequences. The impersonality of an auditorium engenders a different type of encounter than occurs in the privacy and exclusivity of a small conference room.

Different spaces allow for varying levels of speculation, contrasting degrees of technical discussion, and particular expressions of emotions. Among colleagues who are engaged in a dispassionate assessment of public engagement procedures or landfill criteria, planners can be

---

9. Along these lines, Gieryn (2006) claims that the credibility of scientific knowledge depends, in part, on the place—the truth-spot—it emanates from, not just who conveys that knowledge.

10. In discussing the places of policy transfer, McCann (2008, 900) writes that "these microspaces frame the ways in which policy actors *imagine* their practice and their policies" (my emphasis).

blunter in their comments, more adventurous in their thinking, and less committed to positions. Intricate technical discussions are best held with fewer people in smaller places and avoided in large public meetings. In the latter, such talk often seems obfuscatory and insensitive to the issues that have mobilized publics both for and against the planning proposal. Additionally, different places convey different degrees of legitimacy on what is said by whom. The planner can speak authoritatively in front of the county planning commission but is challenged at a public forum.[11]

In public places, people want clear answers to questions, not speculation; they want to hear about the fundamental decisions, not details; and they want to know that the planners, elected officials, and other policymakers know what they are doing, even though they will often accuse them otherwise. For the most contentious of issues, members of these publics want to vent their emotions either because something important about their world is being threatened or because they are simply frustrated with government. They are there to express their concerns, not to deliberate. They are there for acknowledgment and validation, not just to gather information. And they are there to discuss the kinds of places in which they want to live, with whom they want to live, and the changes they are willing to tolerate, not technical arguments.[12]

To the extent that the mix of technical talk, reasoned deliberations, passions, and introspection varies by place and needs to be included, then, planning events require many dissimilar places. Just as it is inappropriate to meet only with organized groups in small venues, holding only public meetings is equally detrimental to democracy. Not all meetings need to be open to everyone, nor should they be. Transparency and privacy have to be balanced. People, whether planners, elected officials, protest organizations, or groups lending support, need to be able to meet alone to consider strategies and tactics, deliberate po-

11. What is not being discussed here, and needs to be for a fuller appreciation of the relation of place to talk, is how practice places are constituted by the stories we tell about them and the talk that occurs there (Joyce 2003, 210–214).

12. For an introduction to the relationship of place to democracy, see Jackson's (2008) history of urban renewal in New Haven, Connecticut, that explicitly recognizes "the ways in which social movements are grounded in particular community spaces" (224). Fure-Slocum (2013, 12) offers an evocative description of the relation between place and politics in Milwaukee in the 1930s and 1940s: "As in other industrial cities, a vibrant working-class culture and politics also came to life regularly around kitchen tables, in taverns, in bingo halls, in bowling alleys, in churches and synagogues, on buses and streetcars, in public housing projects, amid election campaigns, at city hall, in workplaces, and on picket lines." Last, on the importance of places where publics are enacted, see Marres and Lezaun 2011.

sitions, and engage the issues. As Sack (1999, 36) remarks, "Occupying space, closing the doors to our offices and laboratories, our homes and businesses is justified . . . if those involved and affected by it undertake it willingly." Transparency that hinders dissent is undemocratic in the same way that a lack of transparency thwarts justice and consolidates power.

In an ideal, democratic world, the public would be fully aware of the information used and all the decisions made. This is not always possible or even desirable (Kaza and Hopkins 2009). Small groups meet alone to discuss the planning issue; key individuals isolate themselves for reflection. In both instances, making their deliberations and thoughts public would be cumbersome. More important, places have to exist where policymakers, experts, and publics can meet without facing the scrutiny of others. Opposition groups need places where they can debate tactics and argue about values and positions. Policymakers require places to consider the political ramifications of their actions. Experts need to engage in technical debates. All these places appeared in the Bluestem landfill planning process.[13]

Places and actors, then, are interconnected, not autonomous factors in the crafting of a planning event. Larger spaces allow more voices to be heard. Smaller spaces are usually more socially selective. Large spaces are often more accessible and more likely to be viewed as public. Because different people are included, diverse kinds of talk occur in one-person offices, conference rooms, council chambers, public auditoriums, and executive suites. Moreover, the various decisions regarding the places (and people) to include are political acts and thus depend on the distribution of power across the groups and organizations involved.[14]

From the beginning, Bluestem committed itself to a countywide public process that would involve as many people as wanted to participate. The objectives were not only to gather knowledge and win support but also to portray the landfill as a public obligation. Public meetings would also enable the residents to imagine themselves as part of a

13. In his well-known article "Ends and Means in Planning," Edward Banfield (1959, 365–366) wrote that it would be imprudent for an organization to publicize a course of action in advance, since doing so would invite opposition and give it an advantage. Staeheli and Mitchell (2008, xx–xxiii) make a related point about the politics of public space. As regards community gardens, they write (108) that "since *difference* was so critical to the function of community, these public spaces were created through acts of exclusion to create safe places in which it was possible to conceive of different kinds of [counterpublics])."

14. Scott (1998, 78) notes that legibility and transparency confer political advantages on those "who have the knowledge and access to easily decipher the new state-created format."

political community. Being inclusive required more effort (and frustration) and more time. It also, the planners hoped, would make the final decision more legitimate while educating the public about the difficulties of solid waste disposal. Implicit in the process was the framing of the landfill site as a common concern and thus one element in the moral cohesiveness of the community.

The array of places to stage the planning process, then, has implications for the inclusion and exclusion of publics and thus for planners' social responsibilities (Smith 2007). People are treated equally insofar as they are allowed to participate equally. Doing so acknowledges their moral worth as well as the social ties that bind them together politically. Meetings craft publics, and through publics democracy unfolds (Dewey [1927] 1954). One of the moral obligations of democratic planners is to strive for inclusion. This means recognizing that not all meetings can sustain full, representative participation and that even meetings designed to achieve this are likely to fall short of the ideal. Consequently, planners must think of a planning process not in terms of individual meetings but in terms of a constellation of places and meeting types that serve different political and social needs and involve a range of participants.

None of this discussion is meant to suggest that the places of this or any planning event automatically become practically or theoretically significant. Was it necessary for the Bluestem planners to have had focus groups, an advisory committee, consultations with a variety of experts, meetings with the city and county planning departments, and information booths, each occurring in a different place? While I suspect that the planners tried to avoid superfluous or trivial meetings, I also suspect that many meetings where little seemed to be accomplished actually served a purpose. Talk does not have to be productive to be useful. Moreover, not all meetings should take place in the planning agency's conference room. Traveling about the city (or county) is something planners need to do. In the midst of such a process, it is seldom obvious which meetings and places are necessary and which can be eliminated. Even after the fact it is often debatable which were the most consequential.

To speculate, a place might be theoretically significant when more publics are involved and more aspects of the issue are being discussed. Here significance would hinge on the transparency and inclusion of place-based activities. Consequently, these places would enable the theorist to assess whether the process was democratic and why planners were successful (or not) in achieving their objectives. Or consider the significance of places in terms of how issues are framed; that is, in terms of the fundamental decisions that shape the resultant public deliberations, even if elusively and often unconsciously (Gualini and Majoor 2007; Schon and Rein 1994). This line of thought confers greater significance on smaller places (and meetings) than if one focused on transparency and inclusion. It is often in exclusive places that planners and policymakers develop the discursive frame of projects. In the landfill case, the decisions to require the advisory committee to accept (without question) the work of the focus group, make the process as public as possible, and impose a farmland quality restriction on site selection were framing decisions, and all were made in relative privacy. Identifying the places of practice, then, is only the beginning. The planning theorist also has to assess their theoretical and practical significance, which, in a practice-based theory, amounts to the same thing.

Site, Place, Context

Throughout, I have used "site" and "place" to refer to where planning occurs. I implied that they are nonoverlapping concepts that contrast the professional knowledge and activities of planners with the knowledge and experiences of people in their daily lives. More appropriate is to think of sites as a type of place. Before being redescribed in technical language, sites were places (and will be again if the planners and developers are successful) and thus are best thought of as places in transition. Thus a site is only temporary, a professional event, and it has to be performed, acted out, to take material form. If Bluestem had been successful in opening a new landfill, that site would have quickly been turned into a place as work crews laid out access roads, trucks dumped waste, bulldozer operators buried the waste, environmental officers measured runoff and toxins, local residents discussed the landfill, and birds and rodents flocked to pick through the refuse. The technical representations that made it a site suitable for a landfill would then fade away.[15]

Critics of planning often accuse practitioners of fixating on sites and failing to acknowledge the importance of place to people's lives (Graham and Healey 1999; Stephenson 2010). Redevelopment initiatives,

---

15. Not discussed here is how planners (and others) move between place and site; for example, turning a derelict waterfront into a development site and then remaking it as a vibrant neighborhood. Useful in this regard might be Callon, Lascoumes, and Barthe's (2011, 48–70; Callon 1986) notion of translation.

inner-city highway construction, and pro-gentrification policies are seen as denying history and a "right to the city" to the inhabitants of a neighborhood. By doing so, they serve moneyed interests and tax-hungry local governments. Essentially, critics accuse government planners of having a view of the world that casts place as an absolute location within a passive and empty space, stripping it of its emotional and cultural meanings and of its people. From this perspective, space serves as a container for objects from buildings to playgrounds whose improvement, planners argue, will result in better places to live, work, and play (Murdoch 2006, 133–138). They propose an alternative understanding of place that infuses it with attachments and meanings, part of an integrated set of social relations involving identity, history, memory, and moral attachments (Gieryn 2000; Smith 2007, 7). From this perspective, place is socially constructed or performed and thus open and fluid. It "gathers things, thoughts, and memories in particular configurations" (Escobar 2001, 143; see also Healey 2005).[16]

A site is a place recast in professional terms such as lot size, zoning designation, distance from a light rail stop, and market value, for the purpose of intervention (Beauregard 2005b). Often the place is being prepared for development by being sanitized and made legible to those who might invest there, much as the Bluestem planners needed to determine the value of the property slated for the landfill so they could borrow the funds to purchase it and assess its geology to ensure that disposal would not damage the surrounding land. The history of planning, in fact, can be organized around the need for stable and actionable representations of space and place: ichnographic maps, GIS displays (Söderström 1996). And although state-supported property boundaries and property tax systems overlay all places in the cities and regions of advanced economies (Scott 1998), only some of these places become targets of state or private-sector intervention and are turned into sites.[17]

From this perspective, the planning relationship between people and place takes three forms: the transformation of places into sites and then into new places; the preservation or conservation of places; and defense. In the first instance, planners design and implement efforts to rationalize landholdings, provide infrastructure, and eliminate unsafe and unsanitary housing while providing state-approved housing or

16. On the need for social movements to generate spatial settings appropriate to them, see Sloterdijk 2008.

17. A similar phenomenon occurs when states turn politically robust citizens into clients or beneficiaries (Krause 2010).

demolishing a slum for commercial development. This is what Söder-ström (1996, 271) terms curative intervention. Planners also appropri-ate sites for public use, thereby eliminating the previous function, as with Bluestem's initiative to replace farming with solid waste disposal. In the second instance, planners protect places from threats to their history and current social uses. Here we find such policy tools as his-toric preservation ordinances, antigentrification laws, housing code en-forcement, and Corn Suitability Ratings. Zoning, one of the most ubiq-uitous of planning tools, is a way of protecting place while at the same time making it easy for places to be bought and sold, developed or rede-veloped, cleared or maintained. The third instance involves people de-fending their neighborhoods and cities from being turned into differ-ent places when their concerns are overridden by a politics from which they are excluded. Here we find opposition, including often-discussed "not in my backyard" (NIMBY) disputes.[18] Planning events inevitably generate controversy around place, with planners found on all sides of these issues.

A place, then, is different from a site and is often contrasted with what is called "space." In Casey's (1997, 3) phrase, space is an "utter void." It is endlessly and essentially ethereal. Place, on the other hand, exists because people and things occupy it, attach shared meanings, and fold it into collective memory. Places are not empty, like space, but congested: thick rather than thin. They are assemblages of human and nonhuman things whose materiality makes for spatial distinctions. The juxtaposition with space is what gives place its definition. This al-lows, for example, critics of faltering downtowns to talk about replac-ing dead spaces with places animated with sidewalk cafés. Representing space and place in this way, however, edges dangerously close to the problematic metaphor of space as container.[19]

One solution to the theoretical quandary posed by space as an end-less void or as a container for places is to approach space relationally. Rather than claiming that space exists before places and that places are produced "in space" by filling it with social relations, the counterargu-ment is that space is the product of social encounters. As Massey (2005, 10) has written, "Space does not exist prior to identities/entities and

18. Planning stories about the defense of place often equate place with empowerment (for the inhabitants) and site with their victimization. In most of them, planners are stripped of place, and this (arguably) empowers them by making them less visible and unreachable, and thus less vulnerable.

19. Confusing matters, much social science writing treats space as a synonym for place, as when Jackson (2008) writes of "community spaces" (the adjective denying the noun).

their relations." Space is "open" to action and not simply a "void" that preexists it. Such a formulation borders on the metaphorical but avoids the assumptions of the container metaphor. Action and the things that act are the forces that give space its material presence, thereby creating places that are less ephemeral than space itself. What this formulation ignores is the way places draw their identity from their relation to other places, a concern central to the practice of planning and to thinking of neighborhoods, cities, and regions as assemblages.

Places emerge as heterogeneous assemblages of humans and nonhuman things come together (Law 2002), much as a potential landfill site identified through map overlays becomes more and more real as tests and studies are done, the owner of the property is approached, the state environmental protection agency is notified, and the site is publicly discussed. Similarly, a public place is manifest through the things—paving, benches, trees, monuments, light standards, water fountains—and the memories, symbolism, and events that have come to define it. As places become thicker in their connections, increasingly networked, they gather even more things to them. A place becomes a landfill as more reports are written about it, more soil tests are conducted, and more time and resources are invested. Similarly, a planning office without controversial tasks becomes isolated and costless to ignore. Occupied by analysts, computers, charts, maps, reports, and plans attending to responsibilities with consequences for publics, it becomes a place to be taken seriously.[20]

Still unaddressed is "context," another way of differentiating space.[21] In the urban literature, the reference is usually to the history, current dynamics, and conditions of a metropolitan region as they impinge on its core city, the nation-state as it influences what happens in the provinces, or the neighborhood as it bounds the prosperity of households (Watson 2008). Context is often presented as external to what is being studied or planned, the background to the planning foreground. In the Bluestem landfill case, multiple contexts were in play: legislation emanating from Washington, DC, state environmental permit policy, city and county zoning regulations, and the agricultural space economy. Context, by definition, cannot be peculiar to a single event; it influences all the events and places that fall within its reach.

The planning literature contains two meanings of context. One has

20. Latour 1987, 63–100 provides a parallel discussion (which I have drawn on) for scientific laboratories.
21. As a supplement to this site-place-context triad, readers might consider the divisions of territory, place, scale, and network discussed in Jessop, Brenner, and Jones 2008.

to do with the actual setting where planning occurs: for example, the conference room where the planners negotiate with the developer, the low-income neighborhood where activists organize to resist gentrification, or the city council chambers where a resident group calls for historic designation of its neighborhood. One acts in a specific place, at a specific time, and within a specific social setting. Abbott (2001, 23) captured this understanding when he wrote, "The social world is made up of situated actions" that are being "continuously embed[ded] . . . in constraining structures." This is the proximate context.

A second meaning of context is represented by Fainstein's (1997) reference to the Dutch welfare state's influence on planning in Amsterdam. This is the distant context; it is the deep background to the proximate foreground. It focuses on the institutions, history, macropolitics, and socioeconomic conditions overarching any single place, rather than the richness and particularities of the place where planning actually happens. Watson (2008, 230) refers to this as the "broader economic and political forces" that encase practice. From this perspective, planning is doubly situated. It happens both in a specific place and in a more encompassing realm of constraints and opportunities.[22]

As a concept, context is not without its critics. Becker (1995) points to its sloppy use in many sociological studies, a failing also prevalent in planning stories. He writes that as scholars we often provide background information "even if we don't specify exactly how it's relevant, even if we don't make what we mention an explicit part of our analysis" (54). Little attention is given to the causal paths that link contextual conditions with actual practices. Becker then argues that "if it belongs in that description [of the social event], it belongs in your analysis" (57). His dismissal of context cautions us against assuming, rather than stipulating, the influence of structural forces on places and events.

Latour (2005b, 191–193) goes even further. He claims that there is no context beyond the action itself. Context, and by this I believe he is referring to distant context, is a theoretical artifice, a social fact that belongs to none of the actors within the network. Using "big" to refer to context, he argues that "the big is never more than the simplification of *one* element of the small" (Latour 2002, 123; emphasis in the original). In Latour's world contextual factors, so called, do not deserve, nor do they have, ontological status. For him, if these forces are operative

---

22. This raises a host of issues having to do with the putative local/global divide and the constituent form we imagine the world to have. See Tsing 2005 on the former and Law 2004 on the latter.

in a particular social event, then they should be treated as such, not relegated to the background. Or to say it differently, if context matters to an actor, it will be incorporated into its actions.[23]

Site, place, and context: these concepts are ubiquitous in practice stories. Often conflated and presented in different combinations with little attention to the distinction between proximate and distant contexts, they are used to explain and interpret how planners think and the consequences that ensue from their efforts. What concerns me as regards practice-based theory is the disregard of the network of places across which practice is distributed. Practice places are fundamental to planning's micropolitics and involve more than the sites for which plans are being developed and reports written. They influence the deliberations, participation, and publicity that are pivotal for a democratic and just planning and contribute to planning's effectiveness. Planning theorists who neglect the places of practice are missing much that is important about what planners do.[24]

The settings where planners act matter, and the closer we approach them, the more unavoidable becomes our shared responsibility for the places and the people and nonhuman things that inhabit them and give them material presence. The issue for planners, though, is not simply one of behaving ethically by treating others as one would want to be treated. It is also a matter of situating planning in relation to the structural injustices that create many of the undesirable conditions with which planners grapple. Here is where the social responsibility of planners surfaces.

23. Latour has also written that "context moves along and flows just as buildings do" (Latour and Yaneva 2008, 87).
24. Readers might notice that I have avoided the issue of scale. Although including it would have enriched the discussion, scale is a problematic issue in actor-network theory, known for its flat ontology (Collinge 2006).

FIVE

Distributed Morality

On Monday morning, August 29, 2005, the center of Hurricane Katrina, heading northward, passed just a few miles southeast of New Orleans. Once a Category 5 hurricane, which would have made it one of most powerful and potentially destructive storms to reach land, it had weakened to a still very dangerous Category 3. The day before, Mayor Ray Nagin had, after some delay, issued a mandatory evacuation order to residents. By that time, 370,000 people had already fled. Most of the approximately 92,000 people left behind had neither the money nor the transportation to leave; many of them were elderly and needed medical assistance to make the journey to safer ground. Despite the existence of a disaster plan that included evacuation procedures, the city government had made no arrangements for moving them to safety. Public transit and school buses, along with drivers, were unavailable. Mayor Nagin encouraged people to go to the Superdome athletic stadium for shelter, using whatever means they could devise.

By early Tuesday morning a large portion of the city was flooded from the rain. The waters were not deep, the levees had held, the winds were dying down, and property damage had been relatively minor. It seemed as if New Orleans had escaped the storm its residents had always feared. This was not to be.

The storm surge that followed Hurricane Katrina was fierce enough to overflow the storm walls and compromise and eventually push through the levees (Shrum 2014). With most of the city below sea level the damage was extensive, the force of the water lifting automobiles and trucks, knocking buildings off their foundations, uprooting trees, and eventually reaching twenty feet deep in too many places. Those still there fled to their rooftops, drowned in their homes, or began making their way, either in boats, on makeshift rafts, or by wading through toxic water, to the Superdome and later the Convention Center. There they found a lack of food, minimal medical services, and an undercurrent of social disorder. The heat and humidity were oppressive, and for days people lingered with little assistance from either the city government or FEMA, the Federal Emergency Management Agency. Families had been broken up and pets lost. Information was scarce. Those cast aside were disoriented, their condition abysmal and their immediate future unknown.

The official toll for those who died as a result of the hurricane and its aftermath has been set at 1,836 people, with 85 percent from Louisiana and most of those from New Orleans. A rough estimate for the city is well over 1,000 deaths, a number complicated by missing persons. Bodies were often left for days and weeks in abandoned homes, floating among the debris, or simply "parked" outside the facilities where people had congregated. More than 200,000 residents were permanently displaced, and in a matter of days the city's population was reduced by 40 percent. By 2010 many who had been forced to flee returned, but overall the city's population was one-quarter smaller. Approximately 70 percent of its housing units were damaged or destroyed. City-owned properties alone sustained over $1 billion in damages, and the overall destruction in the hurricane-struck area was estimated to be between $75 billion and $125 billion. Most important, but not surprising, the poor, the disadvantaged, the elderly, the frail, and African Americans suffered disproportionately. They were the most vulnerable, and their government had failed to protect them.[1]

Clearly this was a disaster of immense proportions, and almost all commentators recognized that even though Hurricane Katrina could not have been prevented either from becoming a Category 3 storm or from making landfall, many of the deaths and much of the trauma could have been avoided. To repeat the cliché, this was not a natural disaster. In the words of sociologist Kai Erikson (1976), "It is obvious that human populations are spread out across the earth in such a way that the most disadvantaged of them are the most likely to be in harm's

1. My description of Hurricane Katrina's impact on New Orleans is based on Bakker 2005; Brinkley 2006; Comfort 2006; Congleton 2006; Gabe, Falk, and McCarty 2005; Laska and Morrow 2006/2007; Olshansky and Anderson 2010; and Shrum 2014.

way. . . . [T]he vulnerable have already been herded into places where disasters are most likely to strike."

Although Hurricane Katrina was an extreme event, the vulnerability of New Orleans and its residents to severe storms and the scope and complexity of the rebuilding echo many situations that concern planners. Consider such issues as climate change, suburban sprawl, shrinking cities, underdevelopment in Africa, and postconflict reconstruction. These complex events weave together a tangle of interdependencies, cut across innumerable social cleavages, and radically disrupt prior commitments. Moreover, they often engender fundamental disagreements regarding the proper roles of states, markets, and civil society. Consequently, any mediation necessitates changes in the way these institutions function, thereby altering the array of opportunities and liabilities experienced by groups in different social positions. In such situations, planners search in vain for an effective response. Because what went wrong is so difficult to articulate and systematize, what to do is elusive: the twin dilemmas of the "wicked problems" Rittel and Webber (1973) warned planners about over four decades ago.

Many wicked problems—racism, poverty—are intractable precisely because they are entangled in structural injustices. That poor African American households in New Orleans disproportionately suffered was in part a consequence of their being more vulnerable to flooding. This vulnerability stemmed from their marginalized position in US society generally and in that city in particular. They were—and still are— victims of what Zizek (2008) labels systematic violence that transcends individual life histories (see also Young 2011, 52–64). Such injustice is maintained through the ways the social distinctions embedded in different institutions and practices reinforce each other, as when discrimination in housing markets lessens opportunities for the children of the affected group to receive a quality education (Tilly 1998).[2] Deeply rooted in how society is constituted, these injustices cannot be traced to specific individuals or organizations, so assessing responsibility and compelling remedial action are fraught with difficulties. Situations of structural injustice, of which Hurricane Katrina was one, thus threaten what planners do best: identifying the factors that have caused the event and designing actions to prevent its future occurrence.

My interest, and the thematic center of this chapter, is the moral

---

2. Both Young (1990) and Margalit (1996) point out that justice is more than a matter of how resources and opportunities are distributed. A just society should also be a decent society; that is, one "whose institutions do not humiliate people" (Margalit 1996, 1).

responsibility planners have for structural injustice. To pose this as a question is to acknowledge our debts to others (Graeber 2011) and ask what planners are obliged to do and with whom they share these obligations. Rather than approach this issue through abstract and formal arguments, I take a more practical political path. To act morally is to become more entangled in the ligatures of responsibility that bind and divide institutions, organizations, and groups. It means acknowledging our place in a material world of tools, technologies, animals, plants, and landforms and responding politically. To this extent, and if understandings useful to planners are to be forthcoming, the discussion needs to be focused on the realities of moral decision making. Consequently, after briefly presenting arguments for an ethical planning and attending to the meaning of political responsibility, I turn to Hurricane Katrina and consider what might be done to prevent such disasters.

Toward an Ethical Planning

I ask about New Orleans in the fall of 2005 not as a policy researcher hunting for causes susceptible to public intervention, but as a moral critic asking where responsibilities lie and who is subsumed within the "we" of those responsible. Planners are "constantly engaged in questions of values" (Campbell 2002, 272), and every issue that planners address—whether it is protecting waterfronts from a rising sea level or enticing developers to build affordable housing in return for density bonuses—entails decisions about what people value and who will benefit (or not) from the results. At the core of planning are questions about the right thing to do and who will bear the consequences (Hendler 1996). Because the intent is to act, planning is "an inherently moral practice" (Friedmann 1989b, 128). And while planners can hide behind their technical analyses and pass along the difficult ethical decisions to others (usually elected officials), doing so is an ethical choice and relieves them of neither responsibility nor accountability. Planners make situated ethical judgments that, because they are a prelude to action, have real consequences for places and people (Campbell 2006; Watson 2006).

Many planning theorists propose that justice is central to what it means to engage in ethical planning. Planning's procedural core is thereby deemphasized in favor of its material consequences. Social justice theorists (e.g., Fainstein 2010; Marcuse 2009) advocate for the greater importance of outcomes that make people's lives better, reduce inequalities, and foster diversity. Here we find proposals for living wages, affordable housing, quality schools, and a broader array of public services such as health care and transit. Many of these theorists also view social justice as inseparable from the right to the city (Dikec and Gilbert 2002; Harvey 2008; Marcuse 2009), that is, people's right to make a place for themselves and their families with the expectation that they will not be displaced. In short, and for these theorists, justice is the contemporary taproot of ethical planning (Campbell and Marshall 2006).[3]

These arguments often draw on moral philosophers who write on ethics, morality, and rights (Campbell and Marshall 1999; Hendler 1996). Such philosophers are concerned with the conditions under which people become accountable for a specific, undesirable consequence related to their actions or inactions (Fischer 1999; Frankfurt 1969). The philosophical reasoning begins by conceiving of and dissecting how fully individuals have free will and are thus able to make choices. The premise is that individual actions are not predetermined. Rather, individuals can decide to do some things and not others; they have what are known as alternative possibilities. To be personally responsible, an individual must act freely and with intent. But because freedom and intent are always problematic qualities, assigning responsibility is itself a puzzle. Numerous mitigating factors have to be considered: whether an individual's decision or action caused or only facilitated the undesirable consequence, whether the person was fully informed and aware of the consequence, and what other options were available. The question also arises whether a person should be held responsible for actions that fall outside the immediate sphere of family and community.

In working toward their conclusions, moral philosophers are often attracted to stylized examples and thought experiments rather than to real-world situations. To take just one instance, Frankfurt (1969, 831) ruminates on alternative possibilities using a single example: "Jones decides for reasons of his own to do something, then someone threatens him with a harsh penalty (so harsh that any reasonable person would submit to the threat) unless he does precisely that, and Jones does it. Will we hold Jones morally responsible for what he has done?" He adds various conditions (for example, introducing Black, who intends to manipulate Jones but does not), but the example never wavers from an abstract and formal language.

---

3. The theoretical implication is that John Rawls (justice) should replace Jürgen Habermas (deliberative democracy) at the core of planning theory, a distinction more blurred than crisp.

The intent of such philosophical exercises is to establish principles that a person could—hypothetically—apply to real-world situations. First solve the metaphysical problems, these philosophers imply, and the actual solutions will be within easy reach (Fraser 2010; Nussbaum 2006). The strategic intent is to impose morality on reality rather than to derive morality from the complexity and particularities of human existence. To critics of this approach, such philosophers are imprisoned in the "illusion of metaphysics."[4]

The deficiencies of this literature in relation to planning are three. First, discussing ethics, morality, and responsibilities at elevated heights of abstraction, thereby decontextualizing them, precludes the kind of practical guidance needed for living a moral life in a messy world. Consequently the literature is generally unhelpful for indicating how we might live with others (Freeman 2012; Hendler 1990). We are pointed in what supposedly is the right direction and then told to make our way down this path as best we can. Readers are assumed to know how to apply abstract principles—what Young (2011, 124) labels parameters of reasoning—to particular cases. What is needed instead, as Toulmin (1988) so eloquently argues, is a practical philosophy that privileges the particular, local, and timely over the general, universal, and timeless (see also Flyvbjerg 2001).[5]

Second, assumed away is the fact that people are deeply entangled with others and make moral decisions not alone but in profoundly social settings. Morality does not reside in autonomous individuals. Particularly as regards structural injustice, our responsibility is both personal and political (Young 2011) and is always inseparable from the networks in which we are located. In such situations, our obligations are to each other as well as collectively to the political community from which we derive support.

Not to be ignored is that people are ensnared in webs of relationships that connect them to diverse others in ways that are moral as well as performative (May 1992). To persist, communities and societies

---

4. Hilary Putnam as quoted in Westbrook 2005, 2.

5. Speculative realists are also critical of this kind of philosophy. Ian Bogost (2012, 110) writes, "For too long, being 'radical' in philosophy has meant writing and talking incessantly, theorizing ideas so big that they can never be concretized but only marked with threatening definitive articles ('the political,' 'the other,' 'the neighbor,' the 'animal')." Along these lines, my favorite comment comes from Edward St. Aubyn's novel *Never Mind* (2012, 83): "Just as a novelist may sometimes wonder why he invents characters who do not exist and makes them do things which do not matter, so a philosopher may wonder why he invents cases that cannot occur in order to determine what must be the case." For a less dismissive treatment of stylized cases in philosophy, see Sunstein 2014.

require a deep sense of mutual belonging. They are held together by rights and obligations, tolerance, trust, and a compassion that draws on empathy and an ethic of caring (Bellah et al. 1991; Selznick 1992). Neither market-based exchange nor state-provided welfare alone is sufficient to maintain the bonds that enable people to live well together for long periods (Judt 2010).

Finally, these moral philosophers and the planning theorists who follow them lead people to believe that moral principles—and decisions—are independent of the constituent forms in which reality is organized. The hypothesis is that one can step into the world (having left the metaphysical seminar room) and easily find one's way. The actor does not need to know how, and if, the world out there is structured in some fashion. With this absence, these writings imply that the world is unorganized until we decide to act on it. Moreover, they suggest that the material world is wholly passive. This is wrong. For planning practice, the material world is active and consequential.[6]

Because societies are built on reciprocity, moreover, any situated ethics has to be constructed around obligations, the dialectic counterpart to rights (Campbell 2006). Rights are conditions (for example, freedom of speech, privacy) that are legitimized by publics and granted and protected by institutions such as governments. For these rights to be realized, obligations must first be acknowledged. Without obligations, rights also disappear. A person who wishes to speak her mind in public must be willing to allow others to do the same. Societies and the communities that compose them flourish when people care for each other. In such ideal settings, people do not allow groups to be discriminated against, individuals to be exploited, or environments to be degraded. In a moral world, we recognize our common humanity and shared responsibilities, and we aspire to be just and democratic. To achieve this, citizens must have rights, but those rights cannot be severed from their corresponding obligations.

To address the obligations and thus moral responsibilities of planners in situations such as Hurricane Katrina, I draw on three important thinkers: the feminist and political scholar Iris Young, the social theorist and historian of science Bruno Latour, and the political philosopher Michael Walzer. Each enables us to solve specific problems related to acting responsibly. Young points to a robust understanding of what

---

6. Sayer and Storper (1997) write that "normative political and ethical theory tends to be sociologically and spatially naïve" (8), and they offer the observation that "ethical principles are not indifferent to forms of social organization" (9).

it means to live together in morally responsible ways by shifting our attention from assessing blame to engaging in collective action. Latour helps us define the "we" and provides a way to think inclusively. And Walzer offers guidance for setting priorities when the possibilities for intervention seem endless. My goal is to situate planning ethics in the sticky material of the world by applying these ideas about moral responsibility to the specific case of New Orleans and the ever-present danger of severe flooding.

Situating Responsibility

If planners are to confront situations of structural injustice, they need to consider who is responsible (that is, who has obligations) and what action this responsibility requires. Such responsibility is seldom immediately obvious. It entails engagement with a reality only partially revealed to us as well as recognition that not all actors share the same goals and values. Responsibility is not a position but a shifting set of relationships. Thus, what we believe we should do must always be subject to doubt. Accepting these conditions, planners can deliberate with those with whom they might then act. This sequence of concerns takes us from social embeddedness as the basis of an appropriate framework for moral responsibility to the notion of assemblage that delimits the sphere of action.

How can we, as planners, think about moral responsibility in terms of actions to realize it? Iris Young has two big ideas for us: that we need to distinguish responsibility from blame, rejecting the latter, and that we become morally responsible when we engage collectively in rectifying injustices (Young 2004, 2011).

Young proposes that individuals become "responsible for injustice by virtue of their structural connections to it" (Young 2003, 40).[7] On this basis she builds a social connection model of responsibility that differs from the liability (or fault) model that blames a single individual or entity for an action or inaction. To be responsible in the liability model is to have caused or contributed to a consequence. Thus, one is blamed. Young, though, considers blame bad politics; it is detrimental to solidarity and corrodes the moral basis of society. She offers five reasons.

---

7. Related, May (1992, 183) writes that "the shared responsibility that we should feel for the harms perpetuated by our communities is precisely the cost we incur by being members of communities."

First, attributing blame to one or another actor contributes to divisiveness and thereby poisons public deliberations. As deliberations become more contentious and cynical, they erode compassion and solidarity. Second, attributing blame narrows responsibility. Only a few people and organizations are selected to carry the moral burden of what happened, leaving unacknowledged many others who also share responsibility. Those not blamed can consider themselves blameless. Structural injustices, however, are conditions to which many of us contribute even as we deplore them. For example, the clothes we wear and the food we eat, not to mention the electronics we purchase, are often produced under exploitative labor conditions.

Third, affixing blame isolates the specific acts of individuals or organizations and thereby deflects attention from structural inequalities and injustices. Blame is not what should concern us. Our attention should be focused on how responsibility for such conditions as poverty, chronic unemployment, racism, or the subjugation of women is shared among various groups. In the liability model, the background conditions that nurture structural injustices are ignored. In the social connection model, by contrast, we become responsible for the "structured institutional relations" (Young 2011, 40) that diminish other people's lives.

Fourth, attributing blame turns our attention to the past—to what has happened—rather than to the future and what must happen for people to live well together. To this extent, Young is less concerned with punishment or compensation than with rectifying the sources of injustice—more concerned with arriving at frameworks for action than with passing judgment. She wants people to carry out the duties their responsibilities mandate. This means, last, that our responsibility, unlike blame, is broadly shared. It is not that we are collectively responsible for injustices but rather that each of us is individually responsible as well as responsible *with* others. And while our responsibilities are not equal—they vary in relation to our social connectedness, capabilities, and positions of privilege—they cannot be dismissed because of this. Even the least responsible person is still responsible. Our responsibility is to rectify injustice "within the limits of other moral considerations" (Young 2011, 143).

Responsibility, then, is distributed. And because it is, our obligations can be discharged only through collective action. We have to join with others to imagine ways we might act together to make the world more just. This will necessitate public conversations. Reminiscent of the pragmatist John Dewey ([1927] 1954), Young argues for the importance of publics that emerge around shared concerns. Engaging with those concerns, people come to understand their responsibilities to each other. Such conversations, in turn, reinforce the moral ties that bind them together in a way that assigning blame and moving on does not. To act politically, as Dewey and Latour (2007a; see also Disch 2008) have argued, is to build publics around shared issues and then to ponder how they might act in response. The first step toward meeting our shared responsibilities is to engage in moral inquiry in which knowledge is produced and grounded in practice (Lake 2014). Moral inquiry cannot occur without a sense of how society is organized; it requires a sense of the attachments among and between humans and nonhumans. For that we turn to Bruno Latour, who offers a framework for situating moral obligations.[8]

In his actor-network theory, Latour proposes the assemblage as the constituent form of reality (Bender 2010; Latour 2005b). An assemblage exists when humans, nonhuman things (whether living or not), and technologies (or tools) are brought together into a functioning whole. These groupings might be fleeting, as in a flash mob made possible by smart phones, or more enduring, as in the military alliances, fighter planes and tanks, policing, ideological support, and foreign aid that often enable dictators to remain in power. Such assemblages are the forms reality takes as people and things come together. They are always heterogeneous, fluid, and constantly evolving as they enroll other actors and lose allies when conditions change and successes or failures accumulate.

Key to the meaning of assemblage are the notions of symmetry and heterogeneity (Beauregard 2012c). Assemblages are not solely the consequence of human intention such that technologies, nature, and ideas exist only to achieve human goals. Latour (1993) rejects a view of the world that distances culture from nature and technology. His intent is to break down the (artificial) barriers between people and the material world of things. For him it is not humans who act and "others" that are manipulated. Rather, because nonhuman things influence how assemblages function and thus what humans can and cannot do, nonhumans are actors as well. Consider how e-mail affects the flow of a person's day, the pace of her decisions, and the opportunities she has to meet face-to-face with others. Nonhumans are complicit in both

---

8. On actor-network theory and issues of moral responsibility, Fuller (2000, 6) argues that the theory has "an aversion to normative judgments" and is indifferent to social betterment (29). In fact, contra Fuller, actor-network theory usefully links morality with materiality in noting how humans create technologies that take responsibility for human actions (Latour 2008, 5–6).

the functioning of these networks and the consequences they produce. This then changes how we think about intentionality, not as centered in an individual but as shared across a network. The symmetry between humans and nonhumans distributes agency across an array of diverse actors. In doing so, it distributes responsibility as well.

Because all things produce effects and thereby modify the relationships within networks, all things are responsible. To quote from one of Latour's publications, an actor "become[s] *responsible* by *responding*" (Hache and Latour 2010, 312). To be responsible is to be sensitive to others and act accordingly (Young 2011, 121). From this perspective, responsibility does not depend on being self-conscious and thus human, but rather is a matter of consequences and reactions to those consequences. In this sense, both humans and nonhumans are members of moral and political associations (Sayes 2014). Responsibility is a way of being in the world that connects them; it is not confined to humans. Neither does responsibility depend on intent. Yet only for humans can we link intentions to morality. Consequently, and deviating from actor-network theory's emphasis on effects, humans both share responsibility with nonhuman things and also have a moral responsibility that nonhuman things lack. That is, we can hold humans responsible in ways we cannot do for nonhumans. Nonhuman living things can act intentionally, but they do so instinctively (without prior reflection) and thus without free will. A beaver can gather sticks and logs and dam a stream, causing property damage and disrupting people's livelihoods, but that is quite different from a government or a landowner doing the same. The government acts after public deliberations and is subject to democratic expectations. The landowner must take into account environmental regulations and the dam's impact on her neighbors. The beaver confronts none of these conditions.

Similar to the way agency is delegated to different actors and throughout an assemblage (Latour 2004b), then, responsibility is also shared. In this sense, keeping in mind the distinction between types of responsibilities noted above, we can speak of a distributed morality. Latour thus extends our moral sensitivity beyond the small contingent of human things.[9] At the same time, he loosens the bonds of responsibility by avoiding such notions as spheres of responsibility (for example, the family, the ethnic group) and embedding that responsibility

9. Bogost (2012, 73) writes that "when we theorize ethical codes, they are always ethics *for us* . . . moral standards sit on the inside of the *human being*" (emphases in original). He encourages us to consider an ethics of objects as well as an ethics for the interaction of ideas.

instead in the way action constitutes the world. Still, humans alone are morally responsible both for their own actions and for the actions they delegate to nonhuman things (Latour 1994).

This commitment to multiple, heterogeneous, and entangled actors poses a challenge for any purposive intervention. No planner or policymaker, no matter how vast the resources at his command, can intervene everywhere at once. But where to begin? Here Latour is not much help. We turn instead to Michael Walzer (1983) and his notion of dominant goods.

Walzer contends that justice is multidimensional; that is, justice is not one thing but a consequence of the intersecting distributions of different kinds of goods such as hard work, money, kinship and love, recognition, and office. Moreover, justice is more likely in some instances (for example, in the distribution of divine grace) than others (such as the distribution of political power). He then offers an obvious but too often overlooked observation—some goods are dominant because they are able to command other goods. This should not be a surprise. A person with money is better able to run for public office, afford more prestigious higher education, be more secure, and garner greater public recognition.[10] Additionally, by emphasizing goods, Walzer focuses our attention on the materiality of justice rather than treating it as a socially disembedded right. This enables a connection to assemblages and nonhuman things.

The idea of dominant goods avoids a nagging problem of actor-network theory in general and the notion of assemblage in particular. Within this perspective all things, human as well as nonhuman, are equal in the realm of action; they are symmetrical. In addition, agency, power, and responsibility are dispersed throughout the assemblage. What matters for the assemblage (and for any understanding of it) is what actors do within it. In a phrase associated with actor-network theory, one has to "follow the actors." This thinking challenges the ontological status of nested scales and produces what is often termed a flat ontology. If actors and assemblages have different spatial (or scalar) effects, it is only as a consequence of their actions. The effects do not precede them (Collinge 2006). All of this so diffuses moral responsibility that it undermines the basis for political action. This is why I have introduced Walzer's notion of dominant goods.

10. Structural injustice thus emerges in the same fashion as Tilly's (1998) systematic inequality; that is, through the coincidence of different distributions of dominant and subordinate goods.

If we apply Walzer's notion of the relative dominance of goods, we can identify those actors who have the potential to be most influential in mobilizing others to act. In almost all planning cases, this will be the actor with the legal, financial, and moral resources that can leverage additional resources. Advocacy and political pressure should be concentrated on this actor, in ways that never lose sight of the assemblage and recognizing that the assemblage can grow stronger the more actors are committed to it and the more stable those relationships become. An assemblage can become weaker as well. In any political action, in fact, it is likely that the intent is to strengthen one assemblage and diminish others. To do this, to intervene in these assemblages, requires awareness of the configurations within them and thus a sense of which actors are critical to their functioning.

Toward Responsible Action

How do these ideas help us to think about moral responsibility in the case of Hurricane Katrina? For planning theory to have value, it has to travel along the connection between ideas and practice. Yet practice is messy, laced with contingency and conducted by actors attempting to fulfill plans that have been incompletely formulated and contain flaws yet to be revealed. Moreover, often each actor harbors a slightly different interpretation of what the plan intends. Thinking about action in the way planning theorists do, however, is designed to produce consistency and to be effective. Contrarily, actually engaging in situated and ethical practice entails inconsistencies, unexpected consequences, detours, unconscious adaptations, and retreats that, judged against the initial goals, produce a sense of failure. Writing about practice is not the same as doing it.

That acknowledged, we can attempt an intellectual exercise that identifies the responsibilities attendant on the destruction caused by Hurricane Katrina and that might also reveal strategic possibilities. So engaged, I ask not who is to blame—following Young (2006)—but who needs to act and in what ways so the injustices endemic to this kind of event can be prevented.[11]

Hurricane Katrina and its storm surge constituted not a single thing

---

11. The historian Douglas Brinkley (2006, xxv) in his thorough and impressive history of the event, claims otherwise: "Any politician involved with Katrina who espouses the cliché that 'the blame game' is unnecessary is probably harboring a chestful of guilt." On the assignment of blame as regards litigation, see Shrum 2014. And, in her foreword to Young (2011, xvii), Martha

but a gathering of interconnected assemblages. There was the assemblage that produced a vulnerable population, an assemblage that placed the city in the path of hurricanes, an assemblage that enabled most residents to evacuate, an assemblage that produced FEMA's incompetence, an assemblage that made the city government irresponsible, and an assemblage that allowed the levees to fail, just to begin the list. People were harmed in so many ways; so many things went wrong. Rather than drift into the maelstrom of comprehensiveness, however, we need to set a more defined task, one that might reveal specific understandings and even advice.

On the premise that being responsible means preventing harm, I have chosen to focus on the flooding caused by the storm surge and to ask which actors need to be mobilized to drastically mitigate, if not prevent, future flooding. Flood prevention in low-lying New Orleans requires dampening storm surges so that damage to life and property is minimized. This can be done if the bayous are restored and human-made barriers—levees, storm walls, storm gates, drainage channels—are properly designed, built, and maintained.[12] To make my task more manageable, I am going to consider only the restoration of the grassy marshlands known as bayous.

Of the many benefits of bayous, one is that they absorb the force of storm surges, essentially functioning as a hydraulic barrier. Salt grasses and other vegetation, including cypress and tupelo trees, slow the flow of water while redirecting the surge away from the river, lake, and ship channels where it can more easily make its way into developed areas (Shrum 2014). Since the founding of New Orleans in 1718, however, the bayous' ability to do this has been successively and severely compromised. Dredging the Mississippi River robbed them of sediment, residential development and the expansion of agricultural land led to the building of levees that reduced their size, shipping canals allowed salt water to seep into their soils and harm the trees and plants that held them together, and leakage from drilling oil and gas wells in the Gulf generated pollutants that further eroded the bonds of water, soils, and organic matter that gave the bayous their integrity (Congleton 2006; Gilmore 1944; O'Neill 2010). These actions and their consequences allowed storm surges—now less impeded—to flow more freely

Nussbaum argues, contra Young, that to engage the future we also need to assess blame for past actions.

12. On plans in New Orleans to address the flooding and subsidence due to pumping stormwater, see Stromberg 2012. As regards technological solutions, Yablon (2009, 198–200) notes that technologies can worsen natural disasters and make cities more precarious.

into the bayous, across Lake Pontchartrain (just north of the city), and up against the levees. Pulled by gravity, the water behaved normally, searching for the lowest-lying areas, and eventually compromised the viability of the human-made flood protection system. To protect the residents of New Orleans, this natural barrier needs to be rebuilt. For every 1.5- to 5-mile swath of wetlands, storm surges are reduced by one foot (Schleifstein 2010, 31). Who is responsible?[13]

We begin not with humans but with nonhumans: the Mississippi River and the grasses and soils that together with the shallow waters define the bayous. Restoration of the bayous will be successful only if the Mississippi deposits sediment, the grasses and shrubs strengthen and spread so as to hold the marshlands together, and organic matter accumulates. Birds (for example, egrets, sandpipers), fish, insects (for example, monarch butterflies), and small animals have to provide additional support, and the water must behave by gravitating to lower elevations (Argonne National Laboratory, n.d.; Berezowsky 1995). To restore the bayous to an adequate level of performance, contractors must add soils that extend the existing bayous, contour those soils, and introduce native vegetation. All this needs to be stabilized with natural or artificial fiber mats accompanied by berms built for water containment. Then the appropriate vegetation needs to be planted, including various types of grasses (for example, cordgrass), shrubs, and trees arrayed in tiers ranging back from the edge of the bayous to best absorb and contain any sudden rise in sea level. Some of the plants might be free-floating while others are rooted. All these elements—water, soils, birds, plants, trees—need to do their jobs if the bayous are to absorb the tidal surges caused by the hurricanes.

Contractors will have to be hired to undertake the rebuilding and to construct additional barriers to diminish storm surges in the canals and the lake. This will necessarily involve the Army Corps of Engineers and the Coast Guard. The businesses that drill for oil and gas in the Gulf will have to be brought into this assemblage, for they must either cease or modify practices that contribute to the weakening and erosion of the bayous. This means adapting current drilling technologies, developing new technologies, and even halting operations (Barry 2014). The channels that allow salt water to invade the bayous need to be reduced in width, and the shipping companies that move goods along

13. Restoration is already under way: see Environment News Service 2009; Save Our Lake: Lake Pontchartrain Basin foundation www.saveourlake.org; Schleifstein 2010; and Wunder 2011.

the river and through the canals and channels need to modify current procedures (Shrum 2014). Ship speed and wake size, preferred routes, the dumping of ballast, and the burning of low-quality fuels might all have to be changed for these bayous to expand and remain viable.

Current intergovernmental relations place the state of Louisiana and the federal government, with their agencies and elected officials, at the center of any discussion of bayou restoration. They control the public funding mechanisms and the regulatory regimes that enable concerted and widespread action. Environmental regulations, land use controls, and property rights related to the bayous and adjacent lands all contribute to the success or failure of this endeavor. However, these government entities will not act without sufficient pressure from advocacy groups and citizens to overcome the counterpressure exerted by lobbyists who represent businesses that use the river, channels, bayous, and nearby Gulf. Publics have to form so that governments can act effectively with sufficient resources and be made accountable. These governments also need leadership within the legislatures and from chief executives, the governor and the president. Legislators and their staffs, executives, lobbyists, planners and policy analysts, and increasingly the courts must also craft policies that can protect existing bayous and construct new ones. These policies then must be embedded in bureaucracies. In effect, responsible action entails political action and is distributed across numerous actors and networks. Critical to these networks is the government.[14]

This way of thinking suggests that the whole assemblage must be mobilized for the bayous to function effectively. That is, all the relevant agencies of the Louisiana state government and the federal government, along with the grasses, the river, the soils, and the water; the drilling companies and shipping firms; and the authorities that regulate water flow in the canals must act in concert. Lacking that, the implication is that it makes no sense to do anything. So while the notion of an assemblage helps us understand why the condition exists and who and what participate in its continuance, it then seems to stymie political action. Networks are not organizations like the US Army. They lack a chain of command—a hierarchy of authority—that enables not just the setting of common goals and their adoption by all involved,

14. Consider Lears's (2013, 17) comment on the adjudication of justice: "Nonstate justice adjudicates disputes between neighbors who must continue to maintain relationships; state justice adjudicates disputes between strangers who (in most cases) will never see one another again."

but also the mobilization of actors to realize those goals. In an assemblage, relationships are contingent.

Consequently, at this point in the process planners should identify a dominant actor that has legitimacy and can influence others within the assemblage. In this case that actor is the government, though it is difficult to say whether the federal or state government is paramount. The federal government has better access to funds, but federal regulatory regimes are not easily imposed on states. At the same time, the principle of subsidiarity suggests that states closer to the actual places and people that need to be remediated and regulated will be better able to do so, more sensitive to local concerns, and more open to democratic input.[15] Proceeding in this manner strays from the nonhierarchical nature of networks and assemblages. Planners need to recognize that while all actors are ontologically equal, this does not mean they are all equally important to the assemblage and its activities and consequences.

Being Responsible with Others

The goal of this chapter has been to approach ethical planning from the standpoint of practical philosophy rather than that of moral philosophy. To do this, I shifted the discussion from ethics to social justice and, specifically, to planners' moral responsibilities for structural injustices. The emphasis was on action rather than indignation, the future rather than the past, and on situatedness rather than distanced contemplation. A practical philosophy contributes to the "reflective resolution of quandaries" such as structural injustice and situates planners in "the collective world of political life and shared human problems" (Toulmin 1988, 352).

Within this, recognizing that any ethical discussion has to be situated, I deployed the concept of an assemblage. This constituent form of reality focuses our attention on the interrelated background conditions that planners must rectify. Ethical planning begins by thinking about how reality is organized and by embedding planners in the material world rather than perfecting their metaphysical framework or mobiliz-

15. Young (2011, 165–170) suggests that relying solely on the government to carry out our shared responsibilities weakens the social connections we have to each other and needs to be accompanied by strong and engaged publics.

ing their ideological biases. By identifying with the assemblage, planners gain a better understanding of who and what are complicit.

Assemblage thinking also encourages planners to recognize that humans do not exist alone in the world. Moral responsibility is distributed. To remediate the erosion of the bayous, humans will have to act, but they will have to act in concert with technologies and nature. Protocols for stabilizing soils, reenergizing grasses, and gently guiding water flow are partnerships between machines, chemical regimes, manufactured products, and natural forms. This pushes us away from the modernist division between the world in-here and the world out-there. According to this distinction, the world in-here is the world of humans with intentions and capabilities, while the world out-there remains passive, awaiting the directives that humans have devised. This, as Latour (1993) has famously argued, is a false distinction. There is no world out-there separate from a world in-here; they are the same world, a world comprising humans and nonhumans, each entangled with and responding to the other. Any intervention, any attempt to rectify a social problem, has to include humans and nonhumans. Encouraging the state government to reconstruct marshlands without considering what the grasses will do in response and how they need to behave for this to be successful simply returns us to the humanist delusion that separates culture from nature.

An essential component of Iris Young's argument is that public deliberations are essential for establishing moral responsibility (Young 2011, 113). To be true to her approach, to release its pragmatic potential, strong publics must form—as they have begun to do—around the reconstruction of the bayous, deciding who and what are responsible, making strategic decisions, and motivating humans and nonhumans to act in a morally responsible fashion. In short, a political strategy has to be devised that mobilizes bodies, symbols, and resources to influence government actors and establishes and maintains committed coalitions.

Furthermore, planners need to recognize how much the material world contributes to their effectiveness. This should not be too difficult. Improving the quality of people's lives is the ultimate goal of planning, but it is not its immediate goal, not the goal that mainly occupies planners' thoughts and triggers their actions. Nonhuman things are what immediately matter. In fact, planners are much more materialistic than they admit.

Truths and Realities

Few planners, I suspect, would dispute the claim that planning is *for people*. At the end of the day, planners measure their success by whether the city enhances the lives of those who live there. If it does not, planning has fallen short of its public obligations. And while planners often influence how elected officials and others think about the city, contribute to better government, and enhance the city's image with their works, these are merely means to an end. Only when conditions have improved and people are living well together do planners realize the promise of the profession. Only then can they justifiably claim that their actions have been worthwhile.[1]

In practice, however, planners mainly emphasize the management of the city's socioecological-technical relations, a task that elevates the functioning of the nonhuman, material world over the lives of individuals. Quality of life for humans thus becomes a consequence of trends and conditions within the physical environment. Nonetheless, "planning for people" remains a dominant value. In fact, calls for less attention to real estate and economic development are unflagging within the profession. In the 1960s, progressive planners in the United States criticized their colleagues in government agencies for elevating "bricks and mortar" over racial disparities and poverty. More recently, government planners have been accused of being too concerned with new commercial construc-

---

1. Flyvbjerg (1998) loses sight of this when he judges the success of the Aalborg project in terms of whether the proposed physical changes were made.

tion and property values and inattentive to the justice to be accorded marginalized and exploited people. Urban redevelopment projects, ubiquitous in cities across the world, are rife with this tension between planning for people (residents and business owners in the path of "progress," according to critics) and planning for growth or (more pointedly) for those who will benefit most.

What planners do best is make cities, regions, suburbs, and small towns physically better by, for example, providing neighborhood playgrounds, improving air quality, and expanding bus service. By doing so, they improve the quality of life for residents. To accomplish this, they set these places within technical and theoretical frameworks that dispense with details and particularities deemed extraneous for how these places can be made better. Unlike social workers counseling individuals or architects transitioning easily between drawings and actual buildings, each working case by case, planners approach the city and its various land uses at a remove. In the language of planning practice, people become population statistics and are folded into categories. Whether the woman in a heterosexual, two-parent household with two school-age children has a business degree and works for a financial services firm or holds a PhD in demography and teaches at a local university does not matter. Policy is made not for specific households and actual people but for the categories they inhabit. Knowing the size of these categories enables planners to set aside land for different types of housing, zone for various amounts of retail and office space, program for school construction, and align transit options with the locations where people and jobs are concentrated.

Although people's lives are the ultimate goal, the intermediate goal of improving the city and its built and natural environments dominates practice. From this perspective, the assertion that planning is for people is disingenuous. No doubt planners are concerned with the daily lives of those who use the city, but in practice these users are subordinated to less human-centric affairs. Planners are not indifferent to people, but people are secondary to what they do.

The intensity of planners' engagement with a material world occupied by actual individuals is mediated by principles of practice that enable planners to act. Such principles connect density to livability, sustainability to climate change, and housing affordability to property values. They are abstractions from real and concrete conditions, and their use distances planners from people's lives and takes priority over them. Principles of practice harbor possibilities; they are not actualities. Planners' core task, then, is to connect knowledge to action by translating between possibilities (what I call truths) and the material manifestations of those possibilities (what I call realities). Only by doing so can they act in plannerly ways to diminish the burdens of structural injustices, contribute positively to how actual people experience and benefit from the city, and fulfill their moral responsibilities.

To explore this relationship between truths and realities in planning, I will draw on three literary worlds: narrative nonfiction, academic writing, and realist fiction. My concern is with storytelling that communicates critical understandings that invite discussion and enable planners to be in the world (Disch 1994, 140). I will use excerpts from specific texts to illustrate the differences between possibilities and actualities, eventually leading us to how planners understand the city, their social responsibilities, and the importance of translation to their work. Insofar as no single discourse, whether science or fiction, photography or hand drawing, has a privileged relation to truth and reality (Rorty and Engel 2007, 36), planners can benefit from engaging with literary genres that portray places and people.

From Provisionality to Materiality

I begin with narrative nonfiction (Lounsberry 1990, xi–xviii). There, truth and reality appear quite explicitly. Writings in this genre convey a sense of what is possible while depicting what actually occurred. Narrative nonfiction describes people and events in their specificity and attempts to do so with "accurate documentation, *sociological insight*, an accumulation of details of material fact, an avoidance of poetic diction, idealization, exaggeration, melodrama" (Drabble 1995, 824; emphasis added). In it, literary forms and styles are mobilized to produce factually accurate accounts and emotionally resonant stories about real people and events. Much like historians, those writing in this genre strive to craft narratives that are "justified" and thus truthful (Megill 2007, 11).

Such writing might describe the building of the Brooklyn Bridge by focusing on the life of the designer, Joseph August Roebling; his daughter-in-law Emily, who supervised construction; technologies such as the innovative multistrand cables and caissons; and local politics (McCullough 1972). It might delve deeply into the relationship between a Hmong family and the American doctors treating its sick child (Lia Lee) and the miscommunications that occurred when scientific medicine encountered Hmong spirituality (Fadiman 1997). Or it might depict the confrontation of two great philosophers, Ludwig Wittgenstein and Karl Popper, over whether philosophy consists solely of "purely linguistic entanglements" or enables statements about the world that can be shown to be false (Edmonds and Eidinow 2001, 5). For Popper, philosophical statements were not simply language puzzles, and when Wittgenstein shook a fireplace poker at him during a debate at Cambridge University on October 25, 1946, Wittgenstein was doing more than emphasizing a philosophical point. In narrative nonfiction we read about real people taking actions and carrying on actual conversations in actual places.

Take two more extended examples. One is from a book that describes the experiences of three African Americans—George Starling, Ida Mae Gladney, and Robert Joseph Pershing Foster—who migrated from the South just after World War II to three different cities: New York, Chicago, and Los Angeles. The other is an essay on heritage planning in Brockton, Massachusetts.

The first excerpt is from Isabel Wilkerson's (2010, 491) much praised *The Warmth of Other Suns.*[2]

George Starling has lived in Harlem for half a century and knows and loves it in spite of itself. Many of the people who came up from the South have passed away. There are fewer and fewer old timers left. Still, he makes his way around with a sense of ownership and belonging. He has lived there for longer than most of the people around him have been alive.

The magnificent brownstones are aging and subdivided. Urban pioneers have only recently begun to turn them around. The streets have been given over to teenagers with boom boxes, to crack dealers and crack addicts, prostitutes and soapbox preachers, wig shops and liquor stores, corner stores selling single cigarettes for a nickel apiece and homeless people pushing their worldly possessions in shopping carts down what is no longer Lenox Avenue but Malcolm X Boulevard.

In these two paragraphs Wilkerson situates Starling in his world. She reveals his long-term relationship to the neighborhood and describes various activities that occur there. On other pages we learn about his life as a Pullman porter, his wife and children, his attempts to organize fruit pickers in the South, and his search for his Aunt Annie Swanson when he first arrived in New York City.

The second excerpt is taken from Carlo Rotella's (2002, 167) essay

2. I have reversed the order of these two paragraphs.

"Rocky Marciano's Ghost," one chapter in his edited collection *Good with Their Hands*:

Patricia Johanson, an internationally prominent landscape artist, was locked out of her house. Not the house she lived in, which was in upstate New York near Albany, but a vacant house she owned on Dover Street in what was once an Italian section of Brockton, Massachusetts. She and I walked around outside, peering in and trying doors and windows, but it was closed up tight. Her keys did not work because someone had changed the locks—on *her* property, which requires nerve. It was hard not to take this situation as indicative of how badly things had turned out for her in Brockton after a promising start.

Rocky Marciano, a prizefighter who was once heavyweight champion of the world and one of Brockton's most famous residents, had grown up in this house. Johanson was hoping to turn it into a museum and a stop along the Rocky Marciano Trail that she had designed to portray the city's industrial and cultural history to visitors and residents. The culprit was Mark Casieri. Casieri had wanted to buy the property but could not obtain a mortgage. He was also soliciting money for renovations; in fact, he was renovating the house at the time. This explained why he had changed the locks. "'It has to be Mark,' she said, wonderingly. 'He's like me'" (169).

Rotella writes about an effort to recover and preserve a city's past and strengthen its shared identity. He brings us two real people—in detail: Johanson—innovative and persistent—was a landscape artist living in upstate New York; she formerly worked as a painter and sculptor and had been hired by the city government to design the heritage trail. Casieri was Italian (like Marciano), a long-term resident, the owner of three pit bulls, and a post office employee. Details also make the house real: two-family, with unyielding windows, wood-shingled, and with a new lock that Johanson's keys do not fit. Rotella adds credibility to his narrative by informing us that he was there with her.

One can easily imagine a planner reading these narratives and finding much in them that is useful. Wilkerson's writing attends to the kinds of concerns that motivate planners: the condition of the housing, the first stirrings of gentrification, the vibrancy of street life, the retail mix, informal activities, and the sense of community signaled by renaming a major avenue after an important black political activist. Planners' interest would also be piqued by the possibility that George Starling is one of a cohort of elderly individuals in the neighborhood who need assistance. Similar thoughts would likely accompany a reading of Johanson's efforts to preserve both Brockton's heritage and Marciano's reputation. The ethnic changeover of a former manufacturing city, the desire to preserve the past, and the quest for a unique city image would all be familiar.

Planners can learn from these narratives; whether they find them *prêt à l'emploi*, relevant to the actions they envision, is another matter. One issue involves abstraction; in such texts, and from a planning perspective, we are overwhelmed with specifics. Do we really need to know that one can buy a single cigarette for a nickel at a corner store? Too much information muddles the forces that set these conditions in motion. When they are combined with the surfeit of comparisons to similar cases, it becomes difficult to generalize. Rotella does not compare Johanson's proposal to heritage trails in Boston or Providence. There are no categories, only specific cases. Layered in actualities, the underlying possibilities are obscured. Unable to generalize, it is difficult for planners to take what they have read and apply it elsewhere; that is, to use these realities to operate at the level of government policies, long-term trends, statistical categories, neighborhood types, and social groups. These narratives put planners close to people and far from the principles through which they understand the city. From a planning perspective, the problem with narrative nonfiction is that it rings true while its reality diminishes awareness of the forces governing development.

In making this claim, I have in mind specific meanings of truth and reality. I am not presenting truth in the classic sense of a correspondence between a statement and an external reality, the facts. Truth is not, for me, a Platonic ideal—immutable or in any sense universal. It is not "independent of our own making" (Latour 1999, 136). Rather, I treat truth as possible states of the world that might materialize but have not yet done so. Many truths exist, and truth is immanent rather than transcendent; it emerges from below rather than hovering above. Devoid of historical contingencies and the accidents of time and place, truths are general rather than particular. Because they are delinked from the material world, without connections that would curtail their meaning, they are formed in negotiation as people contemplate a world replete with limitless variations and overwhelming details (Tsing 2005, 1). In addition, truths are ripe for harvesting as principles of practice. Consider as an example the truth that cities are constantly in flux as regards their economic dominance. Decades hence, Los Angeles might ascend to the top of the US urban hierarchy, be displaced in its region by a city in the thrall of rapid growth or maintain its status. These are three of the realities that might ensue and that matter to planners.

If something is possible and by definition provisional, it represents a truth about the way the world works. Wilkerson did not provide evidence that brownstones were being gentrified in Harlem, but given the time period and the history of neighborhood change in New York City, such an event was possible. And gentrification was possible because it fit a logic—understood by planners—that ties together real estate investment, demographic change, housing markets, and employment patterns. By conceiving of truth this way, we accept the contingency of events. The past could have been different; the future might unfold in divergent ways. This consciousness of "the discrepancy between the real and the possible" (Marcuse 1964, 229) is at the core of critical theory. Behind appearances, critical theorists argue, lie hidden forces. Do not surrender to the appearance of reality. Be open to the logics behind it, but remember that those logics are always indeterminate (Gibson-Graham [1996] 2006).

An approach to truth that emphasizes possibilities reflects a pragmatic point of view. For pragmatists, truth is a well-justified belief that "answers to our experience of reality" (Westbrook 2005, 45–46). The truth of a belief lies in its consequences. Not all consequences are relevant, however, and inquiry—collective deliberation—is required to decide which consequences fit the truth claim and which do not. Truth thus emerges when people and nonhuman actors come together to share their experiences, consider them skeptically, and test them against possible outcomes. No single truth is waiting to be discovered. Rather, truth is constructed (Hacking 1999), although pragmatists prefer a different term—warranted assertibility (Rorty and Engel 2007). It is discursively realized through deliberations that draw on people's experiences. As William James ([1907] 1978, 97), one of the original pragmatists, wrote, "Truth *happens* to an idea. It *becomes* true, is *made* true by events." Bruno Latour (1988) agrees. We speak truthfully when what we say is deemed warranted (and thus plausible) by those who have gathered to thoughtfully measure its credibility against their experience.

Truth is different from reality. Truth exposes us to the world's possibilities; reality appears when possibilities have been substantively realized—entangled in the world's materiality.[3] Reality is the actual-

---

3. This argument is meant to track critical realism in the social sciences (Sayer 2000, 10–28; 2004) and to echo Merrifield's (1997, 421) distinction between metaphors that represent processes and those that "subsume the deep and richly textured space of lived experience."

ization of a truth. Consider one such truth; people who are oppressed often resist. What they will actually do, individually or collectively, depends on the variety of relationships and conditions existing at the time. The realities are many. Faced with severe discrimination and seg-regation in the South in the first half of the twentieth century, African Americans responded in a variety of ways: organizing in protest, reg-istering to vote, accepting their fate, finding a niche in the southern economy, and fleeing north along different paths to diverse destina-tions. Of these possibilities, George Starling selected one. He acted in a specific way—he left for Harlem. And he left for a particular reason—the owners of the orchards where he worked were about to beat him (or worse) for organizing the pickers and forcing wages up. Starling was assertive in a place and time when institutionalized racism (known as Jim Crow) was still intact and African Americans were supposed to be—were coerced to be—docile and servile. What he did before leaving and what he did to avoid being exploited was peculiar to him, yet his reality is comprehensible against a backdrop of truths about life under those conditions.

Unlike truths whose many possibilities have yet to happen and thus can be treated with skepticism, reality is more or less there.[4] Of all the imaginable paths for the heritage trail (a trail that links sites of histori-cal importance), Johanson selected a particular one for New Bedford. She hoped the path would become entwined with buildings, tourist publicity, collective memories, and ancillary services and, as a result, would become stabilized and able to resist being changed or removed. Reality, in this sense, comes into being when alliances are formed among humans and nonhuman things, whether these alliances are centered on ideas, schools of thought, scientific discoveries, tourist sites, local industries, or social movements (Latour 1988). Once formed, saturated with relationships, these alliances (or assemblages) resist "tri-als of strength" even as they fluctuate in stability and resistance de-pending on the shifting interests and possibilities posed to their mem-bers. As Latour (1988, 185) tells us, "The consistency of any alliance is revealed by the number of actors that must be brought together to separate it." Faced with limited success, critics relegate the alliance to the realm of fact, at least until they can find allies sufficient for disas-sembling it (Latour 1987).

4. I am not suggesting that realities are like rocks and thus incontrovertible—"the thugs of epistemology" (Daston 2005, 680). Callon (1986, 203) writes that "reality is a process."

Realities, then, are specific gatherings. "An entity gains in reality," Latour writes (1999, 158), "if it is associated with many others that are viewed as collaborating with it." Because the collaborators are committed to the assemblage and cannot simply be severed from it one by one, the assemblage is not easily unraveled. Thus it is real in its presence and in its consequences. In the terminology of science and technology studies, the entity has become "blackboxed" (Latour 1999, 2), that is, it is now common and accepted wisdom, much as with the current belief, widely held by planners and city officials, that social diversity enhances economic growth. Reality exists when "we can no longer say whatever we please" (Latour 1988, 182) because the thing we refer to is now entangled with many other accepted ideas, material conditions, and actors.

Rather than lurking—like truths—on its margins, real things are in the world. To this extent the real is "permeated by both social relations and material objects" (Hacking 1999, 25). It is "historically, culturally and materially located" (Mol 1999, 75). Reality "speaks the language of daily life" (Merrifield 1997, 419) with its particularities, passions, richly textured lived experience, and immediacy. When we engage the real, we engage with the substantiation, in all its complexity, of a specific thing and its relationships. Reality is not "gentrification" but rather the specific instance of it in Harlem below 125th Street in the 2000s carried out by developers in an area that city planners had up-zoned for apartment buildings.

Here I part company with Bruno Latour, who claims no qualitative difference between the real and the possible (Latour 1988, 159). At one end of his continuum is the real that is highly resistant to change or denial, and at the other end is the possible that is highly vulnerable to change. By treating the real and the true in this way, by conflating them around the notion of stability (Latour 2005b, 118), Latour veers near to the belief that what is has to be. The possible, for him, is simply less real and not an alternative to what exists. He thereby appears as an uncritical, rather than a critical, theorist. Possibilities, utopian visions, and imaginaries are brought into the domain of the real and reduced to lesser versions of it. In Latour's realism, as Harman (2009, 72) remarks, "Reality does not play hide-and-seek behind a veil." Conceiving of all things as real, however, implies withdrawal into a world that is wholly immanent and lacking in the potential for revolutionary transcendence. If it does not already exist, it is unlikely to do so. Imagination and hope fall away.

A last example of narrative nonfiction spotlights the possibilities captured by truth and the disorderly realities that populate the world. For an essay on farmers' markets in New York City, John McPhee (1978, 52) not only interviewed participants but joined the farmers as they sold their produce in the city's Greenmarkets.

One result of the Greenmarket's considerable success is the attraction it presents to street hucksters, not the Sabrett's-hot-dog sort of street vendors, who are licensed by the city, but itinerant merchants of the most mercurial kind. . . . A guy came up to me once in Brooklyn and offered me a case of hot mangoes. I assumed they were hot. What other temperature could they be when the case lot price was two dollars? Another day in Brooklyn, a man pulled up to the curb in an old Chevrolet sedan, opened the trunk, and began selling Finnish porgies. Cleaning them, he spilled their innards into a bucket and their scales fell like snow on the street.

What is impossible about this? Nothing. And what is real about it? Everything. So many opportunities exist for so many erstwhile entrepreneurs when people are gathered together with buying on their minds. But it takes particular individuals with particular commodities and motivations to appear. For planners, more concerned with truths than realities, the hot mangoes and the Finnish porgies are mere embellishments.

Principles of Practice

Planners appreciate reality and learn from it, but they operate more comfortably, I believe, when dealing with possibilities. They look to the future and what might happen, and they want assurance that the conditions they can change will produce the consequences they desire. What gives planners hope are principles of practice.

Consider the following examples from texts commonly found in the academic planning literature and considered more or less essential knowledge for understanding its practice. The first excerpt is from *Phoenix Cities*, a comparative study of former manufacturing and port cities that rebounded from severe job and population loss in the early twenty-first century (Power, Ploger, and Winkler 2010, 325).

Philadelphia has some significant assets and advantages. It has a dynamic downtown area with a well-developed and imposing CBD housing the third largest and most prosperous downtown population in the country; 62,000 people live there, giving the city centre a vitality and diversity of activities unusual in US city centres. The boom of the downtown area is exerting pressure on real estate prices, forcing some back office activities to the suburbs. This suggests urban regrowth. At the same time, the metropolitan area is relatively dense and successful, with several important suburban centres. So recovery within the city is supported.

The second excerpt is from a study of environmental politics in Phoenix, Arizona, "the world's least sustainable city." In it, Andrew Ross (2011) comments that environmental advocates are fascinated with indigenous models of ecological stewardship in rural areas but fail to recognize similar models in cities:

Yet, in cities like Los Angeles, immigrants have distinguished themselves as heroes of inner-city renovation, fixing up decaying neighborhoods with sweat equity and customizing them with the kind of colorful ethnic detail that would mortify the officials of most homeowners' associations. . . . In some shrinking Midwestern and Rustbelt cities, the new arrivals had also been welcomed for stemming a steep population decline and salvaging near-abandoned neighborhoods. These renovations could also be seen in parts of Phoenix, where the swelling Latino population had long spilled out beyond its traditional barrio boundaries into the hastily built first-ring suburbs. Mayvale, Del Webb's 1950 master-planned community for first-time Anglo homeowners, was now predominately Latino, its crumbling shopping mall brought back to life as vibrant marketplaces of small, family-run stores. (113)

My last example comes from the discussion of community land trusts (CLT) in *Making a Place for Community*, a book on progressive, economic development policy in the United States (Williamson, Imbroscio, and Alperovitz 2002, 253). Community land trusts purchase land and use their control over it to avoid the injurious consequences of appreciating property values. The objective is to forestall land speculation and dampen price and tax increases in order to keep the properties affordable for community use.

Land trusts can be used as a base to launch community-owned business endeavors or a portion of the land trust can be leased to private commercial ventures, whose rents can in turn be used for broader community revitalization projects. . . . One example of such collaboration involves the New Columbia CLT of Washington, D.C. New Columbia works closely with the grassroots organization WISH (Washington Inner-City Self-Help), which itself helped found New Columbia in 1990 WISH helps low-income tenants develop [commercial] co-operatives, and then New Columbia purchases the land beneath the buildings to ensure they remain affordable.

Each of these textual fragments refers to realities. The one on Philadelphia mentions the size of its downtown population; the one on immigrants makes note of a particular place (Mayvale); and the excerpt concerning community land trusts cites actual organizations. The particulars confer credibility on the general statements. We have too little detail, however, to know how to help low-income residents establish a residential cooperative. The details are mainly for connecting imaginatively with readers. Nevertheless, for the most part and for most readers, these are real places, people, and organizations.

The things that do travel and resonate with planners are the truths contained in these excerpts. In the United States, it is common planning wisdom that downtown housing contributes to vibrant street life, encourages investment, and raises property values; that immigrants are hardworking and engender neighborhood-based ethnic economies that stabilize once tottering neighborhoods; and that community-based organizations have an important role in fostering local businesses and enabling low-income neighborhoods to resist the destructive property value increases of gentrification. These are the truths—the principles of practice—that planners find useful; they harbor possibilities that enable them to make cities more prosperous and better places to live. Such truths are just specific enough to be understood as possibilities and just general enough to relieve planners of complicating details.

Although realities can spur action and provide planners with moral justifications, planning requires removal from these realities in order to engage with truths. One sees this in the inclination to principles among social justice and right to the city theorists (Fainstein 2010; Harvey 2008). They are concerned for people who have been marginalized, exploited, oppressed, or in any way treated unjustly, while simultaneously directing our attention to the city's buildings and spaces. The physical city and its users are seemingly conflated. The issue then becomes the material conditions that diminish and enhance people's lives. This leads to proposals for affordable housing and inexpensive mass transit options that situate people in the categories of low-income households and transit-dependent workers, thus stepping back once again from actual individuals, households, and families.

The concern with justice and rights has roots both in the Progressive Era reform movement in the early twentieth century that took up the plight of the urban poor and immigrants and the 1970s call to reorient planning toward racial inequality and poverty. During the latter period, progressive planners argued that focusing solely on land use or the availability of decent housing abrogated planning's social responsibilities (Goodman 1972). (The targets of this criticism, you may remember, were planners employed by the local government.) The moral imperative, left critics argued, was first to help people who had few choices, suffered from discrimination, and lived outside the American dream. This commitment gave rise to a social planning that addressed the everyday concerns of specific groups of people: the elderly, the mentally ill, unemployed job seekers, children, and those without access to health care. By the late 1980s, the possibility of social planning had faded from planning education and was a minor dimension of practice.[5]

Planners do their work by searching for principles and thus possibilities, turning away from specificities and the concreteness of actualities.[6] The pull is toward types of knowledge and thus understandings—principles of practice—that isolate the functioning of the city from the lived experiences of its users. People's lives are situated in categories and associated with various logics of development. Although empathy for people is important, it alone cannot support effective practice. The connection to real people is thereby attenuated, and social responsibility is weakened, though not abandoned. Planners thus confront a double bind. Committed strategically to abstraction and generalization that enable them to act in multiple and often poorly understood (or unpredictable) settings, they simultaneously embrace a built environment saturated with intimations of growth, investor concerns with profitability, and state inclinations to standardization. At the same time, they hold on to an ideology of social reform that requires an openness to possibilities and thus a willingness to violate the imperatives of current realities.

Truth without Reality

If forced to choose, I suspect, planners would opt for truth over reality. This suggests that they could learn from fiction, specifically the narrative styles known as naturalism and realism. These styles refer to an imagined world that is meant to be possible and thus truthful. Those who write in these styles, though, have little interest in repre-

---

5. Nevertheless, it did not wholly disappear. See Editors of *Planning* Magazine 2008.

6. To this extent, planners should find much of interest in Janet Malcolm's nonfiction: "The job of the writer, she likes to remind us, is to vanquish mess—to wade onto the seething porch of actuality, pick out a few elements with which to make a story, and consign the rest to the garbage dump" (Z. Heller 2013, 8).

senting what has actually happened—what is real.[7] They are writing fiction, and any reality is outside the text. The literary critic James Wood (2013, 36) remarks that "the real in fiction is always a matter of belief—it's for the reader to validate and confirm. Fiction moves in the shadow of doubt." The novels of Charles Dickens are a good example. Dickens captures what it was like to be lower class and poor in the English industrial cities of the nineteenth century. Not for a moment do we believe that an Ebenezer Scrooge or an Oliver Twist actually existed. Dickens is representing possibilities, not realities.

As illustration I offer three examples. The first is an excerpt from Kate Braverman's (1993) *Wonders of the West*. In it, Braverman tells the story of the teenage Jordan and her mother. It is the 1960s, and they are driving across the country in a broken-down car, paying for their trip by pawning jewelry, and sleeping in cheap hotels along the road. The novel counters the fantasy of California as a land of sunshine and happiness, luxury and opportunities, beautiful people and enchanted scenes. Consider this description of one of the towns they passed through:

Downtown are the train tracks, the water tower, the grain elevator, the old stock-yards, the structures for storing what grows like so many miniature cities. This is a series of repetitions we have memorized.

Then we cross the tracks, the unborn places at the edges. Now there are streets that could be anywhere. They are lined with trees and the sidewalks are torn, uneven. There are two-story houses behind iron and stone fences. There are stacks of wood cut for burning. It is already so hot, the grass looks yellowed. In the backyards behind the wood and the stone houses are picnic tables and swings hanging from trees. The streets are named for trees; Walnut, Pine, Elm, Maple, Spruce. The streets are named for elements: Water, Ridge, Valley, Mountain, River. (247)

The second excerpt is from a novel by Fred Leebron (2000). *Six Figures* is about Warner Lutz, a fund-raiser for a nonprofit organization in Charlotte, North Carolina. He and his wife, Megan, earn modest incomes, and their lives pale in comparison with those of the bankers and investors who are feasting on the region's booming economy. They are falling further and further behind financially and live in a constant state of status anxiety. After a scene in which Warner has taken his two children, Daniel and Sophie, to a local playground, we read:

7. Historical fiction, by contrast, is meant to be both true and real, even as it imagines dialogue, motivations, and actions that are undocumented.

He walked the now docile children to the car and buckled them in their seats. What was another twenty-minute car trip when they were happy and manageable? They drove north, back to the office and the gallery, back toward Uptown, passing back-hoes and piles of orange clay and nearly hidden coves of tightly packed subdivisions and walled enclaves of newly built monstrous houses and then through relatively old Myers Park where the houses were redbrick and the air reeked of plantation money that had fled Charleston at the end of the Civil War and for the briefest of instants you had a sense of history. Here, at $250 a square foot, was a place he'd never be. (83)

The last example is from *Motherless Brooklyn*, Jonathan Lethem's (1999) story of Lionel Essrog, an orphan employed by a mob-related detective agency cloaked as a Brooklyn limousine service. When Lionel's boss, Frank Minna, is fatally stabbed, Lionel, who suffers from Tourette's syndrome, finds himself adrift and sets out to find the killer. Across the brownstone neighborhoods of Brooklyn and into Manhattan, he searches for evidence that will help him make sense of Minna's death. Here Lionel is describing one part of his world:

A block east, on the corner of Bergen and Hoyt, was an elegantly renovated tavern called the Boerum Hill Inn, with a gleaming antique inlaid-mirror bar, a DC jukebox weighted toward Blue Note and Stax, and a Manhattanized clientele of professional singles too good for bars with televisions, for subway rides home, or for the likes of the Men. Only Minna ever visited the Boerum Hill Inn, and he cracked that anyone who drank there was someone else's assistant: a district attorney's, an editor's, or a video artist's. The dressed-up crowd at the inn gabbled and flirted every night of the week until two in the morning, oblivious to the neighborhood's past or present reality, then slept it off in their overpriced apartments or at their desks the next day in Midtown. (238)

Each of these excerpts refers to something that does not exist: a town somewhere in the backcountry, a couple and their children, and a young man lost in a maelstrom of false leads and sudden verbal outbursts. The characters in these novels are not real in the sense of existing outside the text. Yet they are emblematic of categories that are quite familiar: the destitute female-headed and homeless household, the middle-class family slipping into debt, and the outsider who, like a private detective, strives to make sense of the city. The descriptions evoke conditions that planners understand. We read about small towns either left behind or about to be engulfed by the new economy—their landscapes dominated by the remnants of grain elevators and the stockyards that once made them prosperous but are no longer of use. The street names are reassuring. Leebron's description of Charlotte rings true: playgrounds far from where they are needed, denuded landscapes being prepared for residential subdivisions, gated communities, moneyed neighborhoods, and overpriced housing. Any planner can read this excerpt and imagine the issues the local planning department has on its agenda. And then there is the gentrifying neighborhood of Boerum Hill with its renovated bars populated by people who work in Manhattan but cannot afford to live there. Frank Minna, one of the long-term Italian residents of the neighborhood, provides the contrast between what the neighborhood once was and what it has become.

These narrative styles emerged in the late nineteenth century when certain novelists began to reconsider how they could best portray an increasingly urban society. This group of writers rejected the prevailing narrative style, known as romanticism, which focused on a single individual struggling—often successfully—against social constraints. In romantic novels, men and women strive for perfection and, in triumphing over a flawed society, take on heroic proportions. An often-cited example from a later period is Ayn Rand's *The Fountainhead* (1943), in which the architect Howard Roark refuses to compromise his artistic and personal vision and, as an expression of his beliefs, dynamites a housing complex that he designed because it was not built to his specifications. He is brought to trial but acquitted. Immediately thereafter, he is awarded a prestigious commission by one of his admirers.

Romantic authors make heavy use of symbolism. They often draw on religion and mysticism, deploying a corresponding lyrical or sensual language that reflects a belief in the possibility of freeing oneself from the shackles of a debased world. Romantic figures are transcendent. Consider in this regard Herman Melville's *Moby Dick* (1851), in which Captain Ahab hunts a particular white whale whose death, he believes, will release him from his torments. Ahab is heroic and tragic. Saturated in symbolism, the novel is an allegory of the human struggle to tame nature. And while the novel is real as regards the whaling industry of the time, being real is quite beside the point.[8]

Searching for a new style, nonromantic novelists were influenced by the rise of the industrial city, emerging class conflicts based in the factory system, heightened rural-to-urban migration, large-scale immigration, and increasing socioeconomic inequalities. They also re-

8. Ahab will remind many readers of the discussion of Faust in Marshall Berman's *All That Is Solid Melts into Air* (1982). The world Faust aspires to is the world that will destroy him.

acted to the rise of a mass-market publishing industry and the corresponding shift from writing and publishing for a small audience of like-minded upper-class friends and acquaintances—called "belles-lettres"—to doing so for a large and diverse audience (Borus 1989). This meant, among other consequences, thinking of writing as "work" rather than as a gentlemanly or womanly pursuit.

The rise of factories and business corporations, the growth of dense and socially diverse industrial cities, and the emergence of a professional and salary-dependent middle class along with a disenfranchised and exploited working class made romantic novels seem divorced from reality. The life of the mind and the celebration of individual accomplishment were beyond the grasp of most people. The middle class had other concerns—the development of the professions, the formation of a new type of family, the rationalization of institutional life, the fate of the cities—while the working class barely had time to do anything but survive. What were writers to say about this world, and how were they to say it?

In quick succession, two "new" narrative styles emerged—realism and naturalism. Both had as a bedrock idea the importance of creating faithful representations of reality, the "portrayal of life with fidelity" (Cuddon 1998, 729). Or as Fredric Jameson (1971, 200) has commented, the realist wanted to connect life and meaning "in a concrete way in the historical situation itself." He goes on, "Realism is dependent on the possibility of access to the forces of change in a given moment of history" (204). Realists and naturalists would write what was true, or at least strive to do so. Their goal would be to make readers believe that what they read could have happened in their own world. Consequently, characters and events have to be plausible. Such a literature is intended neither to reproduce class position nor to serve as escapism. Rather, it is crafted to reflect back on its readers the world they know, but it never has been a quest for the real as I have been using the term.

Realists wanted to write about everyday life. This led to a narrative style based on "precise descriptions of prosaic details" (Murray 1999, 992) that placed characters in the "historical moment." This is not transcendence but immanence; the "becoming" of characters occurs as a result of engagement with the world rather than rejection of it. Now more deeply embedded in reality, the individual is less likely to triumph—unlike what occurs in romanticism. Constrained by environmental forces, people cope. Defeat and downward mobility are distinct possibilities and are treated without the moral judgment that earlier writers had offered.

Where the naturalists parted company with the realists was, first, in the subjects they deemed important. The early realists, people like William Dean Howells, Theodore Dreiser, and Kate Chopin took the middle class as their subjects, whereas the naturalists like Upton Sinclair or Frank Norris wrote about the working class. Naturalists were also more inclined than realists to see the individual as helpless and as a product of unseen external or biological forces. We might think of them as more pessimistic. Finally, nature and in particular the "energy" of the city—the city as a "character" or force—had more of a role in naturalism than in realism. Overall, realists and naturalists were intent on capturing the truthfulness—the reality in their terms, but not mine—of contemporary society. This often meant writing about life in the industrial cities.[9]

A narrative style, of course, is a distillation of rhetorical devices and assumptions about the relation of individuals to their environment. It emerges from the interplay between how an author understands the world and how she represents it. If an author believes that characters can be known only in an unmediated way, then she will rely more on dialogue than on authorial description. If she believes the world is contingent rather than determinant, events will be portrayed as complex and unexpected, their meanings left unspecified. These choices, however, are peripheral to my main point that fictional realism and naturalism speak to concerns that are central to planning.[10]

From People to Place and Back

One of the ways planners learn about the world is through written texts. Yet for the most part they confine themselves to scientific and technical documents. While they might read fiction or narrative nonfiction for pleasure, my impression is that neither consciously enters into professional deliberations. The former comes across as indifferent to how things might actually happen, and the latter seems too focused on unique individuals and settings and too silent on the structural re-

9. The one exception here is Mark Twain, who famously wrote about life on and along the Mississippi River in *The Adventures of Tom Sawyer* (1876) and *The Adventures of Huckleberry Finn* (1884).

10. No author fits neatly into one narrative style. So, while we can distinguish the transcendentalist Henry David Thoreau from the post–World War II realist Nelson Algren, neither writes in a pure style. Further clouding the issue, literary theorists disagree about what actually constitutes style and whether it is a useful concept.

lations that shape them. Yet novels and short stories written in a naturalist or realist style have much to offer planners. Fiction often casts place—the city, a suburb—as an actor or a force that influences the decisions characters make and the behaviors that follow. Much narrative nonfiction is sensitive to the particularities of place.

These storytelling literatures thus have the potential to reveal imaginatively the interplay between truth and reality and thereby position planners in relation to the city and the people who use it. Clearly, claiming that planning is for *people* is more slogan than practice—an ideal to be pursued through other means. Planning is mainly about the processes and conditions that shape the material world, and this knowledge is of most importance to planners. Knowledge about real people and their daily lives is interesting but not directly useful. Planners dispense with "anecdotes" and "details" and focus instead on coherent and relatively abstract and general arguments whose internal consistency resonates with professional understandings.

This raises the issue of moral responsibility. If planners concern themselves solely with minimizing traffic congestion, heading off the deterioration of neighborhoods, creating opportunities to replace obsolete land uses, fostering assets such as sports stadiums, enhancing waterfronts with parks and marinas, and zoning for growth, this attenuates their responsibility for the people and nonhuman living things—for those that inhabit and use these cities. Because planners privilege the forces of development and the city in its material form, their empathy for the personal lives of the city's residents is muffled. Consequently their social responsibility is at risk. This is a structural condition within the profession and cannot be eliminated or resolved without changing who planners are and what their place is in the world.

One obvious response is for planners to be more sensitive to the kinds of translations they undertake as they search for useful knowledge about the city.[11] One kind of translation involves the shift, to reference an earlier discussion, between place and site in which the planner begins with local and particularistic knowledge and ends in technical frameworks. This is the commonsense notion of translation in which different forms of representation are deployed to portray a given set of conditions. Such moves, as Latour (1999, 30) has written, seem always

11. Zitcer and Lake (2012) suggest another way to "balance separation and connectedness . . . to retain the integrity of difference while fostering unity and conjunction" (606). Their theoretical solution draws on Hannah Arendt to propose a love that leads to collaboration and world building.

to push the world further away; yet they bring it closer to professional concerns. Successive translations create a distance between the reality initially observed and the evidence used to do science. Translations to higher levels of abstraction and generality, Latour suggests, never wholly leave earlier knowledge behind; they are haunted by prior understandings. The scientist can always return to greater concreteness and specificity. General and abstract knowledge, however, is knowledge compatible with the principles that govern practice.

A second kind of translation is found in Michel Callon's (1986; Callon, Lascoumes, and Barthe 2011) and Bruno Latour's (1999, 24–79) writings on public controversies and scientific research. The process involves not so much moving from one language to another as displacing and reassembling "actors whose mediation is indispensable for any action to occur" (Latour 1999, 311). This translation entails a reinterpretation of interests and a rearrangement of network relations, even to the point of adding new ideas and activities. Here planners engage with the way publics form around issues, thereby connecting their truths with the realities that are meaningful to others.

To the extent that planners are constantly involved in translations, recognizing the merits and demerits of doing so can help them grasp whether they are planning for people or for a thing called the city. Part of planners' moral responsibility is to be constantly aware of the tendency for practice to distance them from real things. I have no problem with planners' wanting to make the city, the suburb, or the metropolitan region function better so that people who live there can live well. My misgiving is that planners very often lose sight of one of the main reasons that reformers in the early twentieth century advocated for planning as a government function—to help those who were suffering. This is still a valid motivation and justification for planning. Principles of practice matter, but not at the expense of entanglements with nature and with each other.

Yet practice principles have to confront realities at some point, and their truths are going to have to either yield or be adapted. Here we have another translation, that between abstract principles and the unavoidable obduracy of the material world.

SEVEN

Planning in an Obdurate World

Reality is what has been stabilized and for all practical purposes has become fact: the earth revolving around the sun, rapid urbanization in China during the early twenty-first century, or the relations among supply, demand, and price. Because these beliefs seem inalterable, they resist critique. Holding a contrary belief proves unrewarding, denying the realities to others leads to disapproval, and subjecting them to trials leaves them unchanged. They remain strong and endure while enjoying widespread support among a variety of believers. Such realities might eventually succumb to a challenge (for example, data that show that hosting the Olympics is more costly than economically rewarding) and thereby no longer enjoy their dominant standing, but for this to occur these challenges will have to overcome entrenched relationships. What is real is what cannot, for the moment, be changed.[1]

The word that describes this condition is "obduracy." Obduracy is the resistance realities pose to attempts at modifying them. Realities are hardened, fixed, and intractable, and obduracy is the friction encountered when humans and nonhumans act against the grain of current accommodations. These realities are embedded in relatively strong networks, and changing them requires disentangling numerous relationships. To be clear, obduracy

1. Bruno Latour (1987, 93) has written that "reality[,] as the latin word *res* indicates, *resists*."

is not just about ideas and beliefs. In her seminal book on obduracy, Hommels (2008) describes the blocking of three attempts at urban sociotechnical change in the Netherlands: a downtown shopping mall in Utrecht that resisted reconfiguration, a highway in Maastricht that refused to be relocated, and a massive housing complex (Biljmermeer) in a suburb of Amsterdam that obstructed efforts to demolish it. She thus treats obduracy as a quality linking past policies, material things, current political capacities, and planning frameworks. For the United States, Kirkman (2009) explores the obduracy of the automobile, an obduracy that stems from its entanglement with road networks, gas stations and automobile repair shops, businesses ranging from parking garages to insurance companies, oil refineries, networks of automobile producers and suppliers, and the current form of metropolitan areas. So described, the automobile seems immune to any diminution of its place in everyday life. Hovering over these examples is path dependency, the "causal relevance of previous stages in a temporal sequence" (Pierson 2000, 252).

Obduracy, then, is a consequence of the stabilizing of assemblages by associations brought into play "that last longer than the interactions that frame them" (Callon and Latour 1981, 283). Supportive of ideas, conditions, policies, intellectual positions, and things, these associations have been "blackboxed." In this sense they are (for the most part) unquestioned and, if questioned, able to repel unwanted change. Bijker (1995, 282) has proposed that an artifact (thing) "has become obdurate. . . . [when] . . . the relevant social groups have. . . . invested so much in the artefact that its meaning has become quite fixed."[2] Nevertheless, things and places vary in their obduracy. Obduracy is unavoidable, but it is also unstable and manifest in the act of resistance. Stabilization is a moment, often quite enduring yet still open to disruption.

This way of seeing the world has important consequences for democratic planning.[3] To plan democratically is to engage with publics (Dewey [1927] 1954) with the intent of collectively reimagining the

2. In science and technology studies, fixed meanings are presented as constraints on scientific findings that limit theoretical assertions. Galison (1995, 14) writes that constraints "mark the endpoints of scientific inquiry, the boundaries beyond which inquirers within the community find it unreasonable to pass."

3. A nondemocratic, state-based planning also confronts obduracy, but resistance entails a much different politics. Examples of such nondemocratic planning include the apartheid regime in South Africa (Mabin 1992) and settlement policy in Israel (Norman 2012; Weizman 2007; Yiftachel 1995). Less extreme might be planning in Amman, Jordan, where in 2006–2007 the planners and their consultants developed a strategic plan for the city and faced little opposition because of the absence of participatory mechanisms and the strong political position of the mayor (Beauregard and Marpillero-Colomina 2011).

city and subsequently joining with those publics—and often the government—to realize what has been decided. Planners and their publics are thus mobilized when the world has gone awry or falls short of its presumed potential. "Politics turn around topics that generate a public around them" (Latour 2007a, 814). Without issues there are no publics, and without publics there are no (democratic) politics. When these publics (and their planners) act, however, they face resistance. An attempt to locate bus and commuter rail services in a single facility is confronted by transit companies that want to remain physically separate, transit riders who complain about new inconveniences, businesses and residents that do not want to be displaced, and a government unwilling to provide adequate funding. Faced with an obdurate world, planners and their allies are never fully successful. In a compliant world, their intentions would be embraced and their directives precisely followed. Goals would be realized and objectives attained. The transit facility would be built. In a heterogeneous world, one that is obdurate, unmediated planning success is rare.[4]

Obduracy, then, reveals planning's inherently political nature and its conflictual tendencies. It serves as a barrier to planners' goals and yet, ironically, is an objective they hope to realize. Conceptually, my interest is the positioning of planners such that they function as a source of change for the networks of which they are a part. This means moving away from the micropolitics of interpersonal relations to the macropolitics of public engagement with plans, projects, and schemes and their various proponents and opponents. My foundational claim is that the concept of obduracy captures our relationship not only to each other as humans but to the nonhuman world as well. To demonstrate obduracy's usefulness for thinking more clearly about planning as well as practicing it more effectively, I offer two examples of obduracy in action. But before presenting them, I should say more about what I mean by obduracy. For this I need the help of a herd of goats.

Goats of the Turkana

Northwest Kenya is home to a group of seminomadic pastoralists called the Turkana (Parenti 2011, 40–53). The region is arid, and the Turkana

---

4. Flyvbjerg's (1998) study of the proposed bus terminal in Aalborg, discussed earlier, can be read as a case of obduracy in planning practice even though the concept is absent from his interpretation.

grow only basic crops and only in small quantities. For milk and meat and as a form of currency, they rely on their livestock–goats, sheep, and camels. Their animals are also a source of status. In the Karasuk Hills nearby lives a tribe known as the Potok whose members derive part of their livelihood from stealing the Turkana's cattle. Since the loss of goats and sheep severely diminishes the Turkana's ability to survive, they aggressively defend against these raids.

In 2008 one such raid was particularly violent. Armed with rifles, the Potok descended from their higher elevation with a plan to encircle as many of the Turkana's sheep and goats as possible and herd them toward a narrow opening in the hills. Once through the pass, they could establish positions where they could fire on the Turkana and prevent further pursuit. Any Turkana who attempted to move through the pass would be shot; the goats would be in Potok control. Having been attacked only a week before, the Turkana had sent armed warriors to guard the goats, but their heightened vigilance and presence were a weak deterrent. The raid began in midmorning, lasted about six hours, and ranged over six kilometers of the flat desert. Both sides knew their opponents' strategy: for the Potok, it was to herd the goats through the pass as quickly as possible; for the Turkana, it was to outflank them, arrive at the pass first, and block the theft by scattering the goats across the dry scrubland. As the Turkana warriors headed toward the pass, the rustlers shot at them to slow their progress as they herded the goats forward. Normally the goats and sheep would have obeyed. This time they did not.

Spooked by the shooting and the yelling as well as by the pace at which they were being herded, the goats and sheep stopped moving. They panicked, and "instead of running, they bunched up, each animal trying to hide inside the flock, all of them pressing into a dense, immobile mass. Other animals got tangled up in the brush" (Parenti 2011, 44). No matter how much the Potok shouted and kicked and pushed the goats, they could not hurry them toward their destination. By the time the Potok and the herd reached the pass, the Turkana had already arrived and were able to disperse the raiders (killing six of them while losing three of their own men) and prevent the herd from being taken. Because the goats opted not to run but to resist the efforts of their captors, the Turkana were able to recapture them. The goats were obdurate rather than compliant; unable to overcome this obduracy, the Potok failed.

This story not only renders a vivid image of obduracy but situates obduracy in the material world, pointing out that obduracy is a property of both humans and nonhuman living things. Moreover, it presents obduracy as relational rather than intrinsic to things (Latour and Yaneva 2008). Last, while the goats' obduracy frustrated the Potok, it served the Turkana's interests. Obduracy thus appears as a dialectical condition that exists in the presence of contending interests.

Goat herds, however, seldom appear on the agendas of planning agencies. If we are to understand obduracy's place in planning, we need to look at more immediate examples. To this end, I have selected two planning stories that illustrate obduracy in practice. The first is a common planning event—the attempt to redevelop what a municipal government believed was a blighted area of the city, in this case Willets Point in New York City. The second involves the construction of Israeli settlements on land contested by the Palestinians.

Willets Point Redevelopment

In June 2012, Mayor Michael Bloomberg of New York City announced that the Queens Development Group, a joint venture of the Related Companies and Sterling Equities, had been chosen as the developer for the first phase of the Willets Point redevelopment initiative. The mayor had first proposed this initiative in 2007, and it was now reaching fruition. During this first phase, the developer would construct a 1.4-million-square-foot retail and entertainment center adjacent to a $600 million major league baseball stadium (Citi Field) that had opened in 2009.[5] The center would include more than two hundred retail stores, movie theaters, restaurants, entertainment venues, and public spaces, with both surface parking and a parking garage. Of the 23 total acres of land, 7.5 acres would be set aside as a buffer between this new mixed-use complex and an adjacent industrial area slated for future redevelopment. The developers estimated that the first phase would attract $1 billion in private investment, create 2,700 permanent jobs, and (on completion) bring the city annual tax revenues of $62 million.[6]

Known as Willets West, the first phase is part of a larger project (Willets Point Community) meant to transform this area of northeast Queens, one of the city's five boroughs. There were to be 2,500 dwell-

5. The entertainment complex would be built on mapped city parkland that the city leased to the baseball team that owned the stadium (Finn 2013).

6. Website of the New York City Economic Development Corporation (www.nycedc.com), accessed May 17, 2013. See also DeJohn 2013.

ing units (875 of them below market rate and thus "affordable"), a two-hundred-room hotel, 500,000 square feet of retail space, and the entertainment complex (Bagli 2013; Karni 2013). Designated by the city government as blighted and as an urban renewal district, the sixty-one acres of land on Flushing Bay had been the target of redevelopment efforts for nearly forty years.

At the beginning of this most recent city initiative, the area was occupied by auto repair shops, automotive parts suppliers, scrap yards, a gravel yard, street vendors, a waste processing plant, a diner, and various small industries. The largest property owner was the House of Spices, which produced and distributed Indian foods. One estimate was that Willets Point had 228 businesses employing approximately 1,700 workers (Baldwin 2009, 81; S. Watson 2008, 35), all of which had to be displaced to realize the announced redevelopment plan. Displacement, though, was only one of the challenges Willets Point posed to the city's planning department and economic development agency.[7]

Most of the businesses did not want to move, since it would disrupt their operations and also sever their relations with other businesses in the area. The automotive repair shops, for example, purchased parts from the nearby automotive supply store, while the street vendors sold food to the businesses' customers and to their employees. The announcement that the city was going forward with the complete redevelopment of the area generated lawsuits meant to stop the project. In 2008 a group of ten large businesses and landowners, calling themselves the Willets Point Industry and Realty Association, went to court to prevent the city from using eminent domain to compel them to sell. In the absence of eminent domain, property owners could remain if they wanted to or negotiate with buyers without having the threat of a "taking" affect the negotiations. That group was subsequently joined in 2009 by Willets Point United, which argued that the redevelopment did not constitute a "public use" and thus could not justify the use of eminent domain. Willets Point United also claimed that the city's environmental review assessment was flawed, calling into question its review process and the subsequent string of regulatory approvals. None of the lawsuits were successful.

Even though a majority of the city council had opposed a previous version of the project in 2008, it accepted the recommendation of

---

7. The city was slated to provide $9 million in relocation assistance to displaced businesses, $3.5 million for renting new premises, and job training support to displaced workers. The area had one official resident, living above a restaurant (Nir 2013).

the City Planning Commission and in late 2013 approved the zoning changes necessary for the initiative to proceed. By June 2012, when the mayor announced the selection of a developer and unveiled the plans for the first phase, the city had bought 90 percent of the properties on the site and was negotiating with the remaining nine property owners.[8] At the end of 2013, the city government had purchased 95 percent of the twenty-three acres, invested $400 million in the project, and given the developers a capital grant of $100 million (Bagli 2013).

The proposed redevelopment site was occupied by businesses that were financially viable. However, it lacked sanitation and storm sewers, a water supply, and sidewalks. Moreover, its roads were poorly paved, inadequately maintained, and potholed. One visitor (Nir 2013, 1) described the streets as "pooled with dark, oil-slicked water or rutted with knee-deep holes that suck in a car's tires." Because of the lack of sewerage and the types of businesses that occupied the site, the soil was highly contaminated by petroleum, paint, cleaning solvents, and other toxins.[9] The director of one business group characterized Willets Point as "Queens' biggest eyesore" (New York City Economic Development Corporation 2012). Remediation and cleanup were unavoidable, imposing significant up-front development costs. In addition, Willets Point was subject to noise pollution from being near one of the city's three major airports—La Guardia—and often under the flight path of departing and arriving jets.

That the site is in a hundred-year floodplain imposed an additional cost on preparing it for new construction, since it frequently flooded in rainstorms. The high water table also contributed to the soil and water contamination and posed further difficulties for remediation efforts. One estimate was that the site would have to be raised six feet to avoid both flooding and sea level rise from climate change. Adding to these concerns was that the adjacent area to the south, Flushing Meadows–Corona Park, was built on a landfill—the Corona Dumps—composed of incinerator ashes, horse manure, and garbage, making the soil unstable and drainage questionable.

Willets Point is essentially a cul-de-sac with insufficient automobile

8. In the United States, property owners who refuse to sell commonly are known as holdouts and are defined by Yablon (2009, 131) as "those relics of an older city that stubbornly persist[ed] within the emerging cityscape."

9. The lack of sewers and good roads were two of the factors used to declare Willets Point blighted, a designation needed for officially naming it a redevelopment site and for using eminent domain. The local businesses and property owners argued that it was the city's decision not to invest there that had caused the blight. In response, the city began a $50 million project in December 2012 to provide sanitary sewers and stormwater drainage.

and transit access to serve the planned commercial and residential development. This in part explains why it had persisted for years as a low-rent area with a serious lack of infrastructure. Willets Point is essentially cut off from the rest of Queens. Bounded on the west by a major street and on two sides by expressways having no access ramps onto the area, served by a commuter rail station some blocks away and an overcrowded subway in need of significant maintenance (which meant it was often shut down on weekends), the site has limited accessibility. When the area is redeveloped, and more cars and trucks and transit riders are going to and from the site, these limited transportation options will become even more difficult for shoppers and residents. To rectify these problems, the city government worked with the New York State Department of Transportation and the Federal Highway Administration (which controls the expressway) to build access ramps to the site. The city and the Metropolitan Transportation Authority also planned to upgrade the subway station. The question that lingered was whether this would be enough to encourage retailers and apartment seekers to locate in a somewhat isolated area of Queens.

For this reason the first phase of the project was designed as an entertainment and retail complex that would be adjacent to the new stadium and draw customers from people attending baseball games. Housing for a residential community would follow after the first phase and after the completion of the sewer system, remediation and cleanup of the soil and water, building of expressway access ramps, and subway station improvements. By the end of 2013, the housing plans had been rescheduled for 2025 (Bagli 2013). The "build-out" would also include neighborhood services such as grocery stores and drugstores. Without such amenities, households would be hesitant to live there. One skeptic was not convinced:

Bounded by busy highways, vast parking lots [for the baseball stadium], and a polluted river, directly beneath the La Guardia flight path, with decades of toxic and sewage waste in the ground, [Willets Point] is not well positioned to become a high-value residential neighborhood—even before factoring in a daily influx of tens of thousands of cars and subway riders two weeks out of every month during baseball season. (Baldwin 2009, 85)

None of these challenges—recalcitrant businesses, poor location, contaminated soil, and toxic groundwater—are foreign to the world of redevelopment. Much contemporary redevelopment occurs on brownfield sites (Altshuler and Luberoff 2003), existing residents and businesses are almost always averse to leaving or selling, waterfront sites (particularly those subject to tidal flooding) cannot avoid issues of elevation, and development on peripheral, nonresidential sites has to overcome the lack of essential services (including transit access) that discourages people from living there. Planners, economic development staff, elected officials, and developers know that even when the proposed site is emptied of businesses and residents, contaminated soils and poor accessibility will still resist large-scale investment. Willets Point also has recalcitrant businesses and property owners. For the project to be successful, their obduracy has to be surmounted.

In his 2012 announcement of phase 1, Mayor Bloomberg summed up the city's commitment to improving the city while hinting at another obstacle in the way of redevelopment—a recession that had been lingering since 2008:

Today the "valley of ashes" is well on its way to becoming the site of historic private investment, major job creation and unprecedented environmental remediation. Investing in infrastructure and laying the groundwork for private investment are hallmarks of our Administration's economic development strategy, and projects like this are part of the reason our economy is doing better than the rest of the country. (New York City Economic Development Corporation 2012)

It was not only the physical facts of Willets Point that had to be resolved: sluggish city, regional, and national economies also stood in the path of redevelopment success. Real estate analysts interviewed by one newspaper reporter (Pristin 2011) noted that a project of this scale was "likely to require a great deal of public financing," a clear indication that private investors viewed the project as unnecessarily risky or, to use my terminology, obdurate.

Planning and Obduracy

The Willets Point example reveals planning to be not just deeply political, something that is widely acknowledged, but also inherently adversarial. The politics are clear. One group's obduracy is another group's justified defiance. Planning interventions require dismantling existing arrangements and redistributing resources and opportunities among various groups. Because they rearrange how people live together and with nature, they are political acts (Young 1990). To redevelop Willets Point, the land has to be given to other businesses and, most likely, a

141

new set of property owners. The users of the site have to be changed from low-wage workers to high-wage residents, with the workers now facing unemployment or longer commutes and, in either case, different rhythms to their day and different people with whom to interact. Faced with such disruption and uncertainty, the workers and business and property owners resisted. The politics aligned along divisions of class, residence (workers who live in Queens versus baseball fans and shoppers from the suburbs), immigration status, and ethnicity.

Planners cannot wish away these politics. In the face of contrary evidence, they might argue that their intentions are based on scientific facts about real estate fundamentals, blight's stifling of citywide development, and the contribution of middle-income housing to a city's prosperity; that is, they might claim that their proposal makes unassailable sense—that it is a fact. The realities on the ground, however, dispute this. The businesses there were financially solvent, and providing sewers and paved roads in no way required building a shopping and entertainment complex. For these and other reasons, the assertions of the mayor and economic development officials were treated suspiciously by the users of Willets Point. Consequently, property owners and workers mobilized to challenge the city government and development interests through the courts and with public protests.

As planners and their publics strive to achieve their objectives, they confront conditions and situations that are relatively fixed and enduring. They have to contend with realities around which are deployed individuals, groups, artifacts, and practices that benefit from current conditions. In Willets Point, many of the businesses provided services to each other, their workers were from nearby neighborhoods that had a stake in their continued employment, retailers from around the city depended on the goods sold by its wholesalers, and motorists needing repairs relied on parts stores and body shops. Such networks are what make realities obdurate.[10]

Prying these networks apart requires political action that shifts allegiances and redistributes opportunities and conditions. This often leads to dissension and even overt conflict. Actors deeply embedded in these networks will oppose giving up the benefits they derive from them. The New York City planners were not solving a problem of blight about which everyone agreed or approaching it in a way considered appropriate by all involved. Rather, they confronted business and prop-

10. Of Willets Point, Sorkin (2009, 53) has written: "Its ecology is singular and symbiotic, thriving on the dereliction of the place."

erty owners who cast the city as a major cause of that blight through decades of neglect and as intent on damaging their livelihood. The relationship was inherently oppositional and antagonistic. This obduracy could not be overcome without conflict. The business and property owners of Willets Point filed lawsuits, protested at city council and planning board hearings, and held public demonstrations. They told their stories to newspaper reporters to rally community support. Since the planners hoped to change what was currently there, they had to confront those who wished to remain and deprive them of the benefits they reaped from being there. Those who resisted viewed themselves as victims rather than beneficiaries of planning.[11]

To this extent, obduracy points to a democratic planning that is always resolving problems of its own making—an incitatory operation that contributes to the issue it ostensibly is designed to preempt.[12] Property owners in Willets Point recognized that the lack of a sewer system and paved roads was undesirable, but the blight that triggered the city's targeting the area for redevelopment was a product of planning; it did not precede it. Within a pro-growth framework, the obduracy was self-inflicted. Problems are not naturally occurring; they have to be constructed and, for planners, documented and addressed. To this extent the city and its planners were implicated in the blight of Willets Point as a consequence of decades of neglect and of their efforts to improve it.

Neither does a single public interest await discovery or, for that matter, any public interest that can be stipulated by planning expertise. There are only the interests (often conflicting) of various publics. Intrinsic to democratic planning is "the task of defining the 'we' that we form together" (Latour 2007b, 7). Many planners, however, might claim to the contrary that a single public interest exists. They might argue that cities and regions and neighborhoods, as well as transit systems and ecologies, have an organic public interest related to their capacity to function in an effective, efficient, and sustainable manner. When these assemblages malfunction, from planners' perspective, they do so independently but require planners to intercede. Moreover, it is planning expertise that lets problems be identified and addressed. Consequently, planners assert that they are innocent of constructing

11. For a much different and ostensibly apolitical view of planning, see Davoudi 2012, 304: "Planning is thus about being prepared for innovative transformations at times of change and in the face of inherent uncertainties."
12. The phrase "incitatory operation" and its definition come from the philosopher Brian Massumi as cited in Weizman 2007, 309n11.

obduracy—it preexisted them. In response, consider this statement by Iris Young (2011, 54): "The inert materials, things and constraints we encounter bear marks of past praxis, but we experience this praxis passively as having objective properties of their [sic] own." In effect, what planners take to be inherent is actually a dubious framing of the past into a "given." The past is fetishized, pulled away from the actors who created and perpetuate it, so that it can then be viewed as obdurate. Such an argument strips the world of human intention by failing to acknowledge that current conditions and trends are socially constituted (Hacking 1999) and that various groups benefit from them. Additionally, it supports the false belief that a single public interest exists and that it can be revealed through technical analysis. A politicized planning would give explicit recognition to which groups benefit from the status quo and which are harmed by or reap the rewards of its "improvement."

Moreover, obduracy is both fixed and not fixed; there are degrees of obduracy.[13] The world is made up of realities that are settled and difficult to change and realities that are disputed and open to modification (Daston 2005; Latour 1987), resulting in a world comprising "those that resist for long and those that do not, those that resist courageously and those that do not, those who know how to ally or isolate themselves and those that do not" (Latour 1988, 159). Planners are constantly assailed by contested facts, unresolved arguments, ill-formed practices, eroding landscapes, and decomposing buildings. Not everything planners confront is obdurate. Willets Point was obdurate, sea level rise is obdurate, and in the United States suburban sprawl is obdurate but not public parks (increasingly managed through a variety of public-private arrangements in New York City), zoning regulations, or inclusionary housing policies. The latter have a malleability that the former lack. The latter are relatively compliant.[14]

The implication is that not all issues planners engage in will encounter resistance. Many facts and practices are in flux, and their proponents are not yet strong enough to defend against what they might view as a hostile act. Here is where planners can make a difference. And

13. On different forms and reasons for obduracy, see Hommels 2008 and Kirkman 2009. Bijker (1995, 285) proposes that "Artefacts can have different shades of obduracy for actors with different degrees of inclusion" in an assemblage.

14. In 1995 the New York City government launched a program to convert obsolete office buildings in Lower Manhattan to residences (Beauregard 2005a). Property owners, financiers, and the real estate industry complied. But many, but not all, buildings resisted. With floor plates on the lower floors too large for all apartments to have windows to the outside, they became nearly impossible to convert.

while planners alone have never been known to be powerful, when joined with publics they can be influential and often successful against weak opponents.

What planners and their publics hope to accomplish is a different obduracy. It is not obduracy in itself that they object to, but obduracy that blocks them from achieving their goals. Much of what planners do involves turning a place (with its many resistances) into a professionally framed site so as to produce another place with new resistances (Beauregard 2005b). The planners in New York City, for example, were determined to replace the blight of Willets Point—a blight that seemingly prevented new and large-scale capital investment—with a multi-story retail and entertainment complex, paved roads, high-rise apartment buildings, and a stormwater drainage system. The hope was that these new structures would withstand physical and economic deterioration and stylistic obsolescence and be in demand for decades by high-end retailers and middle-class households. Willets Point would become so enmeshed in Queens, so entangled in real estate markets, so valued as a shopping and entertainment destination, so important for the city's tax base, and so engrained in the identity of its users and inhabitants that it would resist deterioration and the incursion of undesirable uses, maintain its now high property values, and stave off threats to the integrity of the site plan. Obduracy would make undesirable change unlikely. Thus, while planners might embrace the notion that the city should be resilient and constantly adapt (Shaw 2012), this belief has not led to proposals to plan for multiple transformations. Planners want their creations to endure.[15]

The notion of obduracy, then, not only amplifies the political nature of planning, it also connects planning to the world in two ways. First, obduracy requires that we think in terms of heterogeneous assemblages of technologies, ecologies, ideas, and things, all having the potential to be actors—sources of influence—within them (Latour and Yaneva 2008), including the possibility of being obstructionist. The goats owned by the Turkana and coveted by the Potok became obdurate as a consequence of their forcible herding and the simultaneous shooting and yelling of warriors from both tribes. Obduracy was not inherent in the goats. The business and property owners of Willets Point could not have resisted city-led redevelopment efforts over the past four decades were it not for the periodic flooding, the potholed streets, its somewhat

---

15. Cairns and Jacobs (2014, 15) point to a similar bias in architecture against consideration of "wasting, obsolescence, decay, decrepitude, ruination."

isolated location, and the low-lying land that impeded the aspirations of the city and developers.

Second, the worldliness of obduracy also appears as a bridge between the micropolitics of planning and the city as a macroproject. This is an important issue in planning theory, though it often appears in rather basic form. That form is the debate between the proceduralists and the consequentialists (Fainstein 2000). The former emphasize the processes of planning: the rational model of decision making, interpersonal communications (as in communicative action), public participation, and collaborative planning. With the exception of the rational model, all these ways of thinking involve interpersonal or group relations and speak to the desire to ensure that planning practice is democratic. The latter, however, are apprehensive that democratic processes will not achieve acceptable, substantive results. They fear a tyranny of the majority or a highly vocal, reactionary, and powerful minority. Their focus is on planning's material consequences; for example, households that have a right to place and can resist displacement in rapidly appreciating neighborhoods, public transit options that allow easy access to metropolitanwide employment, neighborhoods with sufficient recreational facilities, and local businesses protected from national retailers. The issue for consequentialists is substantive, not procedural, justice, not democracy. Neither justice without democracy nor democracy without justice makes sense, though. A way must be found, then, to translate between them.

Obduracy resolves this conundrum, in part, by drawing forth the political nature of planning and then positioning planning in a heterogeneous world. There the mandate for planners is to organize—with others—assemblages that serve publics. Planners are not morally, intellectually, or ontologically superior to other actors in assemblages, but they do have the potential to be a source of change that leads to collective benefits. Their ideas and practices are meant to span the city. Of course, they will have to earn their privileged position and, once it is earned, should not expect their powers and legitimacy to be uncontested. Planners must still behave democratically, enroll allies, and make their arguments in public. Planners have the potential to be agents of transformation, exposing and resisting the obduracy of entrenched interests.

One more example involves Palestinians and the state of Israel. Unlike the Willets Point case, government planners here are not working to overcome resistance but rather embedding it in the land. Injustice is obdurate in part because it is entangled in the material world (Hayward and Swanstrom 2011), and critics of the Israeli planners have accused them of doing precisely this. This is also an instance of planners engaging with macropolitics where contentiousness extends beyond the boundaries of the city and the nation. Obduracy helps us understand this politics.

Israeli Settlements and the "Two-State Solution"

In December 2012 the Israeli government announced that it was undertaking "preliminary zoning and planning preparations" for the development of 3,400 units of housing northwest of Jerusalem in an area of the West Bank known as East 1 (E1) (Rudoren 2012; Rudoren and Landler 2012). A 4.6-square-mile area of rocky desert, E1 was largely empty except for a few Bedouin camps and an Israeli police outpost. It is also one of the most politically sensitive and disputed pieces of land in the ongoing conflict between the Israeli government and the Palestinians. The settlement would continue a policy of occupying land in order to assert control over it and the Palestinians who live there (Yiftachel 1995, 2005).[16] Confronted by "geographic borders that have never been demarcated clearly" (Yiftachel 2002, 3), the intent was to create "facts on the ground" in much the way the Israeli state has used archaeology to establish historical continuity with the region (Abu El-Haj 2001).

The Israeli government believes it has a right to this land. And it was particularly interested in E1 because establishing a settlement there would forge a physical connection between an earlier Israeli settlement town (Ma'ale Adumim) and Jerusalem, thereby providing mutual access between these two places. The Palestinians oppose settlements in the West Bank because they believe the land belongs to them and, most important, that Israeli settlements there threaten the "two-state solution" to the conflict between them and the Israelis. The more land settled by the Israelis, the less land is left to be divided between Israel and Palestine, thereby constraining negotiations and making fewer land resources available for the Palestinians (Weizman 2007, 1–5).

A previous government plan for E1 included 3,910 housing units, 2,192 hotel rooms, an industrial park, and a police station. Except for the police station, the plan was not implemented as designed. More-

16. Opponents of Israeli policy toward the Palestinians characterize it as colonialism (Margalit 2013; Weizman 2007, 105).

over, the Israeli government and conservative religious groups have also been constructing settlements on the West Bank and in East Jerusalem since Israel took these areas from Jordan in a war in 1967.[17] A United Nations report estimated that Israel has built 250 settlements in the disputed territories, and approximately 520,000 Israeli citizens have been relocated there amid 2.5 million Palestinians (Cumming-Bruce and Kershner 2013). The settlements are usually gated and guarded and wholly separate from the surrounding Palestinian villages.[18]

Not only do the Palestinians view such settlements as hindering a two-state solution, they also condemn them as illegal. They claim the settlements violate various United Nations resolutions along with a general understanding that has emerged from negotiations between the Israeli government and Palestinian representatives. Of particular importance are the Oslo Accords of 1993 that set a framework for defining areas that could not be further occupied, allowed for interim Palestinian self-governance, and mandated the withdrawal of Israeli defense forces. Also pertinent is the Annapolis Conference of 2007 involving the Israelis, the Palestine Liberation Organization (PLO), and the United States that led to an agreement to pursue a two-state solution.

Additionally, the Palestinians condemned the proposed E1 development because it would block their access to East Jerusalem and the West Bank, where many Palestinians live, while also precluding the creation of a north-south route through the West Bank connecting Bethlehem with Ramallah, a town of approximately 28,000 inhabitants that serves as the administrative center for the Palestinian National Authority (Erlanger 2012). The Israeli government countered these concerns by arguing that it would build a system of "protected" roads and tunnels through Israeli-occupied areas so the Palestinians would have the access they need. ("Protected" here means that Palestinians traveling on these roads and through these tunnels will be unable to exit to adjacent Israeli lands.) The Palestinians also hope the disputed territories will become part of a newly created Palestinian state and thus be available for housing the large number of Palestinian refugees who have fled these areas for Jordan and other nearby countries.

The decision to go forward with the planning for E1 was made public a day after the United Nations had voted to raise the status of the Palestinian delegation to "nonmember observer state" (United Nations

17. That war also involved Egypt and the Sinai Peninsula, a strategically valuable land that Israel invaded and occupied, only to withdraw as part of a 1982 peace agreement.

18. Yiftachel (2002, 3) has claimed that, as of the early 2000s, over 980 Jewish settlements had been established in Israel-Palestine.

General Assembly 2012). The vote was vehemently opposed by the Israeli government, but the resolution passed by a vote of 139–9 with 41 abstentions. And while this was not considered equivalent to official United Nations recognition of the Palestinians as a state or even a state without a sovereign territory, it conferred on them more power to oppose and condemn Israel within the United Nations framework, including the possibility of bringing Israel before an international court. The Israeli government announcement was seen by many countries as retaliation against the Palestinians for pursuing their international rights and, because it ostensibly violated the 1967 accords, as an attempt at illegal occupation, both of which were publicly derided.

The public statement of intent to begin planning for a Jewish settlement in E1 could have been viewed—and was by some people—as mainly a symbolic response to the United Nations vote. The Israeli government declared that it would start preliminary planning work; it did not declare that it would actually begin building a settlement. Plans could be halted or abandoned, and plans are only documents, not "facts on the ground" in the same way as are apartment complexes, roads, protective walls, and infrastructure. In this interpretation, the Israeli government used the symbolism of planning—an intention—to register its dissent. And while the preliminary plans might generate bureaucratic momentum and a popular expectation that an actual settlement would eventually be built, dismantling plans and dismantling communities require quite different magnitudes of effort.[19]

Yet one senior Israeli official commented that "we don't exclude the possibility that E1 moves from symbolic to something real" (Erlanger 2012), thereby making explicit the possibility that this planned settlement could take material form. At the same time, the official minimized the difficulty of erasing symbolic acts and their consequences. Nonetheless, by shrinking the amount of land available for negotiations, Israeli settlements increase the difficulty of arriving at an acceptable two-state compromise.[20]

In January 2013, within a month of the Israeli announcement, approximately two hundred Palestinian activists responded by erect-

19. The Israeli government has dismantled Israeli settlements. In 2005 it evacuated and wholly demolished 1,500 homes in the Gaza Strip that Israel had captured in the 1967 war (Weizman 2007, 221–235). The Gaza Strip borders Egypt on the southwest and sits on the eastern coast of the Mediterranean Sea. The 1993 Oslo Peace Accords turned control of the land over to the Palestinians.

20. Symbolic acts, of course, often are significant and obdurate and are frequently accompanied by material acts (Edelman 1964).

ing twenty tents in E1 and establishing their own village, which they called Bab al-Shams, Gate of the Sun (Al-Jazeera 2013; Kershner 2013a, 2013b). Simultaneously, they sent lawyers to the Israeli Supreme Court to argue that any attempt to remove them should require the Israeli government to explicitly state the grounds for such a move. The Israeli government counterargued before the court that the occupation could lead to rioting (that it was a national security issue) and that the land belonged to the Israeli state. The court overturned the injunction, allowing the protesters to be expelled. Having warned the protesters that they were trespassing and would be evicted, the next day the Israeli security forces removed twenty Palestinian activists and all the tents.[21]

Israeli planners were politically engaged, enmeshed in an ongoing conflict, and instructed to establish different forms and levels of resistance in the landscape. As they filled hilltops with housing and valleys with roads, the lives of both Israelis and Palestinians were altered and local ecologies reconfigured (Norman 2012). The Israeli planners were thus instrumental in increasing an obduracy that many observers believe blocks a diplomatic and geographic solution to the conflict. For the Israeli state, including its planners, such obduracy was an acceptable consequence of exercising its right to appropriate land to house its people. Finding this obduracy to be oppressive and disempowering, the Palestinians protested through diplomatic channels and with bodies, tents, and banners.

In this and the other examples in this chapter, place is joined to action. The plains and hills were critical for the success of Potok raids and Turkana resistance, the location and material conditions of Willets Point had a major impact on the politics of redevelopment, and the planned settlements in E1 reverberate into peace negotiations. Obduracy was inseparable from place. But place is also inseparable from another key concern of planning—time. Not only is place enacted in time, but its conditions are framed by an inclination to improvement involving an undesirable "present" and a better "future." But while place is scrutinized in the planning literature, time is treated uncritically and even dismissively. It is to "time," then, that we now turn.

21. Three months later, another group of Palestinian activists erected fifteen tents near the site of the earlier occupation. See International Solidarity Movement, "As Obama Lands, Palestinians Erect New Bab al-Shams Neighbourhood," www.palsolidarity.org, accessed May 17, 2013. By the end of 2013, Israeli construction plans had been suspended in an effort to dampen political tension with the United States (Rudoren 2013).

EIGHT

Temporalities

A few decades back, the planning theorist John Friedmann (1993, 482) proposed a non-Euclidean mode of planning that would bring "knowledge and practice to bear directly on action itself."[1] Concerned that rational-comprehensive planners had lost touch with the lives of the people for and with whom they planned and had become satisfied with proposing imagined futures, he argued for a more action-centered planning. Consideration of the future would still be important, but the time of non-Euclidean planning would be the *"real time* of everyday events" (482). Friedmann thus posed two notions of time: one of grand leaps forward and the other of the incessant demands of daily life. The morally responsible path is to focus on the inequalities and injustices people face in the present. It is irresponsible to offer problem-free futures that might never be realized.

Conceiving of time in this way, as if the present and the future are distinct states, leaves too much unsaid (Kern 1983). I appreciate the moral impulse that motivated Friedmann, but planners need a more nuanced understanding of time if they are to achieve planning's promise of a better life for all. Time is more than the public time of standardized days, months, and years that unfold chronologically. As represented by calendars, airline schedules, clocks, and state-regulated working hours, public time is

1. "Euclidean" refers to the Greek mathematician Euclid of Alexandria, who is purported to have developed geometry, not to the famous court case *Village of Euclid v. Ambler Reality Co.* (1926) that made zoning ordinances legally justifiable.

fragmented with electoral cycles, fiscal years, tax periods, and university semesters, all parts of what it means to be in the world. To this we might add moments of discovery (for example, landing humans on the moon) and social accomplishments such as the Nineteenth Amendment to the US Constitution, ratified in 1920, that granted women the right to vote. A variety of heterogeneous, nonpublic times also exist: careers, marriages, the pursuit of educational degrees, and home relocations, to name just four. Many of these public and nonpublic times are commingled, and we negotiate among them.

Diverse temporalities are mostly unacknowledged in the planning literature and, if acknowledged, treated superficially.[2] For a profession so concerned with the future, this is a significant absence; there is more to planning time than past, present, and future—themselves hardly naturally occurring categories. Temporalities are manifest in highly varied ways and deeply influence how planning is done. Planners, of course, are hardly passive in the face of time, and their accomplishments create a public time that stabilizes and legitimizes planning as a function of local governments.

To give theoretical weight to how time functions within the world of planners, I draw on Bruno Latour's insight that it is the stabilizing of relationships that distinguishes one moment from the next. Time passes because an event has occurred, a condition has become established, or an idea has fended off its critics. This insight is used to explore how time helps us understand the history of city planning in New York City. Before delving into these matters, we first need to consider how time has been treated in planning practice.

Time in Planning

Time is inherent to the concept of planning. Deeply embedded in any understanding is that planning is meant to be done before taking action. This implies time as duration (the time it takes to plan) and time as sequence: the planning itself—a before—and then the actions that follow—an after. The city council decides to build a reservoir to expand the water supply, so a dam must be constructed. Where the dam is located, how big the reservoir needs to (and can) be, when pumping

---

2. As an example, Brooks (2002, 9) makes this claim about time: planning is "the process by which we attempt to shape the future. The future, in this definition, refers to anything beyond the present," whether short-run or long-run. This begins and ends his discussion.

stations need to be built, and what size pipes will deliver the amount of water needed after the reservoir is operable must be determined before contracts are signed, funds expended, and implementation launched. Time must elapse for planning to have any hope of being effective, and planning must occur before actions are taken. To plan afterward is illogical.

If planners are successful, we will know that time has passed; the consequences produced by their actions will differ from the less desirable conditions that existed before them. The difference represents the passage of time and, for some, progress as well. However, other temporalities are also in play. Three deserve attention. The first involves time as it appears in the making of comprehensive and long-range plans, arguably the defining activity of city planning. Here we find multiple temporalities being considered, not just the future when the plan will ostensibly be realized, but the developmental times of different land uses. Second, time is an integral part of determining which areas of the city need planned intervention. For the future place to be realized, it is often necessary to confront the past and erase what exists. And finally, time is inseparable from the impulses (often associated with modernism) that established planning as a pervasive activity of governments, militaries, corporations, and other large organizations.

We begin with what was once the major function of local government planners—writing comprehensive, long-range plans (Kent [1964] 1990). These plans are meant to establish the appropriate land uses, transportation, public facilities, and open spaces for a city's future. Planners consider in advance how the city might absorb population and employment growth without generating imbalances between, for example, the size and location of the school-age population and the number and location of classrooms. In effect, they allocate future growth across the city—creating new places—so as to minimize, if not eliminate, negative externalities and functional inefficiencies, particularly as the latter relate to the movement of people and commerce and the access required by interdependent land uses. Moreover, since these master plans "provide directions for the future betterment of the city and its residents" (Keating and Krumholz 1991, 136), growth is ostensibly accommodated with minimal disruption.[3]

In producing these documents, planners work with different temporalities. One has to do with how far into the future planning consider-

---

3. For an informative discussion of contemporary, comprehensive planning, see Schilling and Vasudevan 2013.

ations should be extended. T. J. Kent Jr. ([1964] 1990, 95) wrote in 1964 that "long-range has always meant, in simplest terms, that the plan should be forward-looking. . . . provid[ing] for the future needs of the community insofar as it is possible." A long-range plan, however, needs a chronological target, a time horizon. Is it ten years, twenty years, fifty years? A huge difference exists between thinking about what the city government should do next year to address the lack of affordable housing and what it needs to do over the next twenty years. The choice of a time horizon is thus a critical moment in the master planning process; its specification has to account for developmental trends as well as current and future political support. To the extent that these conditions vary across cities, one would expect time horizons to vary as well. Yet most city plans look equally far into the future—twenty to thirty years seems to be the norm. The recent plan for Amman, Jordan, begun in 2006, looked to 2025 (Beauregard and Marpillero-Colomina 2011), the New York City plan of 2007, *PlaNYC*, was meant to take the city to 2030, and the Berkeley, California, Master Plan of 1955 focused on 1980. The major textbook on the comprehensive, long-range plans of the 1950s and 1960s stipulated, without any discussion, a twenty- to twenty-five-year time period (Chapin 1965, 459).

Time also enters into master plans through the employment and population projections that planners use to calculate future land use needs (Chapin 1965). Employment projections enable the scaling of future industrial and commercial areas through ratios that translate the number of new jobs by industry into the space needed for each worker. Demographic information on family size and composition, in turn, connects population projections to future housing, provision of public facilities (such as schools), and the land use requirements of future retail services.

Such projections present time not as a far-off future condition, but as a flow of workers and households into the city, to be served by a parallel stream of new buildings and structures. They rely on past trends and previously collected data to think about the future. When compared with the time horizon of the master plan, time here is fine-grained. At its most sophisticated, these projections acknowledge the diversity of preparation times for different land uses—a new subway tunnel requires many more years to plan and implement than a new bus route. They also recognize that the flows of workers, households, and capital are cyclical rather than linear (Beauregard 1991b; Olson 1979). Consequently, the city is more likely to grow in spurts than in equivalent increments. A critical concern for planners is how to balance different developmental trajectories to create a harmonious city.

Planners attempt to guide these processes and minimize deficiencies and conflicts by using zoning regulations to stipulate where different land uses will be located and by engaging in capital programming to establish when public facilities and structures, such as new roads, bridges, fire stations, and recreational centers, need to be built (Nunn 1990). Capital programming addresses the development trajectories of the public investments that will move the city into the future. Its time is the time of government funding: the borrowing of capital funds from the bond market to pay for the construction of bridges and sewage treatment plants and the tax revenue streams that will enable these bonds to be repaid. Bonds are often amortized over fifteen to thirty years, while operating budgets are set yearly. The coordination of those two times affects how well the planners can anticipate and guide development, for example, installing sewer systems when developers are most interested in building homes.

Finally, there is the temporal gap between when a plan is formulated and when it is realized. In the "golden" era of comprehensive, long-range plans in the United States, roughly the 1920s through the early 1960s, planners did not (except for capital programming) pay much attention to all the various tasks that would have to be undertaken to implement the plan. As Kent ([1964] 1990, 20) wrote, a plan is not a program; it "does not specify the means of achieving the desired ends." A plan is a device for guiding decisions, and the expectation is that appropriately written zoning regulations, carefully considered public investments, and thoughtful decision making by elected officials will realize what planners have proposed. Otherwise planners neither stipulate nor became involved in managing those tasks (Altshuler 1965). The time between the adoption of the plan and its implementation has always been a concern, but planners have been reluctant to give it their undivided attention.

The absence of any sense of "what to do next" gave rise in the 1970s to strategic planning, one purpose of which was to shorten the time span of the plan by focusing on specific actions in the next two to five years (Albrechts 2004). As frameworks for action, strategic plans would compensate for the inattention to implementation and be more flexible and responsive to prevailing conditions. When strategic plans subsequently became intertwined with project-based planning and displaced the concern with the future that comprehensive, long-range plans had provided, planners reacted with public "visioning" exercises (Klein et al. 1993).[4] Visioning encourages residents of the city to imagine what they would like in their ideal city, thereby returning to the planning process the long-range future that strategic planning has minimized.

These ways of thinking about the future hide how far contemporary planning, at least in the United States, is involved with the past.[5] This is particularly the case for planners working in places where cities are built out and new growth is mostly occurring in the suburbs. Here planners confront how to adapt already developed areas to new technologies, changing resident populations, and a diverse array of users. The primary issue is redevelopment, whether through rezoning or through megaprojects on former industrial sites (Altshuler and Luberoff 2003). Constantly pressured to maximize their tax base, local governments are intent on ensuring that land produces its highest tax revenues and that ample sites are available for upgrading the city's office buildings, shopping areas, and housing. For these reasons, planners have to decide whether an area is obsolete and how to balance this decision against social concerns and calls for historic preservation. If the area remains in its present state, will it impede the city's ability to attract investors and desirable households? Will it be a drain on tax revenues? And if it is to be redeveloped, what new land uses will make the area sustainable?

Such assessments have been a significant part of city planning in the United States since the mid-twentieth century (Teaford 1990). After World War II, the large industrial cities needed to compensate for nearly fifteen years of disinvestment. This involved identifying blighted central business districts and slums, neither of which functioned effectively to retain office and retail activities or provide decent neighborhoods. The planners' job was to determine what areas of the city had become financially dysfunctional or unhealthy for their residents. To do so, planners engaged in various representational strategies to define areas as obsolete (or not) or as harmful for future growth. Along with elected officials and real estate interests, they argued that close-knit, ethnic neighborhoods of tenements and narrow streets were incompatible with the contemporary city. Similarly, beginning in the late 1990s, planners deemed the single-use, automobile-friendly districts planned

---

4. Albrechts (2004, 746) argues that project planning is the antithesis of strategic planning. I view them as compatible.

5. Mandelbaum (1985, 185) presents the most common understanding of how the past fits into planning: planners "looked upon the past as a time of more or (characteristically) less interest; the future was theirs to shape."

in the 1950s and 1960s as obsolete. In their place they proposed diverse, multiuse neighborhoods with peak densities centered on public transit stations. These new neighborhoods would best accommodate the prevailing dynamics of urban growth. Here time appears as a rejection of the past and recognition of the obduracy of previous decisions and investments.

These temporalities of planning have their roots in the modernist project that institutionalized planning in governments and corporations in the late nineteenth and early twentieth centuries (Holston 1989). Modernism turned away from the past and replaced tradition with progress, the "time-consciousness of modernity" (Disch 1994, xi). What mattered for existing cities was their ability to remake themselves for a future shaped by science and technology, whether in the form of time-saving kitchens or automated vehicles moving swiftly across the metropolitan landscape. Planning would enable a break from how things were once done. A planned city would be radically unlike existing cities. Decisions would be made by experts scientifically trained to uncover and manipulate the forces of development and by governments that endorsed coordination over unregulated competition. Planners had no need for history. At the same time, given the unknowability of the future, they could hardly be certain their proposals would succeed. Unacknowledged was that modernist planners encased themselves in a contradiction. Progress is nothing if not restless, and whatever planners proposed would eventually be obsolete.[6] To grasp this, planners need a better sense of both past and future histories (see Mandelbaum 1985 and Abbott 2007, respectively). History, however, has never had much of a presence in their world.

Marking Time

Above, I described planners as users of preexisting temporalities. They set their plans within chronological and developmental time, undertake redevelopment in response to past burdens and future potentials, and view themselves as contributing to the progressive evolution of the city—in contemporary terms, a city moving closer and closer to livability and sustainability. Time confronts planners, and they act within its constraints.

---

6. Deeply embedded in this commitment to progress is the forward projection of desire (Berman 1982).

This characterization is much too one-sided. Planners are not puppets pulled this way and that by the politics of development, cycles of capital investment, and electoral shifts. Much of planning has to do with creating time and place together. Planners are engaged in crafting a history of the city and of a planning that makes the passage of time meaningful. To this extent, they are active agents not only in shaping development but also in reproducing the support they need to be legitimate representatives of the interests of publics, developers, and the government. The dynamics and conditions of the city have to be experienced and documented as having changed as a result of planners' proposals. In short, if planners are going to claim that the world is different and better, they must make it move through time. It is not enough for them to propose; their proposals must enter a flow of events that they are seen to control (Throgmorton 2000). To think more systematically about this, we turn once again to Bruno Latour.

Time, Latour (1988, 50) tells us, is "the distinction between moments." It passes when moments have formed, each distinct from the others; that is, when things are gathered together such that knowledge, relationships, and materials become fixed and realities are stabilized. Stabilized, these arrangements or assemblages are less open to debate and transformation. For example, in the early twenty-first century, most people began to believe in climate change (Bulkeley 2010). Although not universally embraced, it became the common wisdom. To question it was a form of willful ignorance, a denial of science, or simply deviant. Widely accepted as fact, it became real by being "associated with many others that are viewed as collaborating with it" (Latour 1999, 158). Since weakening climate change as a reality requires disentangling all the alliances that have formed around it, it has become more and more difficult to dislodge (Latour 1987). Once climate change was not a matter of concern—that time no longer exists.

Events, then, mark moments of time; they make time. As Latour has written (1999, 200), "the arrow of time is *still there*," and the "mechanism [that] makes it tick" is the ever-greater entanglement (and intimacy) of humans and nonhumans. Thus we experience a time before the recognition of, say, climate change, women's suffrage, or the Internet and a time after because each is enmeshed in the material world. Subsequent events and conditions—the continuing shrinkage of glaciers and increasing levels of CO_2 in Earth's atmosphere—are also part of these temporal frameworks. And while new events and conditions produce new understandings, the past defined by such dominant moments is left intact. In this way time is created by stabilizing assemblages in which certain actors are victorious (Latour 1988, 51). It thus appears as a series of moments embedded in an ever-changing history: "Time does not pass, it has to be made to pass" (Latour 1988, 112). It is situated not "with respect to a regulated set of dates" but with respect to "events in relation to their intensity" (Latour 1993, 68).[7]

For time to elapse, time-defining moments must be irreversible. It has to be impossible for the things that have been gathered to be returned to their original states. If the present can revert to the past, then we lack markers that set one moment off from the next, and time ceases to be. All moments blend into each other. Even if we are able to reduce CO_2 levels and stop glaciers from shrinking, halt sea level rise, and bring down rising ambient temperatures, we will still not erase climate change. Any reduction in these measures will be seen instead as a validation of it. Climate change is so rooted in geology, the atmospheric sciences, popular imagination, and public policy that we cannot return to a time of ignorance. And while it can be weakened by subsequent scientific findings and ideological attacks, it cannot be forgotten.

Stabilizing realities has two important consequences: one involves the past and the other, possible futures. First, fixing a moment rewrites history. Because a particular reality has become durable, the past now looks different. Events make clear what the past means to the present. To this extent, as Latour (1999, 172) points out in his inimitable fashion, the year 1944 becomes "subject to what happens in 1950." Even as he acknowledges chronological time as represented by calendars and clocks, he also understands that earlier times change owing to events and moments that occur later. This seeming reversal of the widely accepted notion that causes must precede effects is meant to be neither teleological (that is, arguing that actions in the future cause things to happen in the present) nor a rejection of the sequential relation between a force and the reaction to it. Latour still believes in the latter—to act in his world is to produce an effect—but he rejects the former as too simplistic. How an earlier year is represented is what changes, not what happened in any real sense.

Latour (like historians) thus recognizes that the past is constantly being reinterpreted and mediated by current concerns. The building of the interstate highway system in the United States in the late 1950s and 1960s, once considered an engineering feat bringing a great advance

---

7. Riis (2008, 300) claims that Latour believes time has intentionality, a claim related to how time is created.

in mobility, looks quite different from a present in which automobile pollution depletes the ozone layer, contributing in turn to sea level rise and increasingly severe storms. As seen from 2013, the 1956 passage of federal highway legislation takes on different meanings than it had during the golden years of highway construction and automobile use: 1956 has changed.

The second consequence of stabilization concerns its impact on the future. As things are stabilized, the possibilities for subsequent actions are diminished; action is path dependent (Mahoney 2000). By becoming entangled with and committed to assemblages, things are fixed. So committed, actors find it difficult to extract themselves and change their allegiances. Modifying a highly stable assemblage is difficult. After elected officials have obtained popular approval and dedicated the departments of public works, finance, city planning, economic development, and recreation to counteracting rising sea levels through waterfront development, a subsequent political regime that denies climate change faces a nearly insurmountable task in disentangling these commitments. Once these government activities are literally in place, nongovernment actors react with compatible investments and actions that reinforce them while enhancing the buildings and landforms devoted to this goal. Public agencies, advocates, berms and wetlands, and raised building foundations all resist diversion from this path. Doing so would renege on prior arrangements and abandon the benefits—the prestige, the protection, the funding—that actors enjoy by being so entangled. And although assemblages are always provisional and require constant maintenance, once stabilized they have a momentum that favors their continuance.

To this extent, stabilizing moments makes time go by and also slows its passage. By limiting the possibilities for forming other assemblages, time is arrested. This is precisely what is meant to happen. Planners involved in combating sea level rise want to act to protect the city from the future. Their goal is to eliminate events that might threaten it and its residents. They seek an obdurate, more functional city. This means stabilizing the reality we know as climate change.

The Stabilization of City Planning

With these ideas in mind, we can reflect further on the ways planners use time to place planning in the world. Planning not only must be done, it must be seen to have been done.[8] To ground the discussion, I draw on a history that tracks city planning's evolution from stipulating property boundaries and surveying streets to serving as a legally sanctioned, formalized, and continuously supported function of local governments. Before this, city planning was ad hoc, episodic, and narrowly focused—it was preinstitutionalized (Benevolo 1971). By the 1930s, at least in the United States, planning had become a durable government activity regulating the physical development of cities and suburbs. In considering the specific case of New York City, my objective is to explore how institutionalization was achieved and how those achievements made time pass and planning seem necessary.[9]

For planning to become institutionalized, it had to convince elected officials and various publics that it could improve the city by enhancing investments, reduce environmental problems, minimize conflicts over land use, and make the city livable for as many people as possible. Once local governments accepted this, planning prospered by adapting to the city's changing patterns of development. When their initiatives became part of the calculations made by investors, developers, households, businesses, and the local government, planners realized a temporality that sustained their endeavors.

Left to individuals, cities grow chaotically, with little thought given to the proper alignment of streets, the incompatibility of land uses, the relation between infrastructure and new buildings, and the necessity of setting aside land for public use and ecological sustainability. Consequently, as cities have formed, various individuals and organizations have attempted to bring order to their development, hoping this order will yield a host of beneficial effects, from preventing land disputes to making traffic flow efficiently. This concern required strengthening government's ability to stipulate property ownership, designate public spaces such as streets, and levy taxes. Lacking discipline, the city was unlikely either to generate wealth (except for a few) or to be livable for the many (Boyer 1983).

Numerous technologies such as property markets, building insur-

8. This is a paraphrase of a famous quotation by the jurist Gordon Hewart in *Rex v. Sussex Justices ex parte McCarthy* (1924): "Not only must justice be done; it must also be seen to be done."
9. My focus is the trajectory of events, with each event a building block of an institutional time of planning. Together these events in New York City constitute a "whole story" (Abbott 2001, 181) whose sequence is comparable to what has occurred elsewhere, for example in Amman, Jordan (Beauregard and Marpillero-Colomina 2011), Philadelphia (Beauregard 1996a), and Reykjavik, Iceland (Reynarsson 1999).

ance, real estate appraisal, restrictive covenants, fire safety codes, social pressure, and even violence have been deployed to regulate the growth of cities. Beginning in the late nineteenth century, as local governments in the United States expanded their activities, city planning has become more and more stable and influential. This trajectory, from the platting of estates to the formation of city planning agencies and the crafting of strategic plans, took up time, set planners in it, and shaped the phasing of the city's development.

New York City (initially called New Amsterdam) was settled in the early seventeenth century as a free trading post of the Dutch West India Company (Shorto 2005). The governor of the trading post made an initial attempt to regulate where people built their homes by erecting a large fort where everyone could live. Relationships with the natives being good, however, the post's inhabitants chose to live outside the fort. Buildings were constructed nearby and along meandering paths that eventually became streets. The Company made no additional attempt to control where people lived or set up shops. "At first, the city [sic] was allowed to grow without any definite plan. Each settler was permitted to build his house where he pleased" (Real Estate Record Association [1898] 1967, 4).

When the trading post became established and developed as a town, the Company granted estates to those who would farm them. These estates were on Manhattan, across the river to the east in what is now Brooklyn, and to the northeast in what is now the Bronx. In 1625 Governor Peter Stuyvesant appointed a surveyor of streets and buildings with the power "to prevent the erection of unsightly and improper buildings and to regulate street lines according to land patents" (Real Estate Record Association [1898] 1967, 9). Yet "streets and blocks were developed haphazardly for the next century and a half" (Grava 1995, 1130).

Not until 1807, long after the Dutch had ceded the colony to the English and the Americans had fought a war to gain their independence, was another attempt made to control the city's development. In that year the state legislature authorized the local government to develop a street plan (Scobey 2002, 120–131). Adopted in 1811, the plan overlaid a grid of 12 north-south avenues and 155 east-west streets on an area of Manhattan just above the current settlement and extending to the northern tip of the island. The surveyors created 2,028 blocks of similar size while allocating land for squares, a parade ground, and a municipal market. This grid plan made it easier to regulate development and established property lines that let a local real estate market emerge.

By the late nineteenth century, the city had expanded beyond the grid, and the density of development had increased in response to new building technologies, rapid population growth, and the limits that existing transportation placed on the dispersal of jobs and households. Densities were regulated after 1860 by a superintendent of buildings within the fire department, whose task was to enforce laws related to building construction. To address expansion, in 1898 the presidents of the five boroughs that made up New York City were given responsibility for mapping streets and setting aside land for public parks. Until 1936, when a citywide department of buildings was established, each borough was responsible for enforcing fire, safety, and health codes.

By the early twentieth century, planning had become embedded in the landscape. Legally mandated streets and a commitment by the local government to control the location and quality of buildings were more than regulatory technologies; they were also material conditions. Still, these were only rudimentary planning tools. Even to the civic leaders at the time, government control over development seemed inadequate, given its fast pace. Of particular concern were the increasing building heights and the migration of manufacturing buildings northward into low-density residential areas, many with significant concentrations of large, detached middle-class homes. And although the city's Improvement Commission had been asked in 1903 to develop a comprehensive plan, the request was ignored (Grava 1995, 1131).

To address these issues, in 1913 the city government created the Commission on the Heights of Buildings and the Committee on the City Plan.[10] The commission recommended expanding the police powers of the government to allow it to control the location of different land uses, much as Los Angeles was already doing with its division of the city into industrial and residential zones (Scott 1969, 76). Zoning regulations would restrict where different types of buildings and structures could be constructed depending on their compatibility with each other and the negative externalities they might generate. Within a year this commission was replaced by the Commission on Building Districts and Restrictions, whose purpose was to draft zoning regulations. The proposed zoning ordinance divided the city into residential, commercial, and unrestricted districts and also placed controls on building density. In 1916 the Board of Estimate (essentially, the city council) adopted the proposal and it became law.

10. My description of New York City's history of city planning in the twentieth century relies greatly on Eugenie Birch's (1995) excellent encyclopedia entry on the topic.

Two years earlier, in 1914, the Committee on the City Plan had issued its report *Development and Present Status of City Planning in New York City.* The report called for a permanent planning commission, but political support for a dedicated public agency was lacking. As a consequence, the committee was charged with overseeing the zoning ordinance. Although by 1916 New York had a relatively strong and innovative zoning ordinance and a way to control the location of streets, it still lacked an entity to develop plans for the city and integrate them with policies essential for regulating growth.

Not until 1926 were the politics favorable for establishing a city planning agency. Acknowledging this possibility, Mayor James Walker appointed a Committee on Plan and Survey to draft a bill for doing so. Two years later the committee proposed a City Planning Commission that would take responsibility for development. This required that the state legislature amend the city charter (the document that stipulates the powers available to the local government). This did not happen. Other complications arose, but Walker persisted, and in 1930 he issued Local Law No. 16, which created a planning department with power over zoning. Still, the law was barely approved by the Board of Estimate, and the department was denied any real authority. When the country entered an economic depression in the 1930s, the department became a victim of budget cuts, and in 1933 it was abolished. Political support for control over the city's developmental future was still anemic.[11]

A few years later—in 1936—the new mayor, Fiorello La Guardia, proposed another amendment to the city charter that would allow for a permanent planning commission to regulate land use and take responsibility for capital improvements. The commission would develop a master plan, maintain the official map, oversee the zoning ordinance, and produce a capital budget (Birch 1995, 232). The amendment was successful, and the mayor appointed seven members to the City Planning Commission.[12] The commission employed a full-time technical staff of planners—the planning department. In 1940 the city issued its first comprehensive plan for the city's development, titled *Master*

11. Earlier, in Philadelphia, a similar event occurred, with the city government establishing a planning board in 1912 and then eliminating it in 1919 (G. Heller 2013, 40).

12. In its official history of the Planning Commission, the New York City planning department notes that its creation "provided the structure for comprehensive planning in New York City, replacing a haphazard planning and zoning system that functioned principally through the interaction of interest groups and political forces." See www.nyc.gov, accessed September 11, 2013.

Plan for Land Use (Schwartz 2007). It imagined the transformation of the land use pattern of 1938 to 1965 and then to 1990 and focused primarily on new development in the boroughs outside Manhattan. In the face of opposition, the plan was never adopted by the Planning Commission. Although the politics were favorable for having a planning commission oversee zoning, they were insufficient for coordinating future development through an official plan.

Attention turned back to zoning as the chief planning mechanism for the city, and in the late 1940s an architectural firm was hired to study the current ordinance, which had become unwieldy with the addition of numerous overlapping maps and "fourteen hundred amendments" (Birch 1995, 233). Moreover, the ordinance was based on a projected population of 70 million residents, far greater than the 8.2 million the city reached in 2010. The *Plan for the Rezoning of the City of New York* (1950) eventually led to a new zoning ordinance that became law in 1961, superseding the 1916 ordinance. One of its innovations was the use of the floor-area ratio (FAR) to determine densities within different districts. With that ratio and other zoning regulations, the Planning Commission could influence the height and bulk of buildings by type. This gave planners an important tool for controlling development and further solidified their position within the government. The new ordinance proposed a high modernist planning approach compatible with the prevailing style of redevelopment in cities across the country (Marcus 1991). However, critics considered it "highly inflexible and incompatible with the traditional pattern of attached buildings in the city" (Kwartler 1995, 1288). To mediate between the zoning regulations and current development patterns, over the next few decades the Planning Commission utilized special districts (basically a zoning overlay) and instituted incentive zoning devices. Soon thereafter the city planning department produced another comprehensive plan that would address the zoning ordinance's deficiencies. For a number of reasons, including the lack of public input and excessive attention to developing an inventory of the city's assets, the six-volume *Plan for New York City* (1969) was highly controversial, never adopted, and quickly put aside.

Planning was further anchored in the government by the 1963 charter revision that decentralized public services (Marcuse 1990). It established community boards (comprising mainly citizen volunteers and a small paid staff) to coordinate services within community districts and provided a public forum for comment on zoning changes and development proposals. In effect, the boards would advise the Planning

Commission. This role was strengthened in 1975 with another charter revision that established the city's Uniform Land Use Review Procedure (ULURP).[13] It stipulated levels of citizen and government review and mandated specific review periods for zoning changes, housing and redevelopment plans, and subdivision maps. ULURP formalized and systematized the relationship between the planners (and the government) and the city's residents while decentralizing planning decision making. These new procedures mandated input at the community district level, the borough president level, the Planning Commission level, and the city council level, where the Planning Commission's recommendations were approved or disapproved. The mayor makes the final decision. While this increased oversight of the planning department's decisions and recommendations, it also rooted planning in the neighborhoods in a new way. Here was an opportunity to add popular support to the political backing of elected and appointed officials and the legal support provided by charter revisions.

About the same time, a series of actions was under way that would eventually weaken the city planning department's control over development and its place in local government. This sequence of events started in 1966 with the Public Development Corporation, a quasi-public entity responsible for economic development. Its mandate was relatively narrow: to dispose of city property and develop programs to encourage the leasing of industrial space within the city. Fourteen years later, in 1980, the city created the Financial Services Corporation to provide financial subsidies (usually low-interest loans) to promote business expansion. By 1991, economic development in the United States had moved away from industrial development to land development, with economic development agencies becoming active in large multiuse real estate projects and redevelopment initiatives. This led these agencies into the planning world, where their projects came up against both comprehensive plans (now fading in importance) and existing zoning regulations. Responsibility over major land use changes (for example, large redevelopment projects) that would redefine areas of the city became the purview of the economic development agency, not the planning department. This division was strengthened in 1991 when the city government merged the Public Development Corpora-

13. www.nyc.gov/html/dcp/html/luproc/ulpro.shtml. The new charter also allowed community boards to produce plans for their districts that, if approved by the City Planning Commission, would become law, thereby enabling the further decentralization of city planning. Few such 197-a plans have been produced, and fewer have been approved (Angotti 2008).

tion and the Financial Services Corporation into the nonprofit Economic Development Corporation.[14]

In 2006 Mayor Michael Bloomberg further restricted the scope of the city planning department when he established the Office of Long-Term Planning and Sustainability in the mayor's office. Its mandate was to produce a strategic plan that would enable the city to absorb approximately one million new residents and 800,000 jobs by 2030, strengthen the local economy, enhance the quality of life, and adapt to climate change. Released in 2007 and updated in 2011, *PlaNYC* focused on environmental sustainability, affordable housing, transportation, and energy use (City of New York 2007). Never intended to be a comprehensive plan, it was designed to influence the fundamental decisions shaping the city's future development. That it was not written by the planning department and substituted for a master plan suggests a marginalization of both the planning agency and the idea of comprehensive planning. Meanwhile, the Planning Commission focused on rezoning large areas of the city to accommodate the projected population growth. With strategic planning and project planning the prerogative of the mayor's staff and the Economic Development Corporation and displacement of long-range, comprehensive planning from the city's agenda, the role of the planning department was constricted. Still institutionally embedded, city planning's influence over the future of the city had, for the moment, ebbed.

From Contingencies to Possibilities

What you have just read is a standard history. In it, events appear in a chronological sequence—first one thing happens, then another. Each event, moreover, seems to prepare the way for subsequent events, and the overall arc of the story is one of progress. Planning moves from being an episodic activity of governing elites to a significant and permanent presence within local government. There it influences much of the city's development and enters the lives of the city's users in multiple (though often unseen) ways. Its institutionalization, though, was not smooth. The city planning department established in the 1930s

14. It could be argued that the Landmarks Preservation Commission established in 1965 to oversee historic preservation also weakened the prerogatives of the city planning department by adding another strong voice to development decisions (Marcus 1991, 710). Neither economic development nor historic preservation, though, is inherently incompatible with planning.

was defunded and closed. In more recent years, planning's influence has been eroded by economic development agencies, historic preservation regulations, project-driven development, and the move to strategic planning within the mayor's office. Nevertheless, the history celebrates the rise of city planning as a government activity against the backdrop of a very public and chronological time.

This history can be read differently. A critical reader might strive to be more sensitive to the hidden side of planning and less susceptible to the teleological allure of progress. That hidden side includes planning's complicity in prevailing structures of power and injustice while encompassing how we think about time and the city. To be more influential, planners and their advocates pursued more allies, legal support, an administration presence, and dedicated public funding. By being active in persuading others about how to think about improvements to the city, planners affected the passage of time. Healey's (1993, 247) comment that planning should "be *future seeking*, but not, like its physical blueprint and goal-directed predecessors, *future defining*" speaks to this relationship. But because planners' actions shape a collective understanding of time, contra Healey, they are always defining the future.

Time passes when events and assemblages are configured, maintained, and reconfigured. From this perspective, the institutionalizing of planning is a process by which successive events prevent time from being reversed. Once the 1916 zoning code was in place, supported by the New York City government and recognized as legitimate by developers and property owners, dismantling it and returning to an earlier time was unimaginable. All that could be done was to modify these regulations with special districts, exceptions, and density bonuses or to substantially rewrite them. Because alliances had been successfully formed and stabilized, subsequent actions were more or less dependent on this defining moment. The zoning ordinance also marked the "advance" of planning in New York City. It and other planning events stabilized the world and caused time to pass. A time of no zoning ceased to exist except as a historical artifact.

Key to this stabilization is both the incorporation of a planning mentality (Boyer 1983) in the minds of elected officials, agency directors, private businesses, developers, and property owners and its material manifestation as facts on the ground. As long as planning remains in the form of proposals, plans not adopted, or regulations unenforced, it lacks the substantive presence to mark time. Consequences have to ensue, and the strongest and most influential of them are the public plazas maintained by owners of office buildings, the waterfront promenades used by local residents, the neighborhoods with block after block of preserved late nineteenth-century housing, and subway stations adjacent to employment centers. Entangled with these consequences are official street maps, forms for applying for a zoning variance, real estate lawyers, websites, and building code inspectors. If planning were only about ideas, it would hardly matter.

These changes in the materiality of the city also have to be linked to more widely accepted notions of what it means for a city to be contemporary or modern. (In New York City, the preferred term is "global" [Birch 1996].) This requires planners to show how their plans release people and cities from a debilitating past. Consequently, planners are mesmerized by before-and-after notions of time, with the rhetoric of planning mainly directed at replacing one with the other. The trope is central to their pronouncements. *PlaNYC*, for example, was part of a whole series of government initiatives designed to make New York the leading city in sustainability, transportation, affordable housing, technology, real estate investment, and urban design. Other cities would struggle to make the present better; New York City would leap into the future, leaving behind both the present and the past as well as its global competitors.

Working within this agenda, planners have to commit to the future while redefining the present. Both are necessary for time to elapse and change to occur. As New York City, for example, celebrates its openness to immigrants, the slums of many yesterdays are being replaced by diverse and vibrant neighborhoods on the cusp of the middle class. Aspiring and forward-looking, native newcomers are joined by highly educated immigrants taking up positions in science, technology, and finance. These new arrivals are no longer the "huddled masses" of an earlier era. And while city planners continue to praise historic neighborhoods (mainly as enclaves for the affluent and sites for gentrification), they focus as much if not more on the neighborhoods of young, educated, and ostensibly innovative people. In this and many other instances, planners participate in a perverse form of creative destruction in which the past is infused with substance (its richness a source of its fascination), even though rejected, and the future is stripped of complexity, determinateness, and informality, even though embraced. This issue haunts planning. The slum is portrayed in all its detail, even if formally represented in statistics and maps, and the future is portrayed schematically and in quasi-utopian language. Without the former, however, the latter is less compelling. Even as the past is being discarded, it is being incorporated into the future.

Planners' control over the future, however, is very limited. This applies both to the city's development and to the ongoing stabilizing of planning as a key function of local government. Important here is the progressive abandonment of master planning since the late 1940s. New York City did attempt a new comprehensive plan in the early 1960s, but it was the last gasp of this technique. Project planning replaced the master plan and happened outside the city planning department. The rhythm of city planning became transformed. The long-range master plan was part of a methodical and reflective process meant to unfold at a pace encompassing, but not subservient to, building cycles and time-dependent investment opportunities. Developers and investors, however, want public decisions to be made quickly and the planning commission to conform to the fast pace of real estate innovation and the unrelenting imperative of growth. Planners resist by championing a longer-range perspective for public and private decisions. The battle seems to have been lost, though, particularly with the emergence of strategic planning and the ascendance of economic development as the ostensible key to the city's future.

If planners abandon their need to control the future, they might see opportunity in moving away from comprehensive planning. The new commitment would be to possibilities. Whereas comprehensive planning considers and then discards a range of options, aiming for an exclusionary outcome, grafting project planning onto a planning mentality might open planners, and planning, to the anomalous, the informal, the deviant, and the unexpected.[15] Project planning is opportunistic, with time conceived less as the difference between fixed moments than as the absence of those moments; that is, as a field of contingencies. There is no reason, beyond the usual political impediments, that planners cannot turn project-based planning to just ends.

Consider in this regard Albert O. Hirschman's idea of possibilism (Hirschman 1985). Public intellectual, development economist, Latin American scholar, and political activist, Hirschman was a critic of modernist planning.[16] More accurately, he rejected a planning that assumed that the desired future was a product of a probable sequence of events and that the planner's task was setting that sequence in motion. Believing that social change was mostly unpredictable and that policymakers had limited control over events, Hirschman gazed upon a world

15. Project-based planning has the additional benefit, not to be dismissed, of situating planners closer to implementation.
16. Hirschman not only was an agile and insightful scholar, he also lived a fascinating life. See Adelman 2013.

of unanticipated reactions, unintended consequences (some beneficial and some not), and failures that turned into opportunities. Consider an example from planning practice. New York City's 1916 zoning ordinance was written in part to prevent the mansions along Fifth Avenue from being overtaken by loft factories that had been moving northward (Page 1999, 21–67). Yet the ordinance made the area more desirable for alternative uses, resulting in the displacement of mansions by apartment houses and office buildings. Fifth Avenue became more rather than less susceptible to high-density development.

Planners and policymakers need to be open to these and other possibilities. Hirschman urges them to embrace the "multiplicity and creative disorder of the human adventure" (Hirschman 1985, 27). To put it bluntly, as he did, he refused to be "realistic" (28). Focusing only on what is probable, Hirschman believed, dampens the imagination.[17]

Hirschman thus thought of time not as linear but as discontinuous, social change not as predicable but as unanticipated, and control over the future as illusory. All planners can hope to do is launch events whose legacy will emerge from the way people and things react to them—that is, from their effects. Time is fragmented, with the planner joining a flow of actions whose consequences are only partially known and, even then, known with little certainty. Rather than lamenting this, Hirschman proposed that such an understanding of time and change should be not merely tolerated but adopted. Unanticipated, the unintended consequence and the serendipitous moment can often be favorable. As an additional benefit, when confronted with a world of capabilities and ingenuities yet to be imagined, planners are more likely to be humble. Planners should neither define nor seek the future in its substantive reality but should be open to its possibilities. This means being hopeful about opportunities to do good and about the promise of planning itself to contribute to a more just, equitable, and democratic society. When hope disappears, time ends as well (Lear 2006).

17. Hirschman's (1958) insights into the hidden benefits of imbalanced development—in which the lags between different sectors of the economy draw forth slack resources and untapped creativities—could usefully be applied to the earlier discussion of planners' efforts to coordinate the different developmental trajectories of land uses within the city.

NINE

Unfulfilled Promise

To be a planner in the United States is to be diminished, to be made to feel smaller. Among the rich and highly developed nations of the world, few have such a wide gap between planning's promise and its realization. It is difficult not to envy the control that French planners have over real estate investment, the Singaporean government's capacity to build "public" housing, and Finnish land policy. Of course no country has fully realized this promise. Some, such as the Netherlands and Sweden, have come tantalizingly close. When they did, they offered a glimpse of a world where publics matter, people's welfare was a major concern of state policies, and residents of cities, suburbs, and small towns had access to robust public services and affordable private ones, enjoyed amenities from parks to good libraries, and could live in diverse neighborhoods. The promise of planning in the modern era, like the promise of the twentieth-century welfare state, is that cities will function efficiently and effectively and that people will live well.

Planning's promise in the United States has been thwarted by an indifferent civil society and a political economy that is deeply capitalist and tenuously democratic (Forester 1989, 3). More tolerated than embraced, planning has been limited in so many ways. Obduracy seems to be everywhere. Private property rights are elevated over public stewardship, unrelenting growth trumps preservation, financial investments dominate community development, and the pronouncements of economic elites have more weight than the interests of whole communities. Planning has mainly been confined to local issues, blocked from operating across political jurisdictions, and more and more restricted to issues of land use and such regulatory activities as zoning. Relative to its promise, planning in the United States is a disappointment.

This discrepancy between the promise and the reality enables us to understand what planning is and is not and what can effectively, equitably, and justly be done in its name. In exploring the gap, however, we must avoid the lure of utopian pronouncements and instead ground the discussion in the material conditions with which planners have to contend. Neither should we lament the failure of states and their citizens to recognize planning's inherent benefits or complain about the restrictions placed on local planning. The philosopher Michael Walzer (1988, 3) might convincingly claim that complaint—"one of the elementary forms of self-assertion"—can be prelude to effective criticism, but within planning it should never take the place of careful and critical assessment of current realities.

Planning can best realize its promise if the state is strong and democratic and local governments are given legal and financial support, develop the capacity to mediate private and public investments, and have equal status in intergovernmental relations. My dual concern is the relative silence in planning theory and practice regarding the importance of a robust, welfare-oriented state and an overreliance on civil society among progressive planning theorists.[1] No matter how much popular support planners have, it will be of little value if the state—at all levels—fails to maintain a substantial planning policy and to address structural injustices (Young 1999). The state has to be a countervailing force to capitalist markets and a defender of collective compassion for less advantaged people and places.

Below, I present three examples of a major issue with which planners grapple: capital's ability to move freely across political boundaries. Of the issues that stifle the promise of planning in the United States, capital mobility is the most obdurate. The examples come from the policy worlds of business attraction and retention, shrinking cities, and state growth management plans. With baroque complexity, an idea I will explain later, they will lead us back to the promise of planning and what can be done to realize it. That path involves reformulating the

1. In a 1997 article, Fainstein (1997, 306) praises planning in Amsterdam as compared with that in London and New York City and attributes its virtues to the Dutch state's maintenance of a high level of equality through physical planning and social welfare expenditures. In *The Just City* (2010), however, she gives little attention to the state as a source of social justice. In this Fainstein is not alone among planning theorists.

relation between planning and the state around a political discourse that "imagines a new eloquence" for planning (Latour 2005a, 21). It also requires delving into the relationship between the activity of planning and the distribution of public responsibilities across the various levels of the state.

Planning and the State

Planning in the United States owes much of its legitimacy and influence to its adoption by local governments in the early twentieth century (Hancock 1967; Scott 1969). These governments provided the regulatory powers that enabled planners to attack the slums, organize the street system, coordinate land uses to protect public health, ensure that the city sidewalks had ample daylight, and minimize the negative externalities of textile factories, meatpacking plants, and garbage dumps. Planners, in turn, expanded the capacity of local governments to manage growth and deliver services. State governments, relatively anemic at the time, saw little benefit in planning, and the federal government, also small, was detached from local affairs. Planning thus started as local and for the most part it has remained so.

As the federal and state governments grew in resources and capacity, however, they flirted with adding planning to their list of functions (Biles 2011; Gelfand 1975; Graham 1976). In the 1920s the federal Department of Commerce provided model zoning legislation that state governments could adopt and that would aid municipalities in writing zoning ordinances and controlling land use. During the Great Depression of the 1930s and the New Deal that followed, the federal government deployed planning in a variety of ways including, but not limited to, providing public works, regulating interstate commerce, overseeing food quality, and reclaiming agricultural land. Of particular importance was the National Resources Planning Board that produced reports on regional planning and called for more rational use of natural resources. Most lasting from this period was the realization that it was possible to have an activist federal government concerned with the national economy, supportive of local planning, and engaging in significant public development initiatives.

The end of World War II, however, saw the federal government withdraw from its many planning efforts. The price controls, industrial policies, and commodity restrictions instituted during the war were dismantled, and a stronger and growing economy made state intervention there seem superfluous. Nonetheless, the federal government passed legislation to provide public housing, build an interstate highway system, subsidize the redevelopment of blighted downtown urban cores (a program that required comprehensive city plans as a condition for federal funding), and regulated the home mortgage market. Not until President Lyndon Johnson's War on Poverty in the 1960s, though, was planning once again embraced as a tool for improving people's welfare. Much of the legislation passed during this period was designed to combat rural and urban poverty by increasing economic opportunities, addressing educational and health deficiencies among the poor, and blocking discrimination against African Americans in housing, job markets, and voting rights. In addition, and very important to the planning profession, the new legislation required that local governments and other recipients of government funding develop plans for carrying out these initiatives and involve citizens in their deliberations. The War on Poverty was to be fought locally, but with federal assistance, in poor and African American inner-city neighborhoods and rural towns. Support for local initiatives in disadvantaged communities, moreover, established the political and financial basis for the nonprofit community-based organizations that have become critical for local planning. Equally significant was the availability of funding for advocacy planners who were hired by antipoverty groups and related organizations such as health planning and manpower planning agencies.

Much like the relationship between the national state and planning that was forged during the New Deal, the relationship that emerged from the War on Poverty quickly dissipated. One contributing factor was city mayors who viewed these new agencies as threatening their influence by strengthening grassroots groups and bypassing existing city agencies and funding mechanisms. Another factor was a popular backlash against the precipitous rise of property taxes (exacerbated by inflation) and against what many working-class whites viewed as disproportionate assistance to poor African Americans coupled with indifference to their needs. This led to antitax and socially illiberal politics that turned against "big" government. Planners bemoaned the subsequent withdrawal of federal support for planning and the cities. And even though in the late 1970s President Jimmy Carter held out the possibility of a national urban policy and though earlier in that decade Congress had debated a national growth policy that would merge environmental protection with zoning, federal interest in planning remained fragmented and subdued, never directly addressing the processes by which cities, suburbs, towns, and rural areas grow and prosper (Beauregard 2012a). A few states, such as New Jersey and Oregon, attempted statewide control over urbanization, but most left planning to local governments.

Planning's relation to the state unfolded somewhat differently in other countries (Friedmann 2005; Ward 2002). In England the national government took an interest in local planning, and after World War II, spurred by the population growth of London, it established a national commission to address development issues. The Barlow Commission's minority perspective—never adopted—called for a national planning framework with power to control industrial location (Hall 2002, 182). Nevertheless, the national state maintained a regulatory interest in local planning. In France, urban planning was centralized until the 1950s. And even though national controls over local practices were tempered after that, most urban policies still emanate from the national government. Japan has had a similar planning history of central state control. In these and other countries, the national state has been much more involved with cities and local municipalities than has been the case in the United States. Moreover, fiscal arrangements often ensured that national revenues would be redistributed to localities, a rare occurrence for US intergovernmental relations. Yet few countries embraced national planning for either the economy or the country's settlement patterns. Many developed regional policies to counteract rural depopulation resulting from industrial concentration, but except for countries like China and Russia during their initial Communist periods (and to the present for China), most countries have avoided controls over where people can live and where industries can be built.

That said, planning is ideologically compatible with the contemporary state, particularly in its bureaucratic forms. They view the world in similar ways. A rationalist impulse guides each and is manifested in regulatory powers, data collection as the basis of regulation, standardization (as with zoning maps), goal-driven policymaking, and expert knowledge (Scott 1998). More generally, each harbors a distrust or unease with popular democracy (Frick 2013). And yet governments in the United States are reluctant to allow planning a central role in development processes, even as they apply its tenets to trash removal, allocating police services, and writing capital budgets. Popular belief in the inviolability of property rights and the combination of interest-group politics and businesses' reliance on government subsidies and regulations to protect their markets constitute formidable obstacles to any ascendance of planning within the state.

Fischler (1998) also points to commonalities between planning and the state. Focusing specifically on the welfare state, he proposes that zoning, a tool of planning generally associated with local governments, and the welfare state, which is always national in scope, are connected by people's needs: "The shared heritage is the practice of needs analysis" (396). That is, each rests its decision making on assessments of people's living conditions. For planning, it matters whether housing is sanitary or affordable, school-age children live within walking distance of an elementary school, and the elderly can easily visit doctors and friends. For the welfare state to provide public health services, it must have a sense of how many people suffer from cancer or asthma or are disabled or malnourished. Lacking such information about needs, neither can proceed. For Fischler, planning is very much "a vector of action of the Welfare State" (403).

We can approach this relationship from another direction. Instead of asking how planning and the state have been functionally entwined or whether they share values, we might look at what powers the national state has from which planners might benefit. Such discussions are very much a part of local planning. The federal government in the United States has better access to tax revenues than state and local governments do and is not as constrained in borrowing funds. It can also address the many cross-jurisdictional issues with which planners have to deal; for example, river flooding, national and international migration, residential mobility within metropolitan areas, air quality, and corporate relocations. Moreover, numerous local public services (such as police, firefighting, public health, mass transit, and public education) benefit from federal (and state-level) funding streams and operate under federal (and state-level) regulations and laws. In the way they function, local governments are entanglements of intergovernmental relations to the point where all higher levels of government seem collapsed into them—the national government distributed administratively across municipalities and other governmental levels.

States (national or otherwise) can provide for the welfare of their citizens but are also capable of abrogating their responsibilities and depriving them of a decent life. Planning has the same potential to do good as to do evil (Yiftachel 1998), and we can easily find examples where it has done the latter. One is South Africa under apartheid, roughly 1949 to 1994. Government planners were complicit in uprooting black townships and developing policies to maintain the cities as "white by night" (Friedmann 2005, 194–198; Mabin 1992). Critics of the Israeli government point to its use of planning to colonize Palestinians through land use policies, infrastructure provision, and housing investments (Weizman 2007). And in China planners have been involved in uprooting rural villages to make way for hydroelectric dams and demolishing traditional *hutong* neighborhoods to build office towers (Campanella 2008). Within the United States, progressives accuse government planners of fixating on maximizing land values and developing the city for the rich and the middle class while ignoring the resulting inequalities and polarization. This dark side of planning has to be part of any discussion of planning and the state. It indicates the need for a robust welfare state that is compelled to be democratic by a strong civil society (Young 1999).

Capital Mobility and the State

Many of the obdurate issues that planners in the United States face have their origins in the mobility of people and capital and the constraints imposed by intergovernmental relations that bear on fiscal federalism and the paucity of cross-jurisdictional coordination. Hindering the performance of planning, these conditions can be modified by the state; that is to say, although they stifle the promise of planning, they need not do so. Any meaningful change would require a strong national state that can mount regulatory restraints on corporations and financial relationships and foster greater cooperation among governments while ensuring that revenue and expenditure streams are matched with development's consequences. Three brief examples— business incentive policies, shrinking cities, and state-level growth management initiatives—will make these consequences more obvious and tie capital mobility to planning practice.

My first example involves the financial and other incentives that states and localities offer if businesses will move into their jurisdictions or stay rather than relocate elsewhere (Eisinger 1988, 128–172; Zheng and Warner 2010). These incentives include policies aimed at both attracting and retaining businesses, enticing investors into the state or city and hoping to hold on to those already there. Given a federal government disinclined to provide fiscal support to states and localities and fiscal arrangements that require state and local governments to fund themselves from taxes generated within their jurisdictions (own-source revenues), it is perfectly understandable that subnational governments will act to retain the tax-paying businesses they have and hope to lure others as well.

Business incentive policies emerged in the 1920s when southern states sent representatives to the North to persuade firms there to move to the South (Eisinger 1988, 128–129). Their prey was labor-intensive industries such as shoe production and textile manufacturing, and the main incentive was that the southern states had right-to-work laws that made labor unions virtually nonexistent. Relocated businesses would be able to cut their labor costs and strengthen control over their workers. State governments would reduce business taxes for these firms and provide financial and regulatory assistance for constructing new factories. Interstate competition over business attraction became pronounced again in the 1980s, when many state governments lured automotive assembly plants (Bluestone and Harrison 1982). With the decentralization of American carmakers from the Detroit region and the entry of Japanese and German automakers into the US market, numerous opportunities existed for bringing a major employer and taxpayer into a struggling region. States competed to provide low taxes, free or low-cost land, low-interest construction loans, employment training subsidies, and new roads and rail lines to potential sites.

Intensive and well-funded business attraction and retention efforts arrived at the local level with the recession of the mid-1970s. The recession was one consequence of the shift of the US economy away from heavy manufacturing and was accompanied by a reduction in federal funding for cities. Many big-city governments responded by establishing city agencies and nonprofit development corporations to promote industrial and later economic development with initiatives that would retain existing firms and attract new ones. Using tax abatements, land write-downs, industrial parks, and a host of other incentives, they hoped to stabilize, and even enhance, their industrial and tax base.

One of the most egregious of these efforts involved the automobile manufacturer General Motors. In the 1980s it informed the Detroit city government that it planned to build a new Cadillac plant and was thinking of locating it elsewhere. General Motors needed a larger tract of land than was available within the city limits. To create such a site and keep this General Motors plant, the government proposed to clear a neighborhood known as Poletown of its 3,500 residents, 1,500 homes, 144 businesses, a school and a hospital, and 16 churches—465 acres of land. Using eminent domain, the government subsequently condemned and purchased all the properties, relocated the families and businesses, and turned the now-empty site over to the automaker. The plant was built but employed only half the promised number of workers. Similar events occurred in Flint, Michigan, where the city government subsidized a new hotel only to have it go bankrupt a few years later; provided financing for an automobile museum that closed; contributed to a "festival marketplace" that became a nonperforming asset; and fruitlessly expended numerous funds to keep its main employer, an automotive assembly plant.

Not all such efforts fail, and many cities do prevent businesses from leaving and attract firms that contribute jobs and tax revenues while increasing local spending. And though business retention strategies are still widely employed, city governments are leery of strategies for attracting businesses, preferring to focus on nurturing new industries (for example, biotechnology) from within and on ensuring that existing businesses remain. Economic analyses of the costs and benefits of both attraction and retention are generally unfavorable, however.

My second example concerns "shrinking cities," a phrase that came into vogue in the late 1990s and replaced "declining cities," which had been used since the 1950s (Beauregard 2003, 2015). Both terms refer to the persistent population and job loss suffered by cities and the resulting negative effects on housing markets, tax revenues, transit systems, retail establishments, and political capacities. A number of cities that had lost residents, however, experienced a resurgence in the 1980s with residential gentrification, a rise in tourism, and the revitalizing of downtown retail districts and historic neighborhoods. Attitudes changed, and the declining city occupied popular perception less and less, while academic interest waned. With the collapse of the Soviet Union in 1991 and the flight of households from Eastern Europe to the more affluent Western European countries, many post socialist cities began to exhibit some of the same characteristics as the declining US cities of the 1970s. The former East Germany was hit particularly hard. Older manufacturing cities in Japan and France and resource-based communities in Australia also suffered chronic population loss. Scholars in Germany labeled this condition "shrinking cities."

At the same time, urban researchers and policy analysts in the United States were grappling with the persistent shedding of residents, manufacturing collapse, and housing abandonment being experienced by cities that never recovered from the earlier period of decline. Buffalo, Cleveland, Detroit, St. Louis, Baltimore, Philadelphia, and a host of cities in the Northeast and Midwest continued to lose population as their economies became smaller and smaller. Many had experienced reinvestment in the 1980s, but these projects either failed or had little effect on their overall downward trajectory. Camden, New Jersey, built an aquarium, Baltimore developed its waterfront as an entertainment zone, Pittsburgh subsidized office buildings in the commercial core, and Detroit attracted three casinos, but jobs and residents continued to dwindle. Factories were closed, and no new tenants could be found. Stores were shuttered and never reopened. And house after house across large swaths of the city was unoccupied, abandoned by its owners, and soon vandalized. The tax base kept shrinking, severely hindering local efforts to encourage new investment (which would have to be deeply subsidized) or to demolish abandoned buildings in order to manage the fire, health, and public safety hazards they posed.

Planners and analysts became increasingly aware that these cities would never again be as populous or prosperous at they had been at their peak (Dewar and Thomas 2013; Mallach 2012). Few large investors were interested, and the projects those few proposed would require extensive government assistance to make them financially viable. Most of these cities still had assets—one or two decent neighborhoods, a hospital or university or both, museums, and sports stadiums. Moreover, land was cheap. They had jobs in the downtown core and in manufacturing and service-sector firms, though many of the better ones were being taken by commuters from the suburbs. Large, catalytic projects—such as mixed-use entertainment and shopping centers with housing and offices attached—were unlikely to perform well financially. Even when a few of these cities did manage new investment, the projects mainly served suburbanites and contributed too little in tax revenues to have much impact. The cities' problems were just too vast. In the early 2010s, a number of these city governments filed for bankruptcy.

Many commentators began to argue that elected officials had to think about the city's becoming smaller and stop pursuing a former prosperity. Instead, policies had to be developed that would enable the city to "shrink smart," eventually stabilizing the population and returning the local government to fiscal solvency. Government resources would be dedicated to removing liabilities such as abandoned homes and obsolete factories, then directing new investment to areas with existing assets—a hospital district, for example. Managing shrinkage meant thinking strategically about demolitions and new investment opportunities. This is a difficult position for elected officials to take. None want to be seen as capitulating to the forces of decline and giving up hope for a more prosperous future. Yet the most plausible path for these cities seems to be continued shrinkage or, at best, stabilization at a much smaller population size, with the city economy no longer dominant in the metropolitan region.

Shrinking cities are those places that no longer attract enough capital and households to provide a high quality of life for their residents. In the contemporary parlance, they are no longer competitive. They are unable to expand their boundaries to encompass suburban growth, lack the capacity to undertake public-sector investments that will attract major infusions of private capital, and present an image of decline and destitution that is difficult to overcome. Moreover, they are locked into a system of fiscal federalism that makes them almost wholly reliant on their own revenues. Those revenues have to come from a shrinking tax base while the demand for services by a poorer and poorer population expands. With the federal government unwilling to mount a major urban initiative on their behalf, state governments mostly responsive to suburban constituencies, and the cities losing representatives in state legislatures and the US Congress, the options are limited. All the signs point to dwindling opportunities for any significant growth.

My last example has to do with state-level planning. Since the 1920s, land use planning and other attempts to guide spatial development in the United States have mainly been the responsibility of local governments. State governments passed the legislation that enabled local governments to plan and to establish zoning ordinances, but they did not mandate comparable procedures for overseeing the development of the state itself. Similarly, the federal government has avoided systematic efforts to regulate spatial development at the national level. That said, the federal and state governments have engaged in various regional investments (for example, building dams and interstate highways) and supported local planning, but they have not taken up what might be more generally called "settlement" policies.

Looking downward from the level of the state government, this indifference has left important planning issues unaddressed. One is the need for coordination among municipalities when land uses and new development projects affect adjacent municipalities. The consequences of large-scale investment are seldom confined to a single jurisdiction. Take, for example, the traffic generated by a regional shopping mall on the border between two communities, drawing shoppers from multiple municipalities in the region. Traffic congestion is likely to spill into adjacent jurisdictions whose planners have no control over this new land use or the externalities now placed on their agenda. Many environmental issues are of this type; for example, protecting wetlands, channeling rivers, and regulating air quality. Another obvious set of cross-jurisdictional issues is zoning for noxious industries, often placed on the edge of the city where they abut other municipalities.

Development in the United States, moreover, produces communities of varying levels of prosperity and poverty. Communities do not benefit equally from the capital invested in their state. Some do well while others falter, much as occurs across the neighborhoods of a city. New York City thrives while its urban counterparts in the state, such as Buffalo, Syracuse, and Rochester, shrink. Society Hill in Philadelphia is affluent, well maintained, and a desirable place to live, while many parts of North Philadelphia are abandoned. Such differences among cities result in unequal capacities to provide public services, particularly schools. Communities with good schools can attract more affluent households, thereby improving the tax base but also driving up housing costs and making it difficult for low-income families to move there. The consequences also include tax revenues and the fiscal capacities of local governments. In many instances state governments compensate for these disparities by providing additional funds for underfinanced school districts or grants to build playgrounds and community centers in poor municipalities. Each municipality, fiscally speaking, is meant to be self-reliant.

This uneven development inevitably leads to situations where perfectly viable investments in infrastructure, housing, factories, and retail space are left unused as capital flows to areas of the state (or country) where land is cheaper and development is easier and more profitable. The state government subsidizes new schools and sewer systems that would have been unnecessary if investment and households had been directed to existing places.

In the 1970s, governments began to address these cross-jurisdictional and statewide issues (Gale 1992). Spurred by national legislation on environmental protection, states passed laws to regulate development along their coastlines; protect wetlands, estuaries, and rivers; improve air quality; save farmland; and preserve the state's flora and fauna. A number of states also took up the challenge of growth management, hoping to minimize costly urban sprawl, protect their cities from population and job loss, and provide more balanced development that minimized fiscal and social problems. Oregon and New Jersey took different approaches. Oregon established a growth boundary around Portland, its major city, that encouraged new development to locate close to the city so as to increase densities there and stanch the depletion of open space. Concentrating new investment was meant to encourage more compact development, reduce drive times, and enable economies of scale in infrastructure use. New Jersey opted to use state funding to deny financial support for new water and sewer infrastructure in undeveloped areas beyond the metropolitan periphery. This would make it more expensive to build and thus serve as an incentive for developers to turn to urban areas. Existing cities would be strengthened, and existing infrastructure, roadways, housing, and commercial and industrial space would be better utilized. Oregon has had some success; the New Jersey plan was never implemented.

State governments launched such initiatives in the 1980s just as the political climate of the country was becoming more conservative. Taxpayers in California and Massachusetts revolted against rising property taxes, neoconservatives took over the White House, and support for active government dissipated. Nevertheless, from a planning perspective the motivation was sound. For advocates of these efforts, the mobility of capital occurred at great social cost. For neoconservative dissenters, this was the price of progress. For many others, the states had a role to play in protecting public investments and aiding places that were no longer desirable to investors. Doing so would bolster local planning and dampen the spatial conditions that reinforce inequalities.

Baroque Complexity

Any attempt by planners to strengthen the state has to begin at the local level. Planners are primarily local actors; they are not operatives in national and state government. They need a way of acting that builds on their strengths. The local state, though, is neither devoid of regional, national, and even global influences nor divisible from regional, state-level, and national governments. Similarly, planners are not independent of the state but complicit with it. Baroque complexity can help us make sense of these entanglements.

In exploring the meaning of complexity, John Law (2004) offers two conceptions: the romantic and the baroque. The romantic conception assumes that the function of the parts of any object is to serve that object in its entirety. Parts are conformable and make sense only when put together to form the whole—the global or regional economy. Moreover, the whole is greater than the sum of its parts: it has emergent properties. The romantic method thus proposes a particular understanding of how the world is constituted. It imagines a world in which we are always "looking up" toward the true and most important level of action. As illustration, Law offers globalization, a debate very much in the thrall of romantic complexity. Even when denying the homogenizing of local places by the forces of global capital and interstate institutions, the global scale is still deemed supreme. Local activities and places are subsumed within the global. The point of romantic complexity is to produce "the holism of grand narratives" (18).

Planners adopt an analogous viewpoint. They search for a perspective that subordinates the parts to the whole and judges action in relation to a fully formed entity called "the city." Romantic complexity is also very much how the state and capital are conceived in discussions of the welfare state. Each of my examples illustrates this perspective, but it is most pronounced in the case of state growth management initiatives. There the state government is portrayed as the overarching whole that will take responsibility for the interaction of all the parts (municipalities). Additionally, it is assumed to have powers unavailable to local governments. Although the latter is certainly true, such a portrayal overlooks the many powers that local governments have but the state-level government does not, particularly those related to local knowledge and direct access to residents. A similar understanding pervades the discussion of business attraction and retention policies. The underlying assumption is that a global economy exists in which national and regional economies are embedded like Russian nesting dolls. Local economies sum to regional economies, then to national, and onward to the global economy, with capital moving unhindered across their boundaries. The result of such thinking is to situate action and the power to act effectively "above" the local level. Local planners and elected officials are always looking up for solutions to many of their problems.[2]

Law contrasts romantic complexity with baroque complexity. Embracing the latter, we look down rather than up. The parts are neither components of a whole nor insignificant and powerless unless combined into a coherent and emergent entity. The heterogeneity of the world is embraced, with each part containing all the qualities attributed to a romantic synthesis. The "global" is intrinsic to the local. Tsing (2005, 7) succinctly expresses this point of view when she comments that "universals are indeed local knowledge." Baroque complexity embraces the materiality of the world by blurring the distinction between parts and context. There is no context outside the part, and thus the very notion of geographical scale is challenged. Actors do not move across nested and hierarchical levels; rather, they create scale through the geographical reach of their actions (Beauregard 1995). Scale is

2. Further reflecting this romantic view, city planners in the United States are enamored of the possibility of metropolitan (regional) governance and national urban policy. On this discourse of "nested" capitalist economies and globalization, see Gibson-Graham (1996) 2006, 120–147.

contained within the networks where actors reside. As Law (2004, 19) writes, "we are discovering complexity in the detail" rather than in some higher-level order. Baroque complexity is thus disconcerting for the romantic, for it posits a world in which size does not matter. Without emergent properties, all things from the big to the small, the minute to the massive, are equivalent in ontological value.[3]

We can usefully think of shrinking cities in this way. Shrinking cities are not the discards of US capitalism, stripped of the qualities that enable them to confer benefits on and benefit from the national economy. They contain within themselves all the elements of contemporary capitalism. National and even global capital is being performed within Buffalo, Detroit, and Pittsburgh. If we want to understand shrinking cities, we have to delve deeply into their material presence. There we will find connections to all that matters (Buroway 1998). In effect, this does not mean confining oneself to the "part" (a romantic notion) but instead means acknowledging that what happens within Flint, Michigan, extends beyond that municipality's borders, not because these forces enter Flint from the outside but because they are simultaneously inside it and in other places as well. When General Motors made the decision to close its factory there, leaving close to 80,000 local workers unemployed, it did so by looking at its worldwide portfolio, assessing competition from automakers in Japan, Germany, and Sweden, and weighing alternative uses of its capital. These things were inside General Motors. A baroque complexity conception thus sets context in place. Consequently, all of the world and its current realities are considered to be contained within each shrinking city.

This leads back to the promise of planning and the need for a strong pro-planning, democratic, welfare-oriented state with the capacity to act in the interests of its many publics. The argument begins with a single consequential observation: the national state—the key to any multijurisdictional welfare state—is not about to disappear. As Latour (2007b, 2) has commented, more and more things of the world are being made public—"never [has] the State [been] so busy, so overburdened [as] now." States are not shrinking but are changing in form and even becoming stronger, with "the state itself . . . enacting the redistri-

3. Baroque complexity can be compared to fractals, in which each part of an entity (for example, a floret from a head of cauliflower) "echoes the whole" (Holt 2013, 45). It is also compatible with a decentered, poststructural perspective (Gibson-Graham [1996] 2006, 24–45) and actor-network theory. Latour (2007b), however, does not reject a "politics of the whole." Rather, he writes that a complex and interconnected world cannot be assumed or calculated but must be assembled and composed.

bution of functions that some observers interpret as a hollowing-out of the State and a reduction in state power," as Lake (2002, 819) explicitly indicates. The state is still an essential actor. Only it can mobilize the laws and resources necessary for mediating the conditions of accelerated capital mobility and furnish the safeguards that ensure the welfare of all its citizens. Latour and Lake thus deny the myth of a "weak" American state (Novak 2008) that is unable to act coherently or rein in capitalism. In actuality, and although government powers are fragmented in the United States, the capacity of the state to infiltrate civil society and support business interests is significant and seems to be expanding.

The state is particularly important for addressing issues of equality and justice: "Democratic state institutions . . . have unique and important virtues for promoting social justice" (Young 1999, 153). To this extent, it is central to planning's ideological dilemma. If the gap between the lost promise of the twentieth-century welfare state (and planning) and the world we live in is to be closed, we need a state not just strong but liberal (and, I hope, progressive) in its tendencies. For this to happen, publics must form that advocate for and maintain it.[4] Planners, both within and outside the state, must also do their part if planning's promise is to be realized.

Short of casting off their planning identity and running for elective office or engaging in revolutionary disruption, what planners do best is shape attention and uncover hidden realities (Forester 1989, 19). They can create matters of concern, states of affairs that publics can gather around (Latour 2004a). As they do so, they should think about how to move closer to the promise of planning. This means thinking of the state as fragmented and dispersed rather than monolithic, while recognizing the interpenetration of its functions despite the hierarchical way it is depicted. The state is not one thing but many. It does not overarch daily life, it penetrates its very nooks. And since to govern it has to mobilize and demobilize many actors—state and nonstate—numerous possibilities exist for affecting its performance. If planners are to build arguments for a strong welfare state, they must acknowledge the state as distributed rather than monolithic and politics as a matter of creating concerned publics.

Planners should then augment this understanding of the state with an explicit sense of the world's materiality and the importance

---

4. Here I am following Dewey ([1927] 1954), who argues that when institutional arrangements fail to address an issue, the public must "re-make the state." See also Marres 2005.

of nonhuman things to politics of all kinds (Latour 2005a). Both planning and politics are about things, for it is things (for example, limited-access highways, rising sea levels, abortion clinics) that bring people together to act. When politics address the things of the city, there are matters of concern about which planners have a great deal to say. The whole point of political talk (which is what planners do when they present their reports and answer questions at public meetings) is to create political constituencies (Disch 2008, 93). Action begins with "represent[ing] to the eyes and ears of those assembled what is at stake" (Latour 2005a, 18). In brief, planners have to engage in a politics of enunciation (Latour 2003b).[5]

The state is already strong, and its strength is derived in part from ideological constructions. In fact, an ideology of redistribution currently prevails that seems to weaken the state. One of its components is romantic and aimed at protecting individual freedoms. Resistance to government's ostensible interference in people's lives leads, albeit circuitously, to opposition to government supports (such as unemployment insurance) for people in need (often deemed lazy or undeserving). Equally important are arguments that hide the ways the state props up and protects capitalism: pronouncements that cast the economy as an independent sphere burdened by government. For example, taxes to operate the government (with its many regulations) are seen as dampening economic growth by stifling investment while drawing funds away from consumer spending. The welfare state has no place in this ideological framework.

If the promise of planning is to be realized and a strong, welfare state established, such ideologies have to be opposed (Gibson-Graham [1996] 2006; Judt 2010). Certain planners, but not all of them, are in an ideal position to do so. Everything planners do is saturated with state funding and laws. Everything they do displays the contributions the state can make to the collective welfare. This must be said again and again. Planners are good at such talk. Consider how this might happen.[6]

To begin, planners—local actors—should publicly and repeatedly note how national and state governments are implicated in local gov-

5. Lee and Brown (1994) suggest that actor-network theory supports a vocabulary of liberal democracy that enfranchises all actors and consequently fails to acknowledge oppositional "others," thereby minimizing the conflict inherent in planning.
6. Planners who work for the government or as consultants are more constrained in their public talk than planners who work as advocates or in universities. Nevertheless, their technical knowledge of cities, regions, and neighborhoods gives them a good deal of defensible discretion.

ernment activities, at the places where city and regional planning happens in the United States. Too often, federal and state laws and programs carried out locally are viewed merely as additions to or burdens on the local state. This has the romantic effect of assuming a subordinate local state and thus failing to recognize how it is strengthened by these policies. State-level industrial development bonds, for example, enable local governments to better manage the businesses within their territory, thereby increasing the powers of local government and making the state government, in this instance, dependent on local governments' performance. Similarly, state planning legislation that allows municipalities to engage in zoning and develop sustainability plans enhances the powers of those municipalities while inserting the state government into localities. Viewed through the lens of baroque complexity, local governments are not simply nested within the federal and state governments. In addition, planners must also constantly remind various publics that other levels of the state contribute in numerous ways to the quality of their daily lives and their future prospects. This includes the assertion that prosperity is not wholly dependent on private wealth and that much of what passes for private wealth is a consequence of decisions and actions that cannot be attributed to those claiming its ownership.[7]

Another discussion has to take place that is the opposite of this one. Along with talking about how strong and supportive the local state is, planners need to air their concerns about the ways federal and state laws weaken the local state. Legal and financial constraints on city governments that deprive them of the powers they need to manage the city and interact with surrounding and far-flung places are well documented (Frug and Barron 2008). The intergovernmental system seems designed to weaken city governments relative to their suburban counterparts. The offending mechanisms range from laws limiting annexation and taxing powers to those that stifle metropolitan tax-based sharing and land use coordinating councils. Planners thus must include in their analyses and public pronouncements the restraints placed on local governments' actions. The ways local capacity is stifled are as much a part of local planning as the ways federal and state governments enhance it.

To achieve this, planners should add another task, one that reveals

7. The value of a piece of real property is a result of public improvements that serve that site, the decisions of numerous property owners and users of nearby properties, regulations that protect the site from harm, courts that uphold property rights, and improvements made to the site by its owner.

the damage done by the absence of a strong national welfare state, thereby impairing the quality of life for residents and exacerbating the problems planners are attempting to resolve. Here the references are to capital mobility, fiscal federalism, and intergovernmental relations that set cities adrift to fend for themselves. Take shrinking cities as an example. Certainly local planners should manage vacant properties and coordinate the physical and infrastructural downsizing of distressed and depopulating neighborhoods. They also must attend to the needs of residents who have no choice but to live there. However, local initiatives require state and federal support if the forces contributing to structural injustices—entrenched poverty, racial discrimination, degrading and poorly paid jobs, insufficient health care coverage and educational opportunities, crime, and food insecurity—are to be dampened. These conditions need to change if planners are to have any success. Planners have to bring them into the planning conversation, not as an excuse for the limited impact of their efforts but as recognition of the reality where that work takes place.

These conversations should also refer to the destructive consequences of a relatively unmediated capital mobility. The point is not to condemn capitalism in its various guises, but to acknowledge that when capital is mobile, there are detrimental consequences for people and places. These consequences can be mitigated, but they will return and persist until a strong welfare state has laws and regulations, supported by public investments, that either dampen the excesses of capital mobility or compensate for them. Such a state must also dismantle existing policies that encourage and support suburban governments in attracting businesses away from central cities and must be proactive in discouraging businesses from using their mobility to extort concessions from state governments and municipalities. Similarly, a strong welfare state would address home financing and mortgage practices that enable developers to build speculatively on the metropolitan fringe regardless of the financial worthiness of potential buyers or the distance from existing infrastructure and jobs.

In short, planners need to be more publicly outspoken on matters of concern, in ways informed by considerations of justice and equality. Doing so can enhance the political support for their activities. They should neither take this support for granted nor resign themselves to its weaknesses. Rather, they should—and can—deploy the tools they have, tools very much dependent on the relation between knowledge and action and on state involvement, to mount a concerted campaign to make the state and the planning profession stronger.

I realize this places a burden on local planners, asking them not only to undertake analyses, produce reports, and develop plans, but also to publicly attend to the conditions under which they plan. Of course they cannot do this alone. A strong state will endure only if it is "strongly linked to participatory and critical civic organizations" (Young 1999, 161) that constantly monitor its health. Planners thus must not only speak out but also listen and deliberate with the many publics concerned about the city. Without these publics, an effective and inclusive planning practice will atrophy. The promise of planning will be achieved only when planners join with publics to make the state strong, democratic, and just.

TEN

The Worldliness of Planning Theory

One of the most significant works of planning scholarship is John Friedmann's *Planning in the Public Domain* (1987). When he wrote the book, Friedmann was already a well-known planning scholar whose reputation reflected both his seminal thinking on planning theory and his practical engagement in regional development (Friedmann 2002). He wrote about planning as someone familiar with the leading intellectuals of his time. His influences included urban historian and public figure Lewis Mumford, German social theorist Karl Mannheim, and philosopher Hannah Arendt. Friedmann's writings, moreover, were filtered through his experiences as an analyst for the Tennessee Valley Authority in the United States, an expert with the International Cooperation Administration in Brazil, and a development economist with the United States Aid Mission in South Korea. In addition, a few years before the book's publication, he had written with Goetz Wolff (1982) an article on world cities that spurred a still-growing body of research. Magisterial in scope, *Planning in the Public Domain* is the work of one of the planning profession's most accomplished and insightful thinkers. For this reason alone it deserved—and still deserves—the attention of the field.[1]

1. As of late 2014, Friedmann was professor emeritus at the University of California—Los Angeles and an adjunct professor in the School of Community and Regional Planning at the University of British Columbia.

The book is an intellectual history, the first and still the only book of its type in the planning literature.[2] Friedmann divides that history into four traditions: social reform concerned with advocacy and the role of the state in addressing the lives of the marginalized and the exploited; policy analysis, also focused on the state, with its emphasis on technical problem solving in the service of existing institutions; and two traditions existing outside the state and with much less reliance on technical expertise: social learning that embeds planning in practical experience and popular dialogue, and social mobilization that encourages collective action "from below" along with a politics of engagement. He traced the roots of each tradition to the intellectuals whose ideas and worldviews shaped them. John Dewey, Auguste Comte, and John Maynard Keynes appear in the history of social reform; John Stuart Mill, Kenneth Arrow, and Herbert Simon in the evolution of policy analysis; Frederick Taylor and Kurt Lewin in social learning; and as regards social mobilization, Karl Marx, Pyotr Kropotkin, Saul Alinsky, and Herbert Marcuse. Philosophers, economists, utopians, sociologists, organization theorists, anarchists, labor organizers, and critical theorists, their ideas were imported into planning and constituted, for Friedmann, its intellectual foundation.

The significance of *Planning in the Public Domain* lies in the statement it makes about planning as a bounded domain of scholarly inquiry, a discipline (Beard and Basolo 2009, 234). It looks beyond the substantive research conducted by planning academics on regional transportation systems or public housing schemes to consider the ideas that purportedly guide how planning happens. Focusing solely on planning thought, the book reflects on how planning is conceived and what planners generally do. The assumption is that a direct path exists between knowledge and action, theory and practice. As one early planning theorist, John Dyckman (1969, 299), wrote, "The planner must have a theory of action and decision that he can use to defend his intervention."[3] Friedmann took up this challenge.

To this extent the book provides a justification for why planning should be taught in institutions of higher education and deserves to be a profession for educated, middle-class individuals. Planning scholarship, Friedmann implied, is the intellectual equivalent of the scholarship of sociologists, economists, and geographers. By showing that

2. In commenting on a review symposium of the book, Friedmann (1989a, 63) claimed, contrarily, that his intent "was not to write an intellectual history of urban and regional planning."
3. The implication is that practitioners also have theory. Their theories, however, are more practical than scholarly, what Schon (1982) has labeled knowing-in-practice.

planning has intellectual roots and that there exists a coherent collection of readings that define the field, he demonstrated an affinity between planning and the disciplines already ensconced in college and university departments. Planning, he suggested, is much closer to philosophy and history than to carpentry and automobile mechanics. It has thus earned the privilege of being included in the world of higher education. *Planning in the Public Domain* made a strong case for planning as a scholarly endeavor.[4]

This book might not have happened without an event that also made a significant contribution to planning scholarship: the launching in 1946 of the Program for Education and Research in Planning at the University of Chicago (Perloff 1957, 133–173; Sarbib 1983). At that time numerous planning programs were operating at the graduate level, but none offered doctorates in planning. The Chicago program was the first to do so, and in 1955 John Friedmann was one of its earliest graduates. Together with the students, its faculty explored the intellectual bases of planning and began crafting a formal planning theory that would later become the basis for required courses in master's and PhD curricula.[5] By demonstrating how planning could be formulated as an intellectual project and thus made deserving of a doctorate, the Chicago program provided another argument for why planning should be considered an academic discipline.

The granting of doctorates had a major impact on planning education. As the number of PhDs expanded, they displaced the professionals who were doing most of the teaching. From then on, planning was taught less and less by practitioners who conveyed their experience through hands-on studios and more and more by planning academics who spoke in lecture halls and drew on scholarly texts rather than on any planning experience they might or might not have had. That planning programs continue to employ practitioners and that many doctoral-trained professors are involved in practical research and consulting demonstrates the balance always being sought between planning as a practical task and planning as an intellectual endeavor. Within the university, however, only the presence of PhDs and their scholarly writings makes a credible claim for its intellectual relevance.

4. Offering planning at the graduate level rather than as undergraduate education strengthens planning's claim to being a profession, a status much desired by many occupations (Bledstein 1976). More recent attempts to establish a canon of planning scholarship are discussed in Beauregard 1996b and Innes 1995.

5. Friedmann (2008, 247) claims that "the first planning theory seminar ever to be held anywhere" was in this program and was led by political scientist Edward Banfield.

In contrast to previous chapters, this one is about thought rather than practical action. It is also about being in the world and returns us to the distinction between a world in-here and one out-there. In this instance, the in-here is the planning literature and the out-there is the knowledge of all those who are not themselves planners. The main actors are planning scholars and, within that category, a small group known as planning theorists.[6] In their writings, theorists enter into the world in two basic ways: first, by doing research and reflecting on planning practice and, second, by venturing outside the planning literature to engage the ideas of nonplanning scholars and intellectuals. These two tactics enable planning scholars to craft arguments that appeal to practitioners in the first instance and earn academic credibility in the second.

First, planning theorists have multiple ways of being in the world. Theoretically, they can acknowledge the importance of things by inserting materialism into practice and thought. Empirically, they can theorize about practice by using specific examples to give content and resonance to their theories, something many already do. Second, they can reach out to intellectuals beyond planning's frame and pull into their orbit new insights regarding what it means to plan and to be a planner. However, this is not all they can do. There is a third way that extends beyond writing for professional and scholarly audiences. Planning scholars can engage in matters of broad concern to the many publics to which planning ideas contribute. They not only can speak to the interests of academics and planning practitioners but also can speak publicly about the role of planning in producing a better world. Moreover, planning scholars can do so without abandoning their intellectual portfolios. To be worldly, paraphrasing AbdouMaliq Simone, is to imagine that significant contributions to planning thought and practice are occurring somewhere else.[7]

I will focus here on two of these ways of being in the world. One has to do with how planning theorists affiliate themselves with nonplanning scholars through their writings. Reaching into other worlds for ideas that connect planning theory to the larger realm of scholarship

6. Of note, planning theory is a "northern" (or "western") scholarly project more likely to be found in the United States and the United Kingdom than in Eastern Europe, and nonexistent in Asia and Africa for the most part—though South Africa is an exception. On northern theory, see Connell 2006.

7. The quotation from Simone (2001, 18) concerns the "worlding" of residents of African cities: "It involves the production of orientations to, and sensibilities about, the urban that seemed to posit that the salient features of urban life and its accomplishments were always taking place somewhere else."

is critical for the legitimacy of planning as an academic discipline. The other concerns the potential for planning scholars to become engaged with the general public so that planning becomes part of wider conversations. This leads to a consideration of what it might mean to be both a planning scholar and a public intellectual.

Other Intellectual Worlds

Like all theorists, those writing about planning hope to craft compelling arguments that are widely read and discussed by the scholarly community as well as by the broader profession. Their arguments are meant to influence how other scholars think about planning and how practitioners actually plan by emphasizing collaboration or being sensitive to people's memories of place, for example. To achieve this, planning theorists need to address issues practitioners face while often importing established arguments and conceptual frameworks from other academic disciplines. In constructing an argument that can be taken as credible, theorists have to dispel doubts about its validity, neutralize critics, court allies, and create audiences. That is, they must so embed the argument in the scholarly literature and related conference and seminar debates that it can neither be easily extracted nor be effortlessly discredited (Latour 1987, 21–62).[8] A successful argument is one that has become a reality such that critics no longer view attacks as apt to weaken it. Reality is what is unquestioned (Latour 1987, 2). One way to achieve this state is to reach into other worlds. For this reason, importation is the most important tactic for strengthening planning's academic standing.

Central to both the credibility of planning theory and planning's academic status, then, is linking planning arguments to intellectual projects outside the discipline. These intertextual connections (Beauregard 2012b, 482–484) enable planning theorists to simultaneously publicize their involvement with the broader field of scholarship, enhance their scholarly status, and explore ideas that transform the way they think about planning. Planning's presence in intellectual debates is a

---

8. Consider Latour's (1987, 37) summation of what a scientist must do for her findings to achieve prominence: "Weaken your enemies, paralyze those you cannot weaken . . . , help your allies if they are attacked, ensure safe communications with those who supply you with indisputable instruments, oblige your enemies to fight one another . . . [and] . . . if you are not sure of winning, be humble and understated."

powerful way to justify the discipline to university administrators.[9] If planning academics can show that planning knowledge builds on and extends the scholarship of acknowledged disciplines, then progress has been made in establishing their scholarly credentials. If they can show that planning thought permeates these other disciplines as well, their case for inclusion is even stronger. They must combat the characterization of planning theory as insular and thus inconsequential.

Not surprisingly, the outward orientation of planning scholarship is mirrored in planning practice. One manifestation is "best" practices (Dolowitz and Marsh 2000; Vettoretto 2009). Here practitioners borrow ideas from other places rather than developing projects and regulations wholly from local conditions and possibilities. Examples might include Johannesburg's planners' adoption of business improvement districts from New York City or New York City's planners looking to the Netherlands for ideas about how to protect against sea level rise. Another expression of this is the turn to practical or local knowledge whereby planners recognize that their expertise and technical know-how are insufficient for solving public problems (Corburn 2003). Thus planners ask residents to identify point sources of pollution (for example, dry cleaners) or hold a focus group with homeless families to discuss the location of temporary housing. In these instances, practitioners go outside the profession.

What is it, though, that planning theorists are doing when they leave the confines of the planning literature? How does this aid in building publics, enrolling allies, and achieving credibility (Callon and Law 1982)? To answer these questions, we need to delve into the relation between planning theorists and the literatures from which they draw ideas. As illustration, I offer the writings of four contemporary planning scholars—Patsy Healey, Susan Fainstein, John Forester, and Leonie Sandercock. My objective is to identify the otherworldliness of planning theory.[10]

For the most part, the bulk of the citations in the writings of plan-

9. The scholarly accomplishments of planning faculties are conveyed to university administrators in numerous ways: tenure cases, annual reports, collaborative research projects, noteworthy public events, newspaper and magazine articles about people and research findings, and the various interdepartmental committees on which members of the planning faculty sit.

10. I have written on Forester and Sandercock in exploring how different planning theories imagine different types of practitioners (Beauregard 1998). As of late 2014, Healey was professor emeritus in the School of Architecture, Planning, and Landscape at Newcastle University, Fainstein was a senior research fellow in the Graduate School of Design at Harvard University, Forester was a professor in the School of Art, Architecture, and Planning at Cornell University, and Sandercock was a professor in the School of Community and Regional Planning at the University of British Columbia.

ning theorists refer to the thoughts of other planning theorists. Healey (2006), for example, based the introductory chapter of her major book *Collaborative Planning* on the work of such planning scholars as Bent Flyvbjerg, John Friedmann, Charlie Hoch, Tore Sager, and Judy Innes. This is to be expected; that is her reference group. It is the community she must participate in if she wants her arguments to be taken seriously. By enrolling other planning theorists in her arguments, her writings become planning theory and thus available to be referenced in its further development. One of the first steps toward becoming and being considered a scholar is to join ongoing debates with like-minded people. This is the world inside planning.

Planning theorists also draw ideas from beyond the ever-shifting boundaries of the planning literature. This has been true from the early days of planning theory in the 1960s. Paul Davidoff and Thomas Reiner's "A Choice Theory of Planning" (1962), one of the field's first explicitly theoretical articles, referred not only to economist Kenneth Arrow but also to philosopher Rudolf Carnap and sociologist Robert Merton. Back in the late 1970s, Susan Fainstein and her coauthor (Fainstein and Fainstein 1979) drew on Karl Marx and Friedrich Engels along with geographer David Harvey, sociologist Manuel Castells, and political scientists Ralph Miliband and James O'Connor to construct a Marxist perspective on planning. Later, in formulating her argument for a "just city" (Fainstein 2008, 2010), she deemed philosophers John Rawls and Martha Nussbaum, economist Amartya Sen, and social theorist Henri Lefebvre most relevant to her project.

John Forester's early writings on communicative action in the mid-1980s were informed by the thoughts and writings of Brazilian educator and critical philosopher Paolo Freire, political scientist Murray Edelman, and philosophers Martin Buber, John Dewey, and Jürgen Habermas. For Forester, "Habermas provided the intellectual working out (to be further refined, critiqued, transformed, of course) of Freire's radical pedagogy" (Forester 2013, 14). Patsy Healey (2009) has found productive use for the ideas of sociologist Anthony Giddens and pragmatists John Dewey, William James, and Richard Rorty, while Leonie Sandercock has brought into planning thought such feminist thinkers as bell hooks and Gloria Anzaldúa, as well as socialist philosopher Cornel West. For Sandercock (1995), theory in planning must be receptive to intellectual currents from the humanities and social sciences. Her self-identification as a postmodern modernist has led her beyond the world of white, male, and European scholars. She once remarked (1995, 79) that "if [planning] theory is seen as synonymous with practical philosophy—that is, thought crafted to guide action—we can see even greater relevance" for the writings of the radical postmodernists.[11]

Foreign ideas, in the disciplinary rather than the geographic sense (Connell 2006), are brought into planning for a number of reasons. In the late 1970s and 1980s, Fainstein (2010, 19) used David Harvey and Manuel Castells to join planning theory to urban theory so as to move the former away from its fixation on rational procedures; that is, to shift the "discussions of planning and public policy toward the characteristics of urban areas, lessen the focus on process that has become dominant within planning theory, and redirect practitioners from their obsession with economic development to a concern with social equity." Building on her earlier work on urban politics, she argued that planning was primarily a political matter involving the redistribution of the city's resources from one social group to another. It was not an apolitical, technical process. Her goal was to address the way the material consequences of planning were justly or unjustly distributed. To do so, she needed a political perspective anchored in conflict and contradictions; Harvey, Castells, and—lurking behind them—Marx and Engels provided it. Sandercock (1995, 86) cites intellectuals who "have not lost sight of certain key principles of the [E]nlightenment—justice and equality—but they have seen through the exclusivity involved in the application of these principles." In search of a more inclusive, moral vision, she explores literatures outside the field.

Similarly, John Forester has found Jürgen Habermas and John Dewey useful in shifting the core function of planning away from analysis toward interpersonal communications. The prevailing rational comprehensive model of planning relied on experts to advise on public decision making and, because of this, suffered a severe deficit of democracy. Forster recognized that what was most important about planning practice was not what analysis planners did but the way they discussed their ideas in the quest to have their advice adopted. Consequently, he turned to Habermas and Dewey, who placed democracy within the public sphere where individuals could communicate with each other and give rise to concerned publics. Habermas and Dewey provided the intellectual justification for a deliberative planning while having sufficient intellectual weight to convince other planning theorists of the importance of his argument. In a memorable sentence, Forester (1989, 23) wrote: "What gets done depends heavily on what gets said, and

---

11. Sandercock and Forsyth (1992, 49) had noted a few years earlier that "feminist theory has much to contribute to planning theory."

how it is said, and to whom."[12] In his planning theory talk replaces analysis, with this shift defended by an array of nonplanning allies.

To this extent, planning theorists not only are gatherers of nonplanning ideas but also are perfectly comfortable using those ideas in new combinations. Listen to Forester (2013, 13) again: "My interest in Habermas depended substantially on his *integrating* [John] Austin (doing things with words) with Steven Lukes and Murray Edelman (power as selected attention, agenda-setting, and hegemonic talk and practices) into a critique of ideology" and domination. No idea travels without being adapted or distorted, and ideas are almost always juxtaposed with new evidence and applied to concerns previously unaddressed. Fainstein uses the philosophical guidelines of John Rawls to understand the just city, while Sandercock asks how feminist insights into interpersonal relations can aid in empathizing with people's aversion to the sudden changes often imposed on them.

Nevertheless, while theorists pull ideas from beyond the planning literature, they do not rewrite these arguments and return them to their origins. The transfer is one-way. The objective is to use, for example, Iris Young's theory of responsibility and justice to change our thinking about planning, but not to modify Young's theory. The arguments of Giddens, Foucault, Habermas, Marx, Dewey, hooks, Castells, and Latour contribute to planning but are left unchanged. Patsy Healey turns to regulation theory, Giddens's ideas about structure and agency, and Habermas's reflections on the public realm to develop her institutional approach to planning; she has no intention of rewriting them. Similarly, Forester takes what is useful to him from Habermas and leaves what is not. He deploys Habermas's ideal speech argument to explore the relation between misinformation and power and ignores his utopian inclinations. He makes no attempt to reconfigure Habermasian philosophy in light of what he learned by applying that philosophy to planning practice. Few benefits flow from realigning, for example, Castell's argument about consumption and the city and then entering into debates with the discipline of sociology. Such intellectual work falls outside the boundaries of the world from which planning theorists derive their legitimacy and their institutional support. For planning theorists, these intellectuals are a source of ideas but not an object of theorizing.

Consequently, what planning theorists think seldom appears in the

12. Policy scholars (Majone 1989) were also debating the weak democratic tendencies of policy analysis and exploring the role of persuasion in implementation.

writings of the nonplanning intellectuals from whom they draw inspiration. Planning is not just a minor profession (Glaser 1974), it is also, from the perspective of the dominant social science disciplines, a minor scholarly endeavor as well, much like geography and psychology. It suffers from its practical origins and from being brought into the university as a profession. The more stable academic disciplines—sociology, history, economics, anthropology, and political science—had practical concerns but quickly distanced themselves from them, although economics maintains an engagement with public policy and business. Moreover, they entered university settings as the university itself was becoming established as the center of formal and systematic knowledge production (Bledstein 1976; Gulbenkian Commission 1996, 1–32). Not only did planning come later, in the early twentieth century rather than in the late nineteenth, but its first professors were mainly practitioners (many from architecture and civil engineering) and reluctant to sever their ties to the quotidian world of practice. Only with the granting of PhDs in planning did a gap open between those who teach and those who plan. Having attenuated their ties to the professional world, however, planning academics are unlikely to sever them. Their position within the university is predicated on offering a professional education (Beard and Basolo 2009, 235).

Planning theorists, then, rarely join external debates. This is to be expected. Despite the contemporary celebration of interdisciplinarity, disciplinary boundaries are still deeply entrenched (Lamont 2009, 53–106). The challenges to straying onto other scholarly realms are formidable: lack of in-depth knowledge, an absence of appropriate credentials, no prior involvement or recognition, and the unlikelihood that fame attained there can be of value in the planning community. The planning theory project is one of developing an intellectual basis for planning that will enable practitioners to be more effective. This objective is not served by publishing outside this world.

Of course, exceptions exist. Throughout her career, Susan Fainstein has written on urban politics. In fact, she began as a political scientist commenting on neighborhood mobilization (Fainstein and Fainstein 1974) and only later, as she was writing on the politics of urban redevelopment projects (Fainstein 1994), developed a reputation as a planning theorist. Her writings on urban regime theory can be found outside the core planning literature, and she is one of the people to read if one wants to learn about the politics of urban redevelopment in the United States. Similarly, John Friedmann is a central figure in the world city debate, the precursor to the global city literature. Beyond these two, one searches in vain for a planning theorist who is read by the nonplanning scholars they cite. It would be surprising to find Fainstein cited by Amartya Sen or Jürgen Habermas referencing the work of John Forester.[13] This is not meant to disparage the quality and importance of their work. Rather, it is to point to the persistence of disciplinary boundaries and scholarly hierarchies.

As Public Intellectuals

The subordination of planning scholarship within the academy is a starting point for thinking about planning academics as public intellectuals. As a public profession, planning finds its responsibilities unequally divided. Its main obligation is to the public in its many factions, with the care and nourishment of planning scholarship of secondary concern. Consequently, planning scholars have to do more than venture onto foreign intellectual terrain. They also need to attend to the publics that bear the consequences of planning advice and from which—mediated by the university—they ultimately derive legitimacy. Planning is meant to address how people can live well together and is done by almost all governments (democratic and nondemocratic), most organizations, and many households. Moreover, to the extent that cities, regions, and neighborhoods cannot speak for themselves, advocates are needed to speak for them. If planning scholars believe they have a responsibility to contribute to the welfare of publics, then being present in the world of publics is unavoidable.[14]

Beard and Basolo (2009) claim that planners are already worldly. The profession "has been willingly embedded in public affairs from its beginning" (235), with scholars "routinely reach[ing] outside the walls of academia to communicate their work to broader audiences" (239). Practitioners and academics, they imply, are neither modest nor with-

13. This imbalance appears vividly in Michael Frayn's novel *The Trick of It* (New York: Picador, 1989). Its main protagonist, an English literature professor whose life's work is one specific novelist, comments: "Another funny thing when you think about it. I read every word she writes, even though not a single one of them is about me. She reads not a single word I write, even though most of them are about her" (50). That he is married to this woman further thickens the psychological entanglements.

14. The implication is that there are no public intellectuals who are also planning scholars. I think this is empirically true, at least for the United States. On this point, Jacoby (1987) puts forth the proposition that the expansion of academia after the 1960s constricted the pool of public intellectuals by narrowing perspectives and rewarding disciplinary contributions over public engagement.

drawn. Planning already has a public identity, and this seems to obviate the need for public intellectuals. I only partly agree. Practicing planners are involved in activities that put them in frequent contact with various publics; for example, when they testify at zoning hearings or defend the location of a recycling plant to the residents of the surrounding neighborhood. And research done by planning scholars is likely to enter into public discussions, particularly when debate rages around such issues as sprawl or sea level rise. Neither of these, though, is a substitute for having planning scholars constantly advocating for planning in public forums. This is a much more political act.

American pragmatist and educational philosopher John Dewey (1859–1952) was exemplary in the role of a public intellectual (Dykhuizen 1973). Not only was he an accomplished and widely acclaimed scholar, he was also active throughout his adult life giving public lectures, writing in academic journals and magazines, and collaborating on issues from labor unions to academic freedom, unafraid to voice his opinions on current events. His organizational activities were extensive: he participated in the formation of the American Association of University Professors, the American Civil Liberties Union, the New School for Social Research, and the University-in-Exile that provided teaching positions for scholars fleeing fascism in Italy and Germany during the 1930s. He established the Laboratory School at the University of Chicago and helped organize the New York Teachers Union in 1916. Dewey wrote for such progressive magazines as the *Dial*, the *Nation*, and the *New Republic*. And he spoke out frequently on civil liberties, war, academic freedom, religion, public education, and international cooperation. He acted publicly in ways that connected his intellectual interests with public issues. Dewey was a scholar, an educator, and an activist—"a model of engaged intellectual life" (Ryan 1995, 24).

Most striking about Dewey's activism, aside from the sheer scope of his engagement, is the connection he maintained between his intellectual pursuits and his public concerns. Each issue, each activity he took up was one he could speak of with authority. Much in the way the interests of practice-based planning theorists are relevant, his intellectual interests were relevant to the way people live. His lifelong commitment to democracy, social learning, and individual fulfillment led him to become involved in numerous public issues. Dewey built bridges between his specialized knowledge of psychology, pedagogy, and philosophy and issues around which publics were formed.

There is no reason planning scholars cannot enter into mainstream criticism in a similar fashion.[15] Widely characterized as generalists with a specialty (Perloff 1957, 34–53), the path from the rarefied realm of expertise to matters of public concern has already been established within the discipline. Planning scholars have substantive and general knowledge relevant to many of the issues—traffic congestion, environmental hazards, property values—that daily face the residents of cities, suburbs, and regions. They have thought about how to both imagine a shared future and act collectively to achieve it. Consequently, they can speak in public about what it means to live well with others. Moreover, planning scholars share experiences and ambitions with many of these publics and are neither alienated from nor outside the world they want to change. As Walzer (1988, 23) reminds us, "criticism follows from connection." Last, planning scholars are less constrained politically than planners who work for the government.

To speak publicly and critically, planning scholars must have a voice, a way of speaking about planning that is intellectually sound, intelligible, and provisional. The objectives are to shape attention and help publics to form, not to pronounce on what is and what should be.[16] The premise is that public ideas matter, a premise that supports what many planning theorists and practitioners believe to be the core task of the planner: to link knowledge to action (Friedmann and Hudson 1974). They matter because the world is not devoid of altruism, not fully saturated by self-interested individuals and private-regarding interests. Neither is it devoid of a sense of belonging that encourages the preservation and enhancement of communities—the publics—of which one is a part. Ideas often "overcome interests in determining political choices," and obtaining the consent of others in public deliberations requires that arguments be "expressed in terms broader than the self-interest of the individual or the group making the claim" (Kelman 1988, 39, 52).

Ideas matter, particularly as regards enrolling allies and forming concerned publics (Friedmann 1989b). Planning scholars, like intellectuals generally, "believe in the power of ideas to change the world" (Fuller 2004, 479). They do so by joining the publics that come into

15. This discussion mirrors that in chapter 9 on practitioners and publics. My motivation in both instances is Antonio Gramsci's comment that "every revolution has been preceded by an intense labour of criticism" (quoted in Robinson 2005, 473).

16. On shaping attention, Forester (1999, 72) comments that "the design professions are deeply and inevitably political, then, because they reshape our senses of hope and resignation, our shared perceptions of our possibilities, of the way we can (or cannot) respond to . . . the always precarious possibilities, of human flourishing."

THE WORLDLINESS OF PLANNING THEORY

existence when issues are collectively deliberated (Dewey [1927] 1954; Warner 2002, 125–157). Such publics are constituted by recognition of the consequences of action (Dewey [1927] 1954, 47) and, once constituted, represent matters of concern. By talking together and sharing ideas, people imagine themselves successfully opposing the taking of their parkland, establishing a government commitment to affordable housing, and ridding the neighborhood of drug dealers. Publics become further stabilized when they act together and, even if unsuccessful, discover new ways of understanding how the world might be different and better. This is one of the reasons Dewey not only spoke about academic freedom but also worked to create an organization to defend it (the American Association of University Professors). Knowledge has to be linked with action (and action to knowledge). Ideas are strengthened when they are brought into assemblages of humans, objects, and technologies that can act effectively. In this way they become solidified and influential enough to "[establish] the context within which public policy is debated and executed" (Moore 1988, 75; Schon and Rein 1994). Of course, ideas can also be obdurate and block action that might improve the world (Hommels 2008).

Not principles to be obeyed, ideas are instruments for encouraging deliberation. For the public intellectual whose goal is to shape attention and encourage debate, ex cathedra pronouncements are forbidden. The planning scholar as a public intellectual has to eschew the safe haven of specialized expertise (and academic security) for joint discussions that share knowledge of all types in mutually comprehensible ways. She becomes a mediator who facilitates ideas (and actions) and whose "mediation is integrally public, collective, and interactive" (Osborne 2004, 443). The objective is to encourage widespread consideration of issues and the formation of expert understandings held in common, not to offer autonomous and hermetic knowledge (Callon, Lascoumes, and Barthe 2011). Neither is it to adjudicate among dueling experts as a legislator would. Rather, the role of the planning scholar as public intellectual is to engage in political talk that creates publics (Latour 2003b). She must "[bring[ideas quickly and decisively into public focus, brokering those ideas in the context of different spheres of influence" (Osborne 2004, 435).[17]

This does not mean abandoning planning expertise or theoretical interests; it points to the necessity of making the reasoning behind

17. Disch (2008, 93) argues that "the process of representation confers agency on the represented."

expert knowledge accessible to nonexperts and open to debate. Planners become more accessible by engaging matters of concern rather than matters of fact (Latour 2004b). That is, rather than distilling issues until they are reduced to "bare facts," they expand them via connections to other publics, nonhuman things, institutional arrangements, related issues, and other certainties. The expert planner should thus deemphasize analysis in order to engage in gathering "things." The objective is to move closer to reality rather than further away. Expertise thus functions as one of the mediating mechanisms for distinguishing common sense from good sense (Robinson 2005).

Just as planning practice should be ethically based, the talk and actions of planners as public intellectuals should also make their moral stance explicit. To speak of living well together is to address the responsibilities we have to each other and thus to acknowledge the moral basis of these relationships and the institutions that support or weaken them. Speaking and acting in these ways make planning scholars into moral agents (Lake 2014)—individuals responsive to current conditions and events and complicit in their resolution. Motivated by the belief that the world can be better, that concentrated power can be resisted, and that knowledge shared is knowledge useful for action, these scholars are not just speaking truth to power, the classic position of the public intellectual, but forging truth (and publics) from collective experiences. The objective is not to assess blame but to devise ways of subverting the forces that create a deficit of democracy and perpetuate conditions of injustice and inequality. One cannot be a public intellectual without being morally responsible for oneself and others, sharing that responsibility, and looking toward a better future (Young 2011). As the cultural theorist Raymond Williams (1973, 38) wrote decades ago, "There is only one real question. Where do we stand, with whom do we identify?"

As public intellectuals, planning scholars can do no better than to follow the advice of Steve Fuller (2005, 3): "Learn to see things from multiple points of view without losing your ability to evaluate them"; "be willing to convey any thought in any medium"; "never regard a point of view as completely false or beneath contempt"; always see your opinion as counter-balancing, rather than reinforcing, someone else's opinion"; and "in public debate fight for the truth tenaciously but concede error graciously." To this I would add "recognize the moral basis of your worldview and reveal it to others." A last piece of advice: "learn from and share your experiences"—brings this description back to Dewey's ideas about pragmatism and public education.

For planning scholars to engage only in public talk, however, is to deny what it means to be a public intellectual from a discipline where knowledge is judged in relation to the action it inspires. Dewey knew that publishing in the *New Republic*, submitting press releases to the *New York Times*, and speaking before professional associations was insufficient to achieve the kind of cooperative communities and engaged democracies encouraged by his scholarship. He would not be true to himself if he just talked, so he acted as well. Talk has consequences, but it is only one form of action. Other forms of action are also needed: setting up committees, holding rallies, marching in protest or support, and, among other undertakings, volunteering to leaflet a neighborhood (Walzer 2004, 90–109). The world has to be brought into existence and made real. This requires new relationships among people, ideas, technologies, and things. This is what Dewey did. With others, he created organizations that could publicize and protect ideas of academic freedom, Christian charity, and religious tolerance. Unless ideas and arguments were solidified with bylaws, monthly newsletters, membership rolls, public rallies, and lobbying efforts, they would not be strong enough to absorb criticism. If they were insubstantial, their consequences would be few and impermanent.

Organizing and joining organizations is part of the public intellectual's role, and this is no less so for the planning scholar. It is another form of enrollment and thus of strengthening arguments. Effective criticism is possible only if intellectuals are connected; if they act from within rather than from a position of moral indifference (Walzer 1988, 3–28). To create a public of planning academics, for example, a group of planning educators in 1959 formed the Association of Collegiate Schools of Planning (ACSP) and achieved autonomy from the main professional association (the American Planning Association) in 1981. However, the ACSP, like the American Association of University Professors, mainly looks inward. More outward-looking is Planners Network, an organization single-handedly created by Chester Hartman in 1975 to advocate for equality and justice in planning. As a housing expert, planning professor, and activist, Hartman had been working with community groups opposing government plans that threatened their neighborhoods. The main professional association for planners seemed to be complicit, and he saw a need for a left-leaning organization of practitioners and academics that could serve as a counterweight. Operating as a forum for students, practitioners, and faculty members, Planners Network has maintained planning's progressive impulse with a regular newsletter and annual conferences. Moreover, it has sustained connections to community-based groups as part of its organizational identity. Planners Network is publicly engaged by design. It falls squarely within Friedmann's social mobilization tradition.

Many planning scholars, of course, are involved with community groups, national advocacy organizations, and social movements. Joseph Schilling, a lawyer and planning professor at Virginia Tech, was instrumental in forming the National Vacant Properties Campaign in 2003 to work with cities facing large numbers of abandoned properties. With the community redevelopment consultant Paul Brophy and Dan Kildee, a former city councilman from Flint, Michigan, he then put together the Center for Community Progress in Washington, DC, to provide support for local governments and community-based organizations in shrinking cities. Famous for his planning theory article on advocacy planning, Paul Davidoff (1965) taught planning at Hunter College in New York City and was also directly engaged helping low-income and minority groups resist unwanted changes to their neighborhoods. In 1969 he created Suburban Action to challenge exclusionary zoning in the suburbs, and in 1982 he founded the Metropolitan Action Institute to work with inner-city communities.

Peter Marcuse (best known for his writings on housing, segregation, justice, and globalization and for years a planning professor at Columbia University) has dedicated a good portion of his time to speaking at public forums on contemporary issues such as the mortgage foreclosure crisis and the Occupy Wall Street movement of the late 2000s. Marcuse has also served on various boards, including the Los Angeles City Planning Commission, a Community Board in New York City, and an antipoverty agency in Waterbury, Connecticut. Leonie Sandercock frequently works with disadvantaged communities to address the sources of their discontent, including a First Nations village in northern Canada and an inner-city immigrant neighborhood in Vancouver. A few planning professors have even run successfully for elective office; for example, Allan Feldt of Cornell University served on the Ithaca, New York, city council in the 1970s, and James Throgmorton of the University of Iowa was a city councilman in Iowa City in the early 1990s and again in the early 2010s.

My sense is that these people are not exceptions. Many planning academics do more than teach their courses, write journal articles, and reflect on practice from the confines of their offices. They meet with local community groups, respond to queries from reporters, and advise the staffs of various government agencies. For the most part, though, their actions are not widely recognized, and public debates about how people should live and what the city should be like occur without their involvement. The planner-scholar as public intellectual would be a vocal, and hopefully influential, participant in these forums.

Can planning theorists do the same as regards the other intellectual worlds they draw on for inspiration? That is, can they participate actively and consequentially? This might be an even more difficult task. The media are always looking for the (new) spokesperson and contrary (although acceptable) opinions. Academic disciplines, however, are seldom open to outsiders espousing ideas about how to change what has been stabilized to define the discipline. That said, I know of no social science that bans all but card-carrying members from giving papers at its conferences or submitting articles to its journals. The barriers are intellectual and involve what issues are appropriate to discuss, what methodologies count as valid, and how theories are to be treated. It is possible, then, that planning scholars can join debates in other disciplines, and this has likely happened, though I suspect it is rare. The true test is when other disciplines adopt the arguments that planning scholars are making. Few planning theorists write "pure" theory of high abstraction, the kind that can travel from one substantive context to another. Nor should they. Doing so severely limits their influence within the planning profession.

Speaking to Multiple Publics

John Friedmann is one of the towering scholars in the discipline of planning. He was the first to reveal the contribution of nonplanning intellectuals to planning thought, and he has spent his life writing about what it means to plan and how it should be done. Of utmost concern has been the inclusion of a moral discourse that encapsulates the ethical choices at the root of planning conflicts. Still, Friedmann is not a public intellectual. He has not written for general market magazines, produced frequent op-ed pieces in major newspapers, worked to put together organizations that express his ideas, or joined social movements. In this he is not alone among planning scholars, although many have engaged in one or another of these undertakings. The world of planning theorists comprises academics such as John Forester and Susan Fainstein, intellectuals with practical experience (for example, Friedmann and Leonie Sandercock), thinkers with activist credentials, such as Peter Marcuse, and a few activists, one of the best-known being the late Paul Davidoff. Too few planning scholars, however, speak about planning publicly and consistently and in multiple forums. Too few emulate Dewey in being a public voice for their ideas. Too few planning scholars have ventured outside the academy and into less circumscribed, more heterogeneous, and more obdurate worlds.

Planning is meant to be in the world. If it is isolated, the vibrancy of its ideas and the relevance of its actions suffer and will eventually atrophy. For planning theorists to be worldly and to fulfill this promise of planning, they have to engage with practice while acknowledging the intellectual debates that occur beyond the boundaries of the discipline. Almost all theorists do these things. Ideally, planning scholarship would also spawn public intellectuals to make the case for planning in the institutional arrangements that govern everyday life. That this is uncommon is to be expected, even if it is regrettable. The demands of academia—to teach, publish, and conduct research—seem to stifle any inclination to carve out a role as a public intellectual. And while opportunities for speaking publicly have proliferated with social media, the ease of doing so and the number of those now speaking dilute any single voice. Moreover, a certain type of thinker and personality is required. That said, the idea and practice of planning would benefit if more planning scholars could surmount these barriers.

ELEVEN

Planning Will Always
Be Modern

In the world of the new materialists, social facts are a problem. By proposing "the social" or stand-ins such as globalization, democracy, and modernism to explain how the world works, they argue, we assume (but leave undocumented) the control these factors have over the behavior of individuals. Social facts substitute for a critical realist understanding of how actors exist in the world. As Latour (2005b, 97) has remarked, "The social has never explained anything; the social has to be explained." Yet ideas do matter, at least for human actors, and cannot be tossed aside even if they are so thin (such as justice) or so maddeningly vague (as with sustainability or resilience) that they seem of little practical use. People hold values and have ideas and often act in response to them. But the connection between ideas and actions is always tenuous, and ideas are only one of the factors that enable us to grasp the complexity of the world and act within it.

Modernism is one of these social facts and central to our understanding of contemporary planning. Before modernism emerged in the eighteenth century, planning existed in various guises: as fortifications, military camp layouts, and land surveys. But it was only with the rise of nation-states and the social sciences—markers of modernism—that planning came to be a significant part of the daily lives of the city's human and nonhuman inhabitants. As Boyer (1983, 283) has noted for the United States, "Modernism led to the destruction of traditional modes of physical planning and the abandonment of conventional forms of the American city." In its concerns, methods, values, and principles, contemporary planning is a product of modernism. A defining quality of modernism, it is also a force reproducing it.

For planning theorists, knowing whether planning is a modernist project is an important question, seriously debated during the throes of postmodernism in the 1980s (Sandercock 2003). A modernist planning is situated in an array of ideas and practices that give it a particular identity. A nonmodernist planning, whether postmodern or something else, is a much different phenomenon (Beauregard 1991a). At stake is how we practice planning and where we position it in the material world. Consider Flyvbjerg's (1998, 234) assertion that "modernity relies on rationality as the main means of making democracy work," thereby dispelling ignorance and false beliefs and assuming the efficacy of intentionality. For Flyvbjerg, this means that planning is deeply modern and consequently unable to overcome an ostensibly anti-Enlightenment concentration of power at odds with modernity (3). How planning happens, he suggests, hinges on whether we place it within or outside modernism.

In his well-known book *We Have Never Been Modern* (1993), Bruno Latour is less accepting of modernism than Flyvbjerg. He describes modernism as not just a break in the passage of time (such that we can distinguish moderns from premoderns), but also a belief that humans have gained mastery over the natural environment, the implication being that humans and nonhumans occupy separate worlds. Modernism, he argues, is characterized by crisp dichotomies: between humans and nonhumans, culture and nature, and science (the world of objects) and politics (the world of subjects). This means the modern world is sharply divided in terms of ontological status as well. Humans, animals, plants, geological formations, clouds, and bridges are fundamentally different in their capacities to know and to act and thus to influence others. Under modernism, humans are active agents and the rest of the world passively awaits instruction.

For Latour, a modern world is purified—each category is assigned its place, and alliances across boundaries are forbidden. The "urge to aesthetic abstraction reveals an inability of modern man to establish a rapport with material reality" (Boyer 1983, 282). The result is a loss of analytical continuity, a discrepancy between what we believe and what is actually the case. But because reality always appears in hybrid form, purification is incessantly under assault. No airplane flight is unaffected by weather patterns and instrumentation. No restaurant passes inspection by the public health department without electricity to operate refrigerators, chemicals to kill bugs, and soap to ensure that the cooks' hands are free of microbes. We are constantly swapping properties with and learning from nonhuman things. In Latour's world, to assume that humans are modern is to deny the way reality is constituted. Consequently, Latour (1993, 39) has written, "The modern world has never happened."

This final chapter considers the importance of modernism—this social fact—for how planning is conceived and practiced. Despite public condemnation of government planning by leftist activists and community groups in the 1960s and 1970s and a critical intellectual assault by postmodernists in the 1980s and 1990s, modernist planning has adapted and endured. To deny the modernist qualities that had led to its being institutionalized in government would be to deny its very identity. Planners often ignore the dark and destructive side of modernism, however, and I end the chapter reflecting on it and on a new materialist approach to planning.

My discussion, then, is premised on the importance of modernism to planning and on the claim that they are inseparable. This might come as a surprise. Throughout the book I have embraced and used many of Latour's ideas, even if with reservations. It might thus seem like intellectual suicide to reject one of his main tenets and now claim that city planning not only is still modern but is likely to always be so. Yet I believe this is true even after writing a book intended to be read against the grain of what it means to be modern. Despite various modifications to its procedures and shifts in its point of view, planning still clings to certain values (for example, the public good) and certain procedures (for example, a reliance on expert analysis) that mark it as such. Formed as a modernist project and, over the decades, increasingly entangled in this justification—a justification that underlies its adoption by government—it cannot escape its roots. Consequently, while we can expect planners to adapt to current circumstances and embrace new ideas, we cannot expect them to be other than modernist in their approach to the world.

Modernist Planning under Attack

From its first stirrings in the late nineteenth century, city planning as an institutionalized activity embedded in states has considered itself modern (Boyer 1983). Planning's reaction to the physical chaos and social problems of industrialization and urbanization was to offer to discipline the cities—bring order to their functions, mitigate their negative externalities, protect property values, and make rational decisions. Planning was the modernist antidote to an emergent corporate capitalism insensitive to the public good and incapable of coordinating its activities, particularly when it came to land and property development. The city was chaotic, and planning would bring the order necessary for its efficient functioning. Rapid industrialization and urbanization also produced an unhealthful, fire-prone, and dangerous city, and these consequences had to be addressed as well. Not to go unmentioned was the need to help rural migrants adapt to the city of factories, time clocks, streetcar schedules, congestion, and dense living. The modern city would do all these things, and it would come into being through the guidance of planners who understood how to think about and make the future.[1]

The self-satisfaction with which early city planners embraced modernism was essentially unchallenged through most of the twentieth century. Beginning in the 1960s, however, planning came under intense attack for its modernist commitments. Initially the attack was political and focused on the elitism of local government planning and the landscapes that emerged from an indifference to the particularities and rhythms of daily life. No sooner had these left critics withdrawn than planning was attacked again, this time from the self-proclaimed postmodernists who took an intellectual rather than a political line of assault. Planning weathered both attacks, partly by adapting and partly by returning to its core functions. Despite Latour's implicit claim that planners cannot be modern, despite planning's political critics who called for a more democratic planning, and despite the postmodern attempt to undermine the intellectual foundations of modernist planning, planning maintained its modernist roots.

These mid- to late twentieth-century critiques are important. They could have knocked planning off its modernist foundation; they did not. Instead, planning adapted without ceding significant territory. To make this claim credible, I need to fill in a few details. My reference point, once again, is the United States, though similarities exist with events and debates in other countries.

In the 1960s, planning in the United States was robust; it was a growth decade for the profession and for planning education (Beaure-

1. Lehan (1998, 4) claims that under modernism "the subject of the city becomes a defining issue."

gard 1985). Planners in the suburbs were grappling with rapid growth, doing what planners do best, and those in the large cities—also working for local governments—were engaged in remaking the downtowns and adjacent neighborhoods for modern commerce and living. Backed by federal funds for urban renewal projects, slum clearance, and highway construction, these planners were transforming cities with superblocks, convention centers, sports stadiums, office buildings, and middle-income apartment towers, not to mention plazas, highway access ramps, parking garages, and public housing. The stores, office buildings, and neighborhoods of the early twentieth century were being replaced by modern buildings and spaces (Klemek 2011, 83–127).[2] As an illustration, consider this description (Goodman 1972, 18) of two typical planning events of the time: In Boston, "a small beleaguered group of white families [were] protesting the city's plan to tear down their homes in order to sell the land to a private developer for luxury housing. In Cambridge, the people were displaying their outrage at the state's plan to build an eight-lane highway through the middle of their neighborhood, uprooting thousands of poor people from their homes and jobs."

Those who lived in neighborhoods designated as slums and subsequently demolished for redevelopment, those who stood in the path of limited-access highways, those whose businesses were declared blighted and taken by eminent domain, and those who lived in the "urban villages" of the city (Gans 1962)—what was considered premodern—bore the costs (Berman 1982, 290–329). Their lives were disrupted, their businesses forced to close, and their futures altered without their permission. For modernist planners, these were simply the consequences of progress that would lead to a city where all would be middle-class and prosperous.

"Planning's link to modernism," however, as one commentator (Ryan 2012, 18) has noted, "began to collapse during the 1960s." Political resistance focused on the elitist, top-down way planning was being done as well as on the resulting modernist environments—sterile, uninteresting, inhospitable, and lacking liveliness—where displaced residents were subsequently forced to work and live (Jacobs 1961; Relph 1987). The criticism was not simply that residents were excluded from these decisions. People were also angry that the planners represented them as statistics and reduced their lives to technical categories such as

---

2. The "modern" in this sentence refers to the twentieth-century architecture known as the International Style, not to architecture since the Enlightenment in the eighteenth century.

slum dwellers or "the poor." The modernist planners were shocked (Osman 2011, 52–81). They could not understand why people would question the objective analyses of experts or assume that democratically elected governments were not acting in the interests of the city and its people. Moreover, these planners found it difficult to imagine that city dwellers did not want to live in modern environments with adequate light and air, automobile accessibility, uncluttered apartments, and green spaces adjacent to their buildings. And they found it astounding that the residents were upset at being physically separated from the noise and clutter of the small industries and stores that had occupied their former neighborhoods. The proposed changes, planners felt certain, were inherently beneficial.

The opposition picketed renewal sites, invaded professional meetings, and organized community groups to resist government plans. Though at times successful, they were more often defeated. The modern city was meant for an Americanized middle class, not for a mosaic of ethnic villages. Critics engaged in advocacy planning, and many of them rejected government employment in favor of solidarity with African Americans and other ethnic groups and the various community-based organizations they had formed.

This assault on modernist planning did not strike at planning's intellectual roots. Planning's worldview remained unscathed, even though architecture and civil engineering were replaced in the planning curriculum by the social sciences and planning practice began to fragment into various specialties such as planning for the aged, health planning, and environmental planning (Perloff 1957). Not until the 1980s, spurred on by postmodernism and feminism, was a second attack mounted that aimed at the field's intellectual roots (Allmendinger 2001; Beauregard 1989; Goodchild 1990; Hemmens 1992; Sandercock and Forsyth 1992). But whereas the first assault took place in the streets, the second unfolded in university seminars, at academic conferences, and in scholarly publications. Moreover, whereas the first attack had clear political aims, the postmodern political agenda was muddled; it favored those who were marginalized, but at other times it shied away from political commitments and ideological positions. The targets were planning's conceptual hubris, its certainty about knowledge, its ontological simplifications, and a seemingly unrelenting impulse toward discursive dominance.

What aggravated most postmodern critics was planning's embrace of totalizing narratives: singular and all-encompassing conceptualization of the city that tolerated no counterperspectives (Beauregard 1991a).

Postmodernists believed that modernists were attempting to create a world without differences. The comprehensive or master plan was the text through which such control would be exerted, and it was impervious to the multiculturalism of city life. Despite acknowledging that people lived in housing of vastly differing quality and had widely varying incomes, planners seemed to imagine that all residents of the city should live under more or less similar conditions. Equality rather than difference was what they had in mind. In addition, modernist planners believed that a technical and rational language game was most effective for public deliberations. Postmodernists believed this was false.

Technical knowledge, the critics argued, was only one of many forms of knowledge that people used to live their lives (Sandercock 1998). People had experiences whose value was lost if represented in statistics. And contrary to what planners believed, knowledge was not universal and inherently persuasive. Knowledge was embodied and situated, and emotions were as critical to people's behavior as facts about the world. Moreover, the famed critical distance that planners used to shield themselves from accusations of political partisanship was an illusion (Flyvbjerg 1998). The epistemological bases of society are diverse, postmodernists claimed, with local knowledge in tension with state knowledge, experience and emotion juxtaposed to scientific understandings, and personal opinions equal in value to so-called scientific facts. Deploying objective, technical knowledge and hoping people would succumb to the facts and reasonable arguments was viewed as a left over from Enlightenment understandings that stamped planning with modernism. And while planners knew what they did was political, they still, postmodernists asserted, were blind to the impossibility of being nonpartisan. For many postmodernists, critical distance had to be replaced by a commitment to the multiplicity of equally valid perspectives.

Planning's modernist tendencies also reinforced a view of the world in which gender and difference were absent. For modernist planners, it was interests that mattered, not identity. They recognized race but not that the world, ranging from political arrangements to labor markets and university curricula, was constructed as male. Moreover, whereas modernist planners in the early twentieth century had acknowledged the needs of immigrants, they treated them and African Americans as people with interests that were not being met rather than acknowledging their cultural distinctiveness. The goal was to dissolve everyone and these differences in something called the American middle class. In the world of modernist planning, multiculturalism did not figure in the decisions planners made.

The postmodernists, then, attacked modernist planning on a variety of fronts, each a skirmish but together a powerful indictment of planning's modernist qualities. This was not just about what planners did but about how they thought. And since modernist planners prided themselves on knowing the world and intervening in ways guided by that knowledge, the postmodern assault was much more threatening than the previous political assault. It burrowed into the core values and defining practices of the profession.

The Tenacity of Modernism

Planners adapted. They opened their practices to citizen participation, recognized the utility of local knowledge, abandoned (though not wholly) the fixation on large development projects, acknowledged the need for diversity (even if they confined it to mixed-income housing developments and substituted the juxtaposition of complementary land uses for their functional separation), moved away from the comprehensive plan as a master document, and encouraged more women and people of color to enter the profession (Beauregard 1993). Planning, an activity broad in its possibilities, could easily adapt—up to a point. Modernist tendencies persisted.

Consider the qualities that have not disappeared. Planners still work within the state or, when working outside it, remain deeply engaged with state regulations, public programs (for example, coastal-zone legislation), and government subsidies. They use state data—seeing like a state (Scott 1998). And because states are nothing without capitalist markets, planning still holds a view of the city that casts it as essentially a mechanism for generating wealth. Neither the political activists nor the postmodern critics have pried it loose from its original position of mediating between the state and capitalists or erased its other role of mediating between citizens and an ever-elusive and frequently misleading public interest too often defined in terms of economic growth. The effort to become more democratic has not moved planning into civil society; except in isolated and rudimentary forms, a citizen-based planning has yet to emerge.

Planners still rely on technical knowledge, now augmented with local knowledge, for making state policies and, more specifically, for any decision that requires spending public or private funds. And they continue to define themselves by their technical knowledge—of housing markets, of alternative transit options, and of zoning and development regulations—and by their ability to convert places to sites and then, if all goes well, to new places. Evidence-based planning and data-driven governance, the scientific slogans of the early 2000s, are core values. Even as they tout the benefits of public engagement, collaboration, and listening to the public, planners persevere in believing that their recommendations are informed by a scientific knowledge that is superior to opinions, local experiences, and emotional commitments. Like all modernists, planners equate the facts "with the totality of all that exists and happens" (Daston 2005, 681) and operate under the assumption that the world is knowable and susceptible to human intention, with the consequences of public action predictable.

Seemingly unaffected by the political lessons of the 1960s and the criticisms of the postmodernists, planning has remained committed to the power that reason has to influence decision makers and resolve disagreements. In fact, most government planners avoid conflict, regardless of its presence in almost everything they do (Abram 2000; Flyvbjerg 1998, 234–236). They are reluctant to engage in heated debates and assertive actions that antagonize others. In this sense they retain their liberal commitment to "reasonable arguments" and cling to the possibility that good analysis, objectivity, and thoughtful discussion can lead to better plans and policies. Talk and action still culminate in advice giving, even as collaboration has become increasingly prevalent. Planners remain under the influence of modernism's promise that knowledge can overcome ignorance, resolve opposing viewpoints, and motivate those with power to act for the common good.

Neither has contemporary planning wholly abandoned its modernist need to bring order to the world and fix it in a state of equilibrium.[3] Here we find the urge to purification that Latour rejects. Planners have not cast off the possibility of making a singular sense of the world—coordinating its parts, eliminating its deviations, and resolving its ambiguities. They still embrace a romantic notion of complexity and reject any hint of ontography. Contingency is still valued less than determinacy, fluidity less than stability, disorder less than order, differences less than commonalities, and complexity less than simplicity. For all their celebration of the vibrancy and serendipity of urban living, planners nevertheless strive to impose their distinctive form of discipline on the city.

3. Seldom discussed is planning's relation to the formalism of the late nineteenth century, a relation that persists (White 1947). On the quest for order, Latour (2010a, 474) has written: "The common world has to be built from utterly heterogeneous parts that will never make a whole, but at best a fragile, revisable, and diverse composite material."

Not to be overlooked is the way contemporary planning clings to the strict separation of humans and nonhumans. Even as information and communication technologies have become part of the urban fabric in the form of cell phone towers, electronic toll booths, and computerized citizen complaint lines, and even as environmental sustainability has risen to the top of the planning agenda, bringing with it heat island effects, sea level rise, energy conservation, and the carbon filtration virtues of trees, planners continue to act as if nature exists solely for human ends and technology is under their control.

Why does planning retain its modernist tendencies? And what might be the implications for contemporary theory and practice?

Why Modernist Planning Persists

Even as it adapted to changing circumstances and responded to valid and forceful criticisms, planning adhered to a persistent and legitimized understanding of its modernist identity. That identity comprises a commitment to thinking about the future, a belief that coordination of activities trumps a quasi-religious belief in the market's hidden hand, and an inclination to favor empirical evidence and technical analysis over, for example, price signals, bargaining, and ideology.

To understand why planning has retained these modernist qualities, we need to reflect on two critical issues. One has to do with the purity—or not—of modernism. The other concerns the many ways in which professions persist and prosper because they build on the qualities that provided their initial success and established their public identity and because the relations and alliances in which they are entangled support their mission (Latour 1987; Stinchcombe 1968, 101–129).

First, modernism has never been pure (Toulmin 1990). It has never consisted simply of one set of qualities aligned against another that might be labeled premodern or postmodern (Harvey 1989). Historical breaks in social practices are never precise, and broad categorizations of cultural eras are filled with counterexamples (Kern 1983; Thomas 2014). As Berman (1982, 13) has written, modernism is dynamic and dialectical: "To be modern is to live a life of paradox and contradiction." Consequently, one has to think of the premodern/modern/postmodern distinction as less an empirical claim than a conceptual device that organizes our thinking, its value derived not from truthfulness but from efficacy. Metaphorically, postmodernism is the other side of modernism. They exist in a symbiotic relationship, not a chronologically linear one. Similarly, and at any point in time, multiple modern-isms exist, each formed differently in relation to the place, culture, and institutions in which they are embedded (Chakrabarty 2000). Even so, planning has privileged its modernist side over its postmodern side, and it continues to do so.[4]

Second, planning's modernist qualities are what have enabled it to become established as a profession. A profession emerges only after a long period of testing ideas and practices and searching for a societal niche that provides it with legitimacy and influence. Successfully do-ing so led the planning profession to become institutionalized within local governments as a durable public function supported by laws and budgets. Planning became entangled in an assemblage of laws, prop-erty owners, vacant lots, bankers, floodplains, road networks, tax rev-enues, and Census data. Once institutionalized, the basic mechanisms enabling it to persist were in place—one of the most important being its centrality to land markets and real estate development.

In the late nineteenth and early twentieth centuries, many individ-uals were doing something we now call planning, doing it indepen-dently, and forming voluntary associations that might lead to financial and political support for their endeavors. Think of Daniel Burnham and the Commercial Club of Chicago that supported his 1909 plan or Lawrence Veiller's efforts in the 1890s to persuade the New York City government to adopt housing regulations. These incipient planners de-veloped ideas that enabled commerce to flow more smoothly, munici-pal governments to address public health problems, and property own-ers to protect the value of their real estate. They became valuable to the state, property interests, and citizens. With recognition by local gov-ernments that planned cities would be better cities, laws were passed to regulate streets and establish planning commissions, funds were allo-cated, and planners were hired. The subsequent output of master plans and zoning regulations further solidified planning's presence.

The institutionalizing of planning was eased by its commitment to the public interest and an aversion to partisan politics. Key participants in the Good Government Movement of the time, planners wrapped their advice in empirical evidence and scientific reasoning and thus signaled an alternative to decision making based on political calcula-

4. A distinction is often made between modernism in general and high modernism, which privileged rationality over reason, order over contingency, and state institutions over grassroots movements as well as being associated with the International Style of architecture and large-scale planning schemes in which "formal segregation was joined to hierarchy" (Scott 1998, 103–146; quotation on 111). The distinction is useful but tangential to my argument.

tions and ethnic ties. With the support of government and business interests, planners now had powers that could be used to discipline the city and make it more efficient for commerce while deflecting the conflicts that might arise from slums and deep-rooted poverty. By crafting widely acknowledged improvements, planners also enhanced public support for government's role in civic affairs. These qualities enabled them to establish for themselves a permanent place in local governments. The advice and control they offered was meant to make planning seem indispensable. Over time, their ability to rationalize the city triggered a self-reinforcing cycle that further entrenched them locally. Planning changed, but it was also continually rewarded for doing what it had originally offered to do. The most critical reward for its perseverance and influence was to be retained as a government function.[5]

None of this could have happened without the creation of alliances and the enrollment of planning in various practices and intellectual schemata (Callon and Law 1982). The alliance that has endured is the one with the local state, real estate interests, and local businesses, all of them dependent on the unimpeded flow of commerce and investment opportunities. Making themselves necessary to a well-functioning city and recognizing that a well-functioning city serves the political and fiscal concerns of the local state, planners moved away from their initial involvement with civil society (that is, reform groups, business associations) to a comfortable though not always conflict-free affiliation with local government, an affiliation that includes ties to the business community.

After World War II, however, planning returned to its civil society roots and began offering its services to neighborhood groups and other community-based organizations. Planning initiatives confronted by democratic opposition were unlikely to succeed. In response, another set of allies was solicited and put in place. What planning in the United States has not been able to achieve is broad popular support. Individual property owners and residents see the value of planning when their homes or livelihoods are being threatened, but the conservative foundation of American politics, combined with an almost fanatical belief in freedom, the sanctity of property rights, and the "free market," have deprived it of broad cultural backing and stable political protection.

Planning's institutionalization depended on its offering modernist

---

5. This suggests that planning is also a class project. For example, consider the definition of modernism offered by Chakrabarty (2000, 156): "The aesthetic means by which an urban and literate class subject to invasive forces of modernization seeks to create, however falteringly, a sense of being at home in the modern city." See also Berman 1982, 5–12.

benefits, produced by modernist means, to governments and publics. As the years passed, it drew on those initial qualities to protect and enhance its position. These qualities were challenged by critics within and outside the profession, but they endured because they were of use to both planners and those they had enrolled in their endeavor.

To say that planning continues to be modern, then, is to make a complex argument about how we understand history, social relations, and intellectual formations. As a social form, planning is organized around the state and the state's regulatory powers, but it also drifts politically and practically into civil society. Moreover, no metanarrative of planning exists, but rather a constant and continual attempt to negotiate among various qualities. As an example, consider the tension between a belief in scientific objectivity and a desire to plan for an unknowable future. At the same time, planning has not abandoned its reliance on expertise, its relation to the state, its concern with purification, and a commitment to the need for cities to be organized functionally, if not aesthetically. Most important, it has held on to the values—justice, democracy, tolerance, pluralism—that characterize liberal modernism. These qualities are continually emphasized. They enabled planning to be institutionalized, conferred its identity, and signaled political importance. Thus they continue to be nurtured and persist.

This is not to imply that being modern benefits only the planning profession. Modernism and the kind of planning it has spawned have contributed to great improvements in the quality of life for most people. Public health measures, housing codes, land use regulations, environmental legislation, and design guidelines have removed many of the ills that beset the late nineteenth-century industrial city. Scientific and technological advances, government practices, financial relationships, organizational forms, and educational initiatives associated with modernism have also contributed immensely to economic growth and, less so, to its distribution across the population.

Yet these advances should not be celebrated without recognizing the dark side of modernism. Latour (1999, 196) has declared that the adjective modern describes "a deepened *intimacy*, a more intricate mesh" between society and technologies. To this we might add the greater scale of technologies, not only transportation systems such as air travel and communication networks such as postal services, but also means of mass destruction. The historian Eric Hobsbawm (1996) observed that much of the twentieth century was a time of crisis and catastrophe. The list seems endless: two "world" wars, the rise of fascism in the Soviet Union, genocides, the violent breakup of colonial regimes, innumerable regional conflicts, and large-scale politically induced famines only sketch the outlines of the destruction of human life that occurred and continues to occur. To this we might add ecological disasters.

As I write, the world is no less violent. Nonstate terrorism seems to be spreading, too many governments (North Korea being one extreme) deny their citizens political freedoms and social security, famines persist, civil wars continue to be fought, large numbers of refugees roam Africa and the Middle East, and sectarian and ethnic-tribal conflicts kill innocent people and destabilize governments. On the ecological agenda, the glaciers are melting ever faster and the seas are rising, the ozone layer is being depleted, soils are increasingly compromised by chemical waste, and biodiversity is lessening. All these events and conditions are caused or exacerbated and facilitated by technologies from weapons systems to oil production. In the aggregate, many things about modernism have made life better on this planet, but they have neither stopped human suffering nor protected the ecological realm.

While such thoughts might seem alien to city and regional planning, they are not that far afield. Planners have increasingly embraced an obligation to mitigate ecological destruction, and from the other side of the ledger, authoritarian regimes have often deployed planning to control the population. When it comes to violence, however, what planners can do seems to fall well short of what needs to be done. In many such situations, planning is of little use. This comment is not meant to devalue planning. It is a reminder that planning once, in the throes of modernism, promised a much different world, and we somehow have to remain in touch with that aspiration.

Final Thoughts

In ending, I want to reflect on a way of thinking about planning theory—the approach I have been developing throughout the book—that accepts rather than resists Latour's implicit claim that planning has never been modern. I do this knowing that his larger claim—that "we" have never been modern—might be a rhetorical flourish and possibly tautological. However, as I have been doing throughout the book, I am less interested in settling on truth (in the correspondence sense) than in exploring ideas and their limits. Still, it does seem to me that epistemologically and ontologically, planners do (for the most part) separate humans from nonhumans, science from politics, and culture from nature.

Consequently—and this points to a much broader argument—I think planning would benefit from bridging those divides (Beauregard 2012c; Lieto and Beauregard 2013). I am bothered that a profession whose goal is to make life better for people by addressing the relation between their needs and desires and the built and natural environments then marginalizes the material world both theoretically and practically. In the world of planning, people act, and the rest of the world—nature, nonhuman and nonliving things—awaits human command. As a result, planning practice becomes a matter of having humans do the correct analysis and form the appropriate alliances. Landscapes, buildings, animals, and plants are simply there to be manipulated.

This returns me to Latour and his implication that planners need to focus less on purifying and more on hybridizing—on the way all human activity combines culture and nature. He encourages us to consider as appropriate actors those who influence how other actors behave. It could be a GIS map that causes policymakers to see the city's recreational facilities differently, demonstrating the sharp disparities in service from one area to another. Or it could be a highway access ramp that, because of its connection to how people and goods move about the city, resists being demolished and thus hampers the redevelopment of a neighborhood. This line of reasoning suggests that planners should not divide the world in terms of land uses or functions such as residential mobility or economic activity but rather should look to assemblages of people and nonhumans as the appropriate and constituent forms of reality. Planners have to be compositionists who gather things together while respecting their heterogeneity. And they have to assume that "nothing is beyond dispute" (Latour 2010a, 478).

Planning persists in its embrace of the modernist qualities that defined it at birth; it profits little by abandoning this core identity. It cannot escape its defining worldview and still function politically and institutionally as it has done for nearly a century. Planning will always be modern; this matters, and not only to planning theorists. These qualities of the planning profession cannot be changed without wholly erasing what we mean by planning. Yet planning has historically been highly adaptable and seems able to be pulled and stretched to cover a wide range of diverse activities and ways of thinking about cities, regions, and neighborhoods. If relatively unyielding, relatively permanent inclinations exist within planning—if certain core traits are obdurate—this tells us something about our ability to change planning, whether the transformation we envision is radical or reformist.

Planners are certainly capable of self-reflection and of modifying their thinking and behavior. They can—and need to—reduce the separation between themselves and the material world. Only by accepting themselves as one of many heterogeneous actors can planners truly grasp the limits and potential of collective action and the full expanse of their social responsibilities.

I began the book with a call to reject the culture/nature divide and thus, by the criterion put forth by Bruno Latour, to reject modernism itself, not just because it never happened but because it took planners out of the world. And yet here I am in the last chapter proclaiming that planning will always be modern. Of course, planning can continue to function on one side of the divide and planners can continue to believe in two worlds, one of humans in-here and the other of nonhumans out-there. This is possible because so many fellow human beings and their institutions hold to this conceit. If planners want to realize the promise of the profession, however, they must refuse the comfort of humans for the politics of things and become moral agents deeply entangled with the material world.

Acknowledgments

I am indebted to many colleagues who offered advice on early drafts of these chapters or (along with students) listened to my musings on actor-network theory. Meg Holden, Daphne Spain, Susan Saegert, and Turo-Kimmo Lehtenon deserve special mention. Laura Lieto always reminds me (through her writings and comments) of the value of being theoretically precise. She and Bob Lake devoted valuable time to reading multiple chapters. Bob read the whole manuscript and deserves special appreciation; he is my model of a critical and careful thinker. In addition, for years Bob has been the force behind BURG, the Brooklyn Urban Reading Group. My thanks go out to this ever-changing cast of engaged scholars who celebrate the joys of inquiry and the importance of doing one's best. I am also grateful to the anonymous reviewers of the manuscript, who offered much-needed perspectives on what I thought I had done.

At the University of Chicago Press, Tim Mennel saw the potential in the manuscript, and his suggestions forced me to clarify the arguments and tighten the prose. Nora Devlin efficiently managed the production process, and Alice Bennett improved the manuscript with her copy-editing skills.

I wrote the book during a sabbatical year (2013–14) provided by Columbia University and its Graduate School of Architecture, Planning, and Preservation. Having such a large block of time for writing was a gift.

Two of the chapters—now rewritten—were previously published. "Planning with Things" appeared in the *Journal of Planning Education and Research* 32, no. 2 (2012): 182–190, and "Neglected Places of Practice" was published in *Planning Theory and Practice* 14, no. 1 (2013): 8–19. The publishers—Sage Publications and Taylor and Francis (www.tandf online.com), respectively—kindly granted me permission to use the material here.

The arguments were presented in a number of forums. "Planning Will Always Be Modern" began as a talk at the conference Modernita nelle Americhe, held at the Università degli Studi Roma Tre in May 2012 in Rome. "Truths and Realties" had its roots in a paper then titled "Encountering the Real: Narrative Styles in Urban Studies," presented in August 2007 at the RC21 International Conference "Urban Justice and Sustainability" in Vancouver. "Distributed Morality" was originally a lecture given in the Environmental Psychology Program at the City University of New York Graduate Center in September 2012. "Planning with Things" originated as a paper for the AESOP meetings in Helsinki in July 2010. "Planning in an Obdurate World" was first presented at the conference Planning in a Heterogeneous World, held at Federico II University in Naples in June 2013. I also gave this talk at the School of Architecture and Planning at Ball State University in Muncie, Indiana, in February 2014. Related themes were explored at the Laboratorio Expo 2015 Workshop in Milan, sponsored by the Feltrinelli Foundation in December 2013, and the Planning for Preservation conference at Aalto University in Helsinki in December 2013.

Finally, Debra Bilow continues to be tolerant of the concentration and isolation it takes for me to write. For that I am exceedingly grateful.

Works Cited

Abbott, Andrew. 2001. *Time Matters: On Theory and Method*. Chicago: University of Chicago Press.

Abbott, Carl. 2007. "Cyperpunk Cities: Science Fiction Meets Urban Theory." *Journal of Planning Education and Research* 27:122–131.

Abram, Simone A. 2000, "Planning the Public: Some Comments on Empirical Problems for Planning Theory." *Journal of Planning Education and Research* 19:351–357.

Abu El-Haj, Nadia. 2001. *Facts on the Ground: Archaeological Practice and Territorial Self-Fashioning in Israeli Society*. Chicago: University of Chicago Press.

Adelman, Jeremy. 2013. *Worldly Philosopher: The Odyssey of Albert O. Hirschman*. Princeton, NJ: Princeton University Press.

Agovino, Theresa. 2009. "Look Who Remade New York." *Crain's New York Business*, October 12.

Albrechts, Louis. 2004. "Strategic (Spatial) Planning Reexamined." *Environment and Planning B* 31:743–758.

Alexander, Ernest R. 2001. "What Do Planners Need to Know?" *Journal of Planning Education and Research* 20:376–380.

Al-Jazeera. 2013. "Palestinian Activists Build E1 Tent 'Outpost.'" www.aljazeera.com, accessed May 17, 2013.

Allmendinger, Philip. 2001. *Planning in Postmodern Times*. London: Routledge.

———. 2002. "Towards a Post-Positivist Typology in Planning Theory." *Planning Theory* 1:77–99.

Altshuler, Alan. 1965. *The City Planning Process*. Ithaca, NY: Cornell University Press.

Altshuler, Alan, and David Luberoff. 2003. *Mega-projects: The Changing Politics of Urban Public Investment*. Washington, DC: Brookings Institution.

Angotti, Tom. 2008. *New York for Sale*. Cambridge, MA: MIT Press.

Arendt, Hannah. 1958. *The Human Condition*. Chicago: University of Chicago Press.

Argonne National Laboratory. n.d. "Peconic River Remedial Alternatives: Wetlands Restorations/Constructed Wetlands." www://bnl.gov/erd/peconic/factsheet/wetlands.pdf, accessed January 7, 2013.

Badmington, Neil. 2004. "Mapping Postmodernism." *Environment and Planning A* 36:1344–1351.

Baert, Patrick. 2005. *Philosophy of the Social Sciences*. Cambridge: Polity Press.

Bagli, Charles. 2013. "Citi Field's Neighbors to Protest Eviction before All-Star Game." *New York Times*, July 16.

Bakker, Karen. 2005. "Katrina: The Public Transcript of Disaster." *Environment and Planning D* 23:795–802.

Baldwin, Ian. 2009. "A Tale of Two Points." *Places* 21:80–85.

Banfield, Edward. 1959. "Ends and Means in Planning." *International Social Science Journal* 11:361–368.

Barry, John M. 2014. "Why We're Suing the Oil Companies." *Metropolis* 33:40–42.

Baum, Howell. 1980. "Sensitizing Planners to Organization." In *Urban and Regional Planning in an Age of Austerity*, edited by P. Clavel, J. Forester, and W. W. Goldsmith, 279–307. New York: Pergamon Press.

Bauman, Zygmunt. 1991. *Modernity and Ambivalence*. Cambridge: Polity Press.

Beard, Victoria, and Victoria Basolo. 2009. "Commentary: Moving beyond Crisis, Crossroads, and the Abyss in the Disciplinary Formation of Planning." *Journal of Planning Education and Research* 29:233–242.

Beauregard, Robert A. 1980. "Thinking about Practicing Planning." In *Urban and Regional Planning in an Age of Austerity*, edited by P. Clavel, J. Forester, and W. W. Goldsmith, 308–325. New York: Pergamon Press.

———. 1985. "Occupational Transformations in Urban and Regional Planning, 1960–1980." *Journal of Planning Education and Research* 5:10–16.

———. 1989. "Between Modernity and Postmodernity: The Ambiguous Position of U.S. Planning." *Environment and Planning D* 7:381–395.

———. 1990. "Bringing the City Back In." *Journal of the American Planning Association* 56:210–215.

———. 1991a. "Without a Net: Modernist Planning and the Postmodern Abyss." *Journal of Planning Education and Research* 10:189–194.

———. 1991b. "Capital Restructuring and the Built Environment of Global Cities: New York and Los Angeles." *International Journal of Urban and Regional Research* 15:90–105.

———. 1993. "Planners and the City." *Yhteiskunta Suunnittelu* 4:75–81.

———. 1995. "Theorizing the Global-Local Connection." In *World Cities in a World-System*, edited by P. L. Knox and P. J. Taylor, 232–248. Cambridge: Cambridge University Press.

———. 1996a. "City Planning and the Postwar Regime in Philadelphia." In *Reconstructing Urban Regime Theory*, edited by M. Lauria, 171–188. Thousand Oaks, CA: Sage.

———. 1996b. "Advocating Preeminence: Anthologies as Politics." In *Explorations in Planning Theory*, edited by S. J. Mandelbaum, L. Mazza, and R. W. Burchell, 105–110. New Brunswick, NJ: CUPR Press.

———. 1998. "Writing the Planner." *Journal of Planning Education and Research* 18:93–101.

———. 2003. *Voices of Decline: The Postwar Fate of U.S. Cities*. New York: Routledge.

———. 2005a. "The Textures of Markets: Downtown Housing and Office Conversions in New York City." *Urban Studies* 42:2431–2445.

———. 2005b. "From Place to Site: Negotiating Narrative Complexity." In *Site Matters*, edited by C. J. Burns and A. Kahn, 39–58. New York: Routledge.

———. 2008. "Introduction." In *Overlooked America*, edited by Editors of *Planning* Magazine, vii-xv. Chicago: Planners Press.

———. 2011. "Time, Action, Space." *Urban Geography* 32:470–475.

———. 2012a. "National [Urban] Policy." In *The Oxford Encyclopedia of American Political and Legal History*, edited by D. T. Critchlow and P. R. VanderMeer, 344–348. Oxford: Oxford University Press.

———. 2012b. "What Theorists Do." *Urban Geography* 33:474–487.

———. 2012c. "In Search of Assemblages." *Crios* 4:9–16.

———. 2015. "Shrinking Cities." In *International Encyclopedia of Social and Behavioral Sciences*. New York: Elsevier.

Beauregard, Robert, and Andrea Marpillero-Colomina. 2011. "More Than a Master Plan: Amman 2025." *Cities* 28:62–69.

Becker, Howard S. 1995. *Tricks of the Trade*. Chicago: University of Chicago Press.

Bellah, Robert N., et al. 1991. *The Good Society*. New York: Vintage.

Bender, Thomas. 2010. "Reassembling the City: Networks and Urban Imaginaries." In *Urban Assemblages*, edited by L. Farias and T. Bender, 303–323. London: Routledge.

Benevolo, Leonardo. (1963) 1971. *The Origins of Town Planning*. Cambridge, MA: MIT Press.

Bennett, Jane. 2007. "Edible Matter." *New Left Review* 45:133–145.

———. 2010. *Vibrant Matter: A Political Ecology of Things*. Durham, NC: Duke University Press.

Beneviste, Guy. 1977. *The Politics of Expertise*. San Francisco, CA: Boyd and Fraser.

Berezowsky, Miron. 1995. "Constructed Wetlands for Remediation of Urban Waste Waters." *Geoscience Canada* 22:129–141.

Berkshire, Michael. 2003. "In Search of a New Landfill Site." In *Story and Sustainability*, edited by B. Eckstein and J. Throgmorton, 167–182. Cambridge, MA: MIT Press.

Berman, Marshall. 1982. *All That Is Solid Melts into Air*. New York: Penguin.

Bhabha, Homi. 1994. *The Location of Culture*. London: Routledge.

Bibby, Peter, and John Shepherd. 2000. "GIS, Land Use, and Representation." *Environment and Planning B* 27:583–598.

Bijker, Wiebe. 1995. *Of Bicycles, Bakelites, and Bulbs: Towards a Theory of Sociotechnical Change*. Cambridge, MA: MIT Press.

Biles, Roger. 2011. *The Fate of Cities: Urban America and the Federal Government, 1945–2000*. Lawrence: University Press of Kansas.

Birch, Eugenie Ladner. 1995. "City Planning." In *Encyclopedia of the City of New York*, edited by K. T. Jackson, 232–234. New Haven, CT: Yale University Press.

———. 1996. "Planning in a World City: New York and Its Communities." *Journal of the American Planning Association* 62:442–459.

Black, Alan. 1990. "The Chicago Area Transportation Study: A Case Study of Rational Planning. *Journal of Planning Education and Research* 10:27–37.

Bledstein, Burton. 1976. *The Culture of Professionalism: The Middle Class and the Development of Higher Education in America*. New York: W. W. Norton.

Bluestone, Barry, and Bennett Harrison. 1982. *The Deindustrialization of America*. New York: Basic Books.

Boelens, Luuk. 2010. "Theorizing Practice and Practising Theory." *Planning Theory* 9:28–62.

Bogost, Ian. 2012. *Alien Phenomenology, or What It's Like to Be a Thing*. Minneapolis: University of Minnesota Press.

Borges, Jorge Luis. 1964. *Other Inquisitions: 1937–1952*. Austin: University of Texas Press.

Borus, Daniel H. 1989. *Writing Realism: Howell, James, and Norris in the Mass Market*. Chapel Hill: University of North Carolina Press.

Bourdieu, Pierre. 2005. *The Social Structures of the Economy*. Cambridge: Polity Press.

Bowker, Geoffrey C., and Susan Leigh Star. 2000. *Sorting Things Out: Classification and Its Consequences*. Cambridge, MA: MIT Press.

Boyer, M. Christine. 1983. *Dreaming the Rational City*. Cambridge, MA: MIT Press.

Braun, Bruce. 2004. "Querying Postmodernisms." *Geoforum* 35:269–273.

Braverman, Kate. 1993. *Wonders of the West*. New York: Fawcett Columbine.

Brenner, Neil. 2009. "What Is Critical Urban Theory?" *City* 13:198–207.

Brinkley, Douglas. 2006. *The Great Deluge: Hurricane Katrina, New Orleans, and the Mississippi Gulf Coast*. New York: Harper Perennial.

Brooks, Michael P. 2002. *Planning Theory for Practitioners*. Chicago: Planners Press.

Brown, Bill. 2001. "Thing Theory." *Critical Inquiry* 28:1–16.

Bulkeley, Harriet. 2010. "Cities and the Governing of Climate Change." *Annual Review of Environmental Resources* 35:229–253.

Buroway, Michael. 1998. "The Extended Case Method." *Sociological Theory* 16:4–33.

Cairns, Stephen, and Jane M. Jacobs. 2014. *Buildings Must Die: A Perverse View of Architecture.* Cambridge, MA: MIT Press.

Calhoun, Craig. 1995. *Critical Social Theory.* Oxford: Blackwell.

Callon, Michel. 1986. "Some Elements of a Sociology of Translation: Domestication of the Scallops and the Fishermen of St. Brieuc Bay." In *Power, Action and Belief,* edited by J. Law, 196–223. London: Routledge.

———. 2001. "Actor Network Theory." In *International Encyclopedia of the Social and Behavioral Scien*ces, edited by N. Smelser and P. Baltes, 62–66. Oxford: Pergamon.

———. 2002. "Writing and (Re)writing Devices as Tools for Managing Complexity." In *Complexities: Social Studies of Knowledge Practice,* edited by J. Law and A. Mol, 191–217. Durham, NC: Duke University Press.

Callon, Michel, Pierre Lascoumes, and Yannick Barthe. 2011. *Acting in an Uncertain World.* Cambridge, MA: MIT Press.

Callon, Michel, and Bruno Latour. 1981. "Unscrewing the Big Leviathan: How Actors Macro-structure Reality and Sociologists Help Them to Do So." In *Advances in Social Theory and Methodology,* edited by K. Knorr-Cetina and A. V. Cicourel, 277–303. Boston: Routledge and Kegan Paul.

Callon, Michel, and John Law. 1982. "On Interests and Their Transformation: Enrolment and Counter-enrolment." *Social Studies of Science* 12:615–625.

Calvino, Italo. 1974. *Invisible Cities.* New York: Harcourt Brace.

Campanella, Thomas J. 2008. *The Concrete Dragon: China's Urban Revolution and What It Means for the World.* New York: Princeton Architectural Press.

Campbell, Heather. 2002. "Planning: An Idea of Value." *Town Planning Review* 73:271–288.

———. 2006. "Just Planning: The Art of Ethical Judgment." *Journal of Planning Education and Research* 26:92–106.

Campbell, Heather, and Robert Marshall. 1999. "Ethical Frameworks and Planning Theory." *International Journal of Urban and Regional Research* 23:464–478.

———. 2006. "Towards Justice in Planning: A Reappraisal." *European Planning Studies* 14:239–252.

Casey, Edward S. 1997. *The Fate of Place: A Philosophical History.* Berkeley: University of California Press.

Chakrabarty, Dipesh. 2000. *Provincializing Europe: Postcolonial Thought and Historical Difference.* Princeton, NJ: Princeton University Press.

Chapin, F. Stuart, Jr. 1965. *Urban Land Use Planning.* Urbana: University of Illinois Press.

City of New York. 2007. *PlaNYC: A Greener, Greater New York.* New York: City of New York.

Coll, Steve. 2013. "Comment: Options." *New Yorker* 89:19–20.

Collinge, Chris. 2006. "Flat Ontology and the Deconstruction of Scale." *Transactions of the Institute of British Geographers* 31:244–251.

Collins, Harry. 2010. "Humans Not Instruments." *Spontaneous Generations* 4:138–147.

Comfort, Louise K. 2006. "Cities at Risk: Hurricane Katrina and the Drowning of New Orleans." *Urban Affairs Review* 41:501–516.

Congleton, Roger D. 2006. "The Story of Katrina: New Orleans and the Political Economy of Catastrophe." *Public Choice* 127:5–30.

Connell, Raewyn. 2006. "Northern Theory: The Political Geography of General Social Theory." *Theory and Society* 35:237–264.

Coole, Diane, and Samatha Frost. 2010. "Introducing the New Materialism." In *New Materialisms: Ontology, Agency and Politics,* edited by D. Coole and S. Frost, 1–43. Durham, NC: Duke University Press.

Corburn, Jason. 2003. "Bringing Local Knowledge into Environmental Decision Making." *Journal of Planning Education and Research* 22:420–433.

Cuddon, J. A., ed. 1998. *A Dictionary of Literary Terms and Literary Theory.* Oxford: Blackwell.

Cumming-Bruce, Nick, and Isabel Kershner. 2013. "U.N. Panel Sees Violations in Israeli Settlement Policy." *New York Times,* February 2.

Dalton, Linda. 1989. "Emerging Knowledge about Planning Practice." *Journal of Planning Education and Research* 9:29–44.

———. 2007. "Preparing Planners for the Breadth of Practice." *Journal of the American Planning Association* 73:35–48.

Daston, Lorraine. 2004. "Speechless." In *Things That Talk,* edited by L. Daston, 9–24. New York: Zone Books.

———. 2005. "Hard Facts." In *Making Things Public: Atmospheres of Democracy,* edited by B. Latour and P. Weibel, 680–684. Cambridge, MA: MIT Press.

Davidoff, Paul. 1965. "Advocacy and Pluralism in Planning." *Journal of the American Institute of Planners* 31:331–338.

Davidoff, Paul, and Thomas A. Reiner. 1962. "A Choice Theory of Planning." *Journal of the American Institute of Planners* 28:103–115.

Davoudi, Simin. 2012. "Resilience: A Bridging Concept or a Dead End?" *Planning Theory and Practice* 13:299–307.

DeJohn, Irving. 2013. "Land Use Review for Willets Point Development Kicks Off." *New York Daily News,* March 18.

Dewar, Margaret, and June Manning Thomas, eds. 2013. *The City after Abandonment.* Philadelphia: University of Pennsylvania Press.

Dewey, John. (1927) 1954. *The Public and Its Problems.* Athens, OH: Swallow Press.

Dikec, Mustafa, and Liette Gilbert. 2002. "Right to the City: Homage or a New Societal Ethics?" *Capitalism, Nature, Socialism* 13:58–74.

Disch, Lisa. 1994. *Hannah Arendt and the Limits of Philosophy.* Ithaca, NY: Cornell University Press.

———. 2008. "Representation as 'Spokespersonship': Bruno Latour's Political Theory." *Parallax* 14:88–100.

Dolowitz, David P., and David Marsh. 2000. "Learning from Abroad: The Role of Policy Transfer in Contemporary Policy Making." *Governance* 13:5–24.

Drabble, Margaret, ed. 1995. *The Oxford Companion to English Literature.* Oxford: Oxford University Press.

Dunn, William, ed. 1998. *The Experimenting Society: Essays in Honor of Donald J. Campbell.* New Brunswick, NJ: Transaction.

Dyckman, John W. 1969. "The Practical Uses of Planning Theory." *Journal of the American Institute of Planners* 35:298–300.

Dykhuizen, George. 1973. *The Life and Mind of John Dewey.* Carbondale: Southern Illinois University Press.

Edelman, Murray. 1964. *The Symbolic Uses of Politics.* Champaign: University of Illinois Press.

Editors of *Planning* Magazine, eds. 2008. *Overlooked America.* Chicago: Planners Press.

Edmonds, David, and John Eidinow. 2001. *Wittgenstein's Poker: The Story of a Ten-Minute Argument between Two Great Philosophers.* New York: Ecco.

Eisinger, Peter K. 1988. *The Rise of the Entrepreneurial State.* Madison: University of Wisconsin Press.

Environment News Service. 2009. "Louisiana Begins Wetlands Repair with Mississippi River Sediment." http://www.ens.newswire.com/ens/apr2009/2009–04–14–093.asp, accessed January 7, 2013.

Erikson, Kai. 1976. *Everything in Its Path.* New York: Simon and Schuster,

Erlanger, Steven. 2012. "West Bank Land, Empty but Full of Meaning." *New York Times*, December 18.

Escobar, Arturo. 2001. "Culture Sits in Places: Reflections on Globalization and Subaltern Strategies of Localization." *Political Geography* 20:139–174.

Fadiman, Anne. 1997. *The Spirit Catches You and You Fall Down.* New York: Farrar, Straus and Giroux.

Fainstein, Norman I., and Susan S. Fainstein. 1974. *Urban Political Movements.* Englewood Cliffs, NJ: Prentice-Hall.

———. 1979. "New Debates in Urban Planning: The Impact of Marxist Theory within the United States." *International Journal of Urban and Regional Research* 3:381–403.

Fainstein, Susan S. 1994. *The City Builders: Property, Politics, and Planning in London and New York.* Cambridge, MA: Blackwell.

———. 1997. "The Egalitarian City: The Restructuring of Amsterdam." *International Planning Studies* 2:295–314.

———. 2000. "New Directions in Planning Theory." *Urban Affairs Review* 35:451–478.

———. 2008. "Planning and the Just City." *Harvard Design Magazine* 27:70–76.

———. 2010. *The Just City.* Ithaca, NY: Cornell University Press.

Finn, Donovan. 2013. "New York Neighborhoods Fight Land Grabs." *Progressive Planning* 194:4–9.

Fischer, John Martin. 1999. "Recent Work on Moral Responsibility." *Ethics* 110:93–139.

Fischler, Raphael. 1998. "Toward a Genealogy of Planning: Zoning and the Welfare State." *Planning Perspectives* 13:389–410.

Flyvbjerg, Bent. 1998. *Rationality and Power: Democracy in Practice.* Chicago: University of Chicago Press.

———. 2001. *Making Social Science Matter.* Cambridge: Cambridge University Press.

Ford, Kristina. 2010. *The Trouble with City Planning.* New Haven, CT: Yale University Press.

Forester, John. 1989. *Planning in the Face of Power.* Berkeley: University of California Press.

———. 1996. "Argument, Power, and Passion in Planning Practice." In *Explorations in Planning Theory*, edited by S. J. Mandelbaum et al., 241–262. New Brunswick, NJ: CUPR Press.

———. 1999. *The Deliberative Practitioner: Encouraging Participatory Planning Processes.* Cambridge, MA: MIT Press.

———. 2009. *Dealing with Difference: Dramas of Mediating Public Disputes.* New York: Oxford University Press.

———. 2013. "How Much Do We Care about Progressive and Radical Practice?" *Crios* 5:11–15.

Frankfurt, Harry G. 1969. "Alternate Possibilities and Moral Responsibility." *Journal of Philosophy* 66:829–839.

Fraser, Nancy. 2010. *Scales of Justice: Reimagining Political Space in a Globalizing World.* New York: Columbia University Press.

Freeman, Samuel. 2012. "Why Be Good?" *New York Review of Books* 59: 52–54.

Frick, Karen Trapenberg. 2013. "The Actions of Discontent." *Journal of the American Planning Association* 79:190–200.

Frieden, Bernard J., and Lynne B. Sagalyn. 1989. *Downtown, Inc.: How America Builds Cities.* Cambridge, MA: MIT Press.

Friedman, Milton. 1980. *Free to Choose.* New York: Harcourt.

Friedmann, John. 1987. *Planning in the Public Domain.* Princeton, NJ: Princeton University Press.

———. 1989a. "I Am Pleased to React." *Journal of Planning Education and Research* 9:63–64.

———. 1989b. "Planning in the Public Domain: Discourse and Praxis." *Journal of Planning Education and Research* 8:128–130.

———. 1993. "Toward a Non-Euclidian Model of Planning." *Journal of the American Planning Association* 59:482–485.

———. 2002. "A Life in Planning." In *The Prospect of Cities*, edited by J. Friedmann, 119–157. Minneapolis: University of Minnesota Press.

————. 2005. "Globalization and the Emerging Culture of Planning." *Progress in Planning* 64:183–234.

————. 2008. "The Uses of Planning Theory." *Journal of Planning Education and Research* 28:247–257.

Friedmann, John, and Barclay Hudson. 1974. "Knowledge and Action: A Guide to Planning Theory." *Journal of the American Institute of Planners* 40:2–16.

Friedmann. John, and Goetz Wolff. 1982. "World City Formation: An Agenda for Research and Action." *International Journal of Urban and Regional Research* 6:309–344.

Frug, Gerald E., and David J. Barron. 2008. *City Bound: How States Stifle Urban Innovation.* Ithaca, NY: Cornell University Press.

Fuller, Steve. 2000. "Why Science Studies Has Never Been Critical of Science." *Philosophy of the Social Sciences* 30:5–32.

————. 2004. "Intellectuals: An Endangered Species in the Twenty-First Century?" *Economy and Society* 33:463–483.

————. 2005. *The Intellectual.* Cambridge: Icon Books.

Fure-Slocum, Eric. 2013. *Contesting the Postwar City: Working-Class and Growth Politics in 1940s Milwaukee.* Cambridge: Cambridge University Press.

Gabe, Thomas, Gene Falk, and Maggie McCarty. 2005. *Hurricane Katrina: Socio-demographic Characteristics of Impacted Areas.* Congressional Research Service Report. Washington, DC: Library of Congress.

Gale, Dennis E. 1992. "Eight State-Sponsored Growth Management Programs: A Comparative Analysis." *Journal of the American Planning Association* 58:425–439.

Galison, Peter L. 1995. "Context and Constraints." in *Scientific Practice: Theories and Stories of Doing Physics,* edited by J. Z. Buchwald, 13–41. Chicago: University of Chicago Press.

Gans, Herbert. 1962. *The Urban Villagers.* Glencoe, NY: Free Press.

Garvin, Alexander. 2002. "Philadelphia's Planner: A Conversation with Edmund Bacon." *Journal of Planning History* 1:58–78.

Gelfand, Mark I. 1975. *A Nation of Cities: The Federal Government and Urban America, 1933–1965.* New York: Oxford University Press.

Gibson-Graham, J. K. (1996) 2006. *The End of Capitalism (As We Knew It).* Minneapolis: University of Minnesota Press.

Giddens, Anthony. 1982. *Profiles and Critiques in Social Theory.* Berkeley: University of California Press.

————. 1984. *The Constitution of Society.* Berkeley: University of California Press.

Gieryn, Thomas F. 2000. "A Space for Place in Sociology." *Annual Review of Sociology* 26:463–96.

————. 2006. "City as Truth-Spot: Laboratories and Field-Sites in Urban Studies." *Social Studies of Science* 36:5–38.

Gilmore, H. W. 1944. "The Old New Orleans and the New: A Case for Ecology." *American Sociological Review* 9:385–394.

Glaser, Nathan. 1974. "The Schools of the Minor Professions." *Minerva* 12:346–364.

Goodchild, Barry. 1990. "Planning and the Modern/Postmodern Debate." *Town Planning Review* 61:119–137.

Goodman, Robert. 1972. *After the Planners.* New York: Simon and Schuster.

Graeber, David. 2011. *Debt: The First 5,000 Years.* Brooklyn, NY: Melville House.

Graham, Otis L. 1976. *Toward a Planned Society: From Roosevelt to Nixon.* London: Oxford University Press.

Graham, Steven, and Patsy Healey. 1999. "Relational Concepts of Space and Place: Issues for Planning Theory and Practice." *European Planning Studies* 7:623–646.

Grava, Sigurd. 1995. "Streets." in *The Encyclopedia of New York City,* edited by K. T. Jackson, 1130–1132. New Haven, CT: Yale University Press.

Gualini, Enrico, and Stan Majoor. 2007. "Innovative Practices in Large Urban Development Projects: Conflicting Frames in the Quest for 'New Urbanity.'" *Planning Theory and Practice* 8:297–318.

Gulbenkian Commission on the Restructuring of the Social Sciences. 1996. *Open the Social Sciences.* Stanford, CA: Stanford University Press.

Hache, Emilie, and Bruno Latour. 2010. "Morality or Moralism? An Exercise in Sensitization." *Common Knowledge* 16:311–330.

Hacking, Ian. 1998. "Canguilhem and the Cyborg." *Economy and Society* 27:202–216.

———. 1999. *The Social Construction of What?* Cambridge, MA: Harvard University Press.

Hall, Peter. 2002. *Cities of Tomorrow.* Malden, MA: Blackwell.

Hancock, John L. 1967. "Planners in the Changing American City, 1900–1940." *Journal of the American Institute of Planners* 33:290–304.

Haraway, Donna. 1990. "A Manifesto for Cyborgs: Science, Technology, and Socialist Feminism in the 1980's." in *Feminism/Postmodernism,* edited by L. J. Nicholson, 190–233. New York: Routledge.

Harman, Graham. 2009. *Prince of Networks: Bruno Latour and Metaphysics.* Melbourne: re.press.

Harrison, Philip. 2014. "Making Planning Theory Real." *Planning Theory* 13:65–81.

Hartman, Chester. 2002. *Between Eminence and Notoriety: Four Decades of Radical Urban Planning.* New Brunswick, NJ: Center for Urban Policy Research.

Harvey, David. 1989. *The Condition of Postmodernity.* Oxford: Basil Blackwell.

———. 2008. "The Right to the City." *New Left Review* 53:23–40.

Hayward, Clarissa Rile, and Todd Swanstrom. 2011. "Introduction: Thick Justice." In *Justice and the American Metropolis,* edited by C. R. Hayward and T. Swanstrom, 1–29. Minneapolis: University of Minnesota Press.

Healey, Patsy. 1992. "A Planner's Day: Knowledge and Action in Communicative Practice." *Journal of the American Planning Association* 58:9–20.

———. 1993. "Planning through Dialogue: The Communicative Turn in Planning Theory." In *The Argumentative Turn in Policy Analysis and Planning*, edited by F. Fischer and J. Forester, 233–253. Durham, NC: Duke University Press.

———. 2005. "Editorial." *Planning Theory and Practice* 6:5–8.

———. 2006. *Collaborative Planning: Shaping Places in Fragmented Societies*. Hampshire, UK: Palgrave Macmillan.

———. 2009. "The Pragmatic Tradition in Planning Thought." *Journal of Planning Education and Research* 28:277–292.

Heller, Gregory. 2013. *Ed Bacon: Planning, Politics, and the Building of Modern Philadelphia*. Philadelphia: University of Pennsylvania Press.

Heller, Zoe. 2013. "Cool, Yet Warm." *New York Review of Books* 60:8, 10.

Hemmens, George. 1992. "The Postmodernists Are Coming, the Postmodernists Are Coming." *Planning* 58:20–21.

Hendler, Sue. 1990. "Moral Theories in Professional Practice: Do They Make a Difference?" *Environments* 20:20–30.

———. 1996. "On the Use of Models in Planning Ethics." In *Explorations in Planning Theory*, edited by S. Mandelbaum, L. Mazza, and R. W. Burchell, 400–413. New Brunswick, NJ: CUPR Press.

Hirschman, Albert O. 1958. *The Strategy of Economic Development*. New Haven, CT: Yale University Press.

———. 1985. "Introduction: Political Economics and Possibilism." In *A Bias for Hope: Essays on Development and Latin America*, edited by A. O. Hirschman, 1–37. Boulder, CO: Westview Press.

Hobsbawm, Eric. 1996. *The Age of Extremes*. New York: Vintage.

Hoch, Charles. 1984. "Doing Good and Being Right: The Pragmatic Connections in Planning Theory." *Journal of the American Planning Association* 50:335-345.

———. 1992. "The Paradox of Power in Planning Practice." *Journal of Planning Education and Research* 11:206–215.

———. 1996. "What Do Planners Do in the United States?" In *Explorations in Planning Theory*, edited by S. J. Mandelbaum, L. Mazza, and R. W. Burchell, 225–240. New Brunswick, NJ: Center for Urban Policy Research.

Holston, James. 1989. *The Modernist City: An Anthropological Critique of Brasilia*. Chicago: University of Chicago Press.

Holt, Jim. 2013. "He Conceived the Mathematics of Roughness." *New York Review of Books* 60:45–47.

Hommels, Annique. 2008. *Unbuilding Cities: Obduracy in Urban Sociotechnical Change*. Cambridge, MA: MIT Press.

Hrelja, Robert. 2011. "The Tyranny of Small Decisions: Unsustainable Cities and Local Day-to-Day Transport Planning." *Planning Theory and Practice* 12:511–524.

Innes, Judith E. 1995. "Planning Theory's Emerging Paradigm." *Journal of Planning Education and Research* 14:183–189.

Innes, Judith E., and David E. Booher. 2004. "Reframing Public Participation: Strategies for the 21st Century." *Planning Theory and Practice* 5:419–436.

Jackson, Mandi I. 2008. *Model Cities Blues: Urban Space and Organized Resistance in New Haven.* Philadelphia, PA: Temple University Press.

Jacobs, Alan B. 1978. *Making City Planning Work.* Chicago, IL: American Society of Planning Officials.

Jacobs, Jane. 1961. *The Death and Life of Great American Cities.* New York: Vintage.

Jacoby, Russell. 1987. *The Last Intellectuals: American Culture in an Age of Academe.* New York: Noonday Press.

James, William. (1907) 1978. *Pragmatism: A New Name for Some Old Ways of Thinking.* Cambridge, MA: Harvard University Press.

Jameson, Fredric. 1971. *Marxism and Form: Twentieth-Century Dialectic Theories of Literature.* Princeton, NJ: Princeton University Press.

———. 2003. "Future City." *New Left Review* 21:65–79.

Jessop, Bob, Neil Brenner, and Martin Jones. 2008. "Theorizing Sociospatial Relations." *Environment and Planning D* 26:389–401.

Joerges, Bernward. 1999. "Do Politics Have Artefacts?" *Social Studies of Science* 29:411–431.

Joyce, Patrick. 2003. *The Rule of Freedom: Liberalism and the Modern City.* London: Verso.

Jubien, Michael. 2001. "Thinking about Things." *Philosophical Perspectives* 15:1–15.

Judt, Tony. 2010. *Ill Fares the Land.* New York: Penguin.

Karni, Annie. 2013. "Key Hurdle Cleared in Willets Point Redevelopment." *Crain's New York Business,* March 18.

Kaza, Nikhil, and Lewis Hopkins. 2009. "In What Circumstances Should Plans Be Public?" *Journal of Planning Education and Research* 28:491–502.

Keating, Dennis, and Normal Krumholz. 1991. "Downtown Plans for the 1980s: The Case for More Equity. *Journal of the American Planning Association* 57:136–152.

Kelman, Steven. 1988. "Why Public Ideas Matter." In *The Power of Public Ideas,* edited by R. B. Reich, 31–53. Cambridge, MA: Ballinger.

Kent, T. J., Jr. (1964) 1990. *The Urban General Plan.* Chicago, IL: Planners Press.

Kern, Stephen. 1983. *The Culture of Time and Space: 1880–1918.* Cambridge, MA: Harvard University Press.

Kershner, Isabel. 2013a. "Israelis Evict Palestinians from a Site for Housing." *New York Times,* January 13.

———. 2013b. "Palestinians Set Up Tents Where Israel Plans Homes." *New York Times,* January 12.

Khong, Lynefle. 2003. "Actants and Enframing: Heidegger and Latour on Technology." *Studies in History and Philosophy of Science* 34:693–704.

Kingdon, John W. 2003. *Agenda, Alternatives, and Public Policies.* New York: Longman.

Kirkman, Robert. 2009. "At Home in the Seamless Web: Agency, Obduracy, and the Ethics of Metropolitan Growth." *Science, Technology, and Human Values* 34:234–258.

Kirsch, Scott, and Don Mitchell. 2004. "The Nature of Things: Dead Labor, Non-human Actors, and the Persistence of Marxism." *Antipode* 36:687–705.

Klein, William R., Virginia Lee Benson, John Anderson, Pamela Plumb, and Nancy Davis. 1993. "Vision of Things to Come." *Planning* 59:10–15.

Klemek, Christopher. 2011. *The Transatlantic Collapse of Urban Renewal*. Chicago: University of Chicago Press.

Krause, Moniker. 2010. "Accounting for State Intervention: The Social Histories of 'Beneficiaries.'" *Qualitative Sociology* 33:533–547.

Kraushaar, Robert. 1988. "Outside the Whale: Progressive Planning and the Dilemmas of Radical Reform." *Journal of the American Planning Association* 54:91–100.

Krueckeberg, Donald A. 1983. "The Culture of Planning." In *Introduction to Planning History in the United States*, edited by D. A. Krueckeberg, 1–12. New Brunswick, NJ: Center for Urban Policy Research Press.

Kruks, Sonia. 2010. "Simone de Beauvoir: Engaging Discrepant Materialisms." In *New Materialisms: Ontology, Agency and Politic*, edited by D. Coole and S. Frost, 258–280. Durham, NC: Duke University Press.

Krumholz, Norman. 1982. "A Retrospective View of Equity Planning." *Journal of the American Planning Association* 48:163–174.

Kurgan, Laura. 2013. *Close-up at a Distance: Mapping, Technology, and Politics*. New York: Zone Books.

Kwartler, Michael. 1995. "Zoning." In *The Encyclopedia of New York City*, edited by K. T. Jackson, 1288. New Haven, CT: Yale University Press.

Lake, Robert W. 2002. "Bring Back Big Government." *International Journal of Urban and Regional Research* 26:815–822.

———. 2014. "Methods and Moral Inquiry." *Urban Geography* 35:657–668.

Lakoff, George. 1987. *Women, Fire, and Dangerous Things: What Categories Reveal about the Mind*. Chicago: University of Chicago Press.

Lamont, Michele. 2009. *How Professors Think*. Cambridge, MA: Harvard University Press.

Lapintie, Kimmo. 2007. "Modalities of Urban Space." *Planning Theory* 6:36–51.

Laska, Shirley, and Betty Hearn Morrow. 2006/2007. "Social Vulnerabilities and Hurricane Katrina: An Unnatural Disaster in New Orleans." *Marine Technology Society Journal* 40:16–25.

Latour, Bruno. 1987. *Science in Action*. Cambridge, MA: Harvard University Press.

———. 1988. *The Pasteurization of France*. Cambridge, MA: Harvard University Press.

———. 1992. "Where Are the Missing Masses? The Sociology of a Few Mundane Artefacts." In *Shaping Technology/Building Society*, edited by W. E. Bijker and J. Law, 225–258. Cambridge, MA: MIT Press.

———. 1993. *We Have Never Been Modern*. Cambridge, MA: Harvard University Press.

———. 1994. "Pragmatogonies." *American Behavioral Scientist* 37:791–808.

———. 1999. *Pandora's Hope: Essays on the Reality of Science Studies*. Cambridge, MA: Harvard University Press.

———. 2002. "Gabriel Tarde and the End of the Social." In T*he Social in Question*, edited by P. Joyce, 117–132. London: Routledge.

———. 2003a. "The Promises of Constructivism." In *Chasing Technology: Matrix of Materiality*, edited by D. Idhe, 27–46. Bloomington: Indiana University Press.

———. 2003b. "What If We *Talked* Politics a Little?" *Contemporary Political Theory* 2:143–164.

———. 2004a. "Why Has Critique Run Out of Steam? From Matters of Fact to Matters of Concern." *Critical Inquiry* 30:225–248.

———. 2004b. "Nonhumans." In *Patterned Ground*, edited by S. Harrison, S. Pile, and N. Thrift, 224–227. London: Reaktion Books.

———. 2005a. "From Realpolitik to Dingpolitik, or How to Make Things Public." In *Making Things Public: Atmospheres of Democracy*, edited by B. Latour and P. Weibel, 14–41. Cambridge, MA: MIT Press.

———. 2005b. *Reassembling the Social: An Introduction to Actor-Network Theory*. Oxford: Oxford University Press.

———. 2007a. "Turning around Politics: A Note on Gerard DeVries's Paper." *Social Studies of Science* 37:811–820.

———. 2007b. "How to Think Like a State." Lecture delivered at the anniversary of the Scientific Council for Government Policy (WRR), November 22. The Hague, Netherlands.

———. 2008. "A Curious Prometheus? A Few Steps toward a Philosophy of Design (with Special Attention to Peter Sloterdijk)." In *Proceedings of the 2008 Annual International Conference of the Design History Society*, edited by F. Hackne, J. Glynne, and V. Minto, 2–10. Universal Publishers, e-books.

———. 2010a. "An Attempt at a 'Compositional Manifesto.'" *New Literary History* 41:471–490.

———. 2010b. *On the Modern Cult of the Factish Gods*. Durham, NC: Duke University Press.

———. 2013. "Biography of an Inquiry: On the Book about Modes of Existence." *Social Studies of Science* 43:287–301.

Latour, Bruno, and Albena Yaneva. 2008. "'Give Me a Gun and I Will Make All Buildings Move': An ANT's View of Architecture." In *Explorations in Architecture*, edited by R. Geiser, 80–89. Basel: Birkhauser.

Law, John. 2002. "Objects and Spaces." *Theory, Culture and Society* 19:91–105.

———. 2004. "And If the Global Were Small and Noncoherent? Method, Complexity, and the Baroque." *Environment and Planning D* 22:13–26.

———. 2009. "Actor Network Theory and Material Semiotics." In *The New Blackwell Companion to Social Theory*, edited by B. S. Turner, 141–158. Chichester, UK: John Wiley.

Law, John, and Annemarie Mol. 1995. "Notes on Materiality and Sociality." *Sociological Review* 43:274–294.

Lear, Jonathan. 2006. *Radical Hope: Ethics in the Face of Cultural Devastation*. Cambridge, MA: Harvard University Press.

Lears, Jackson. 2013. "The Round World Made Flat." *BookForum* 19:16–17.

Lee, Nick, and Steve Brown. 1994. "Otherness and the Actor Network." *American Behavioral Scientist* 37:772–790.

Leebron, Fred. 2000. *Six Figures*. New York: Alfred A. Knopf.

Lefebvre, Henri. 1968. *The Sociology of Marx*. New York: Columbia University Press.

Lehan, Richard. 1998. *The City in Literature*. Berkeley: University of California Press.

Lehtonen, Turo-Kimmo. 2009. "How Does Materiality Matter for the Social Sciences?" In *The Materiality of Res Publica*, edited by D. Colas and O. Kharkhordin, 271–288. Newcastle upon Tyne, UK: Cambridge Scholars.

Lethem, Jonathan. 1999. *Motherless Brooklyn*. New York: Vintage.

Lieto, Laura, and Robert Beauregard. 2013. "Planning for the Material World." *CRIOS* 6:11–20.

Lindblom, Charles. 1959. "The Science of 'Muddling Through.'" *Public Administration Review* 19:79–88.

———. 1977. *Politics and Markets*. New York: Basic Books.

Lounsberry, Barbara. 1990. *The Art of Fact: Contemporary Artists of Nonfiction*. New York: Greenwood Press.

Lurie, Alison. 2007. "When Is a Building Beautiful?" *New York Review of Books* 54:19–21.

Mabin, Alan. 1992. "Dispossession, Exploitation and Struggle: An Historical Overview of South African Urbanization." In *The Apartheid City and Beyond*, edited by D. M. Smith, 13–24. London: Routledge.

McCann, Eugene J. 2008. "Expertise, Truth, and Urban Policy Mobilities." *Environment and Planning A* 40:885–904.

McCullough, David. 1972. *The Great Bridge: The Epic Story of the Building of the Brooklyn Bridge*. New York: Simon and Schuster.

McFarlane, Colin. 2011. "Assemblage as Critical Urban Praxis: Part One." *City* 15:204–224.

McPhee, John. 1978. "Giving Good Weight." *New Yorker*, July 3, 36–69.

Mahoney, James. 2000. "Path Dependence in Historical Sociology." *Theory and Society* 29:507–548.

Majone, Giandomenico. 1989. *Evidence, Argument, and Persuasion in the Policy Process*. New Haven, CT: Yale University Press.

Mallach, Alan, ed. 2012. *Rebuilding America's Legacy Cities*. New York: American Assembly.

Mandelbaum, Seymour. 1985. "Historians and Planners: The Construction of Pasts and Futures." *Journal of the American Planning Association* 51:185–188.

Mao Tse-tung. 1965. *On Practice*. Peking: Foreign Language Press.

Marcus, George E., and Erkan Saka. 2006. "Assemblage." *Theory, Culture and Society* 23:101–109.

Marcus, Norman. 1991. "New York City's Zoning—1961–1991." *Fordham Urban Law Journal* 19:706–726.

Marcuse, Herbert. 1964. *One-Dimensional Man*. Boston: Beacon Press.

Marcuse, Peter. 1990. "New York City's Community Boards: Neighborhood Policy and Its Results." In *Neighbourhood Policies and Programs*, edited by N. Carmon, 45–63. London: Macmillan.

———. 2009. "From Critical Urban Theory to the Right to the City." *City* 13:185–197.

Margalit, Avishai. 1996. *The Decent Society*. Cambridge, MA: Harvard University Press.

———. 2013. "Palestine: How Bad, and Good, Was British Rule?" *New York Review of Books* 60:34–36.

Marres, Noortje. 2005. "Issues Spark a Public into Being." in *Making Things Public: Atmospheres of Democracy*, edited by B. Latour and P. Weibel, 208–217. Cambridge, MA: MIT Press.

Marres, Noortje, and Javier Lezaun. 2011. "Materials and Devices of the Public: An Introduction." *Economy and Society* 40:489–509.

Marx, Karl. (1867) 1967. *Capital: A Critique of Political Economy*. Vol. 1. New York: International Publishers.

Massey, Doreen. 2005. *For Space*. London: Sage,

May, Larry. 1992. *Social Responsibility*. Chicago: University of Chicago Press.

Megill, Allan. 2007. *Historical Knowledge, Historical Error*. Chicago: University of Chicago Press.

Menand, Louis. 2001. *The Metaphysical Club: A Story of Ideas in America*. New York: Farrar, Straus and Giroux.

Merrifield, Andy. 1997. "Between Process and Individuation: Translating Metaphors and Narratives of Urban Space." *Antipode* 29:417–436.

Meyerson, Martin, and Edward C. Banfield. 1955. *Politics, Planning, and the Public Interest*. New York: Free Press.

Meyrowitz, Joshua. 1985. *No Sense of Place: The Impact of Electronic Media on Social Behavior*. New York: Oxford University Press.

Mitchell, William J. 2005. *Placing Words: Symbols, Space, and the City*. Cambridge, MA: MIT Press.

Mol, Annemarie. 1999. "Ontological Politics: A Word and Some Questions." In *Actor Network Theory and After*, edited by J. Law and J. Haggard, 74–89. Oxford: Blackwell.

Moore, Barrington, Jr. 1973. *Reflections on the Causes of Human Misery and upon Certain Proposals to Eliminate Them*. Boston: Beacon Press.

Moore, Mark H. 1988. "What Sort of Ideas Become Public Ideas?" In *The Power of Public Ideas*, edited by Robert B. Reich, 55–83. Cambridge, MA: Ballinger.

Murdoch, Jonathan. 1998. "The Spaces of Actor-Network Theory." *Geoforum* 29:357–374.

———. 2004. "Humanizing Postmodern." *Environment and Planning A* 36:1356–1359.

———. 2006. *Post-structural Geography: A Guide to Relational Space.* London: Sage.

Murray, Chris, ed. 1999. *Encyclopedia of Literary Critics and Criticism.* Vol. 2. London: Fitzroy Dearborn.

Needleman, Martin, and Carolyn Needleman. 1974. *Guerrillas in the Bureaucracy: The Community Planning Experience in the United States.* New York: John Wiley.

New York City Economic Development Corporation. 2012. "Mayor Bloomberg Announces Historic Deal to Transform Willets Point into a Vibrant Destination and Mixed-Use Community." Press release. June 14.

Nir, Sarah Maslin. 2013. "The End of Willets Point." *New York Times.* November 24, Metropolitan Section, 1, 6.

Norman, Julie M. 2012. "The Role of Planning in the Occupation of Palestine." *Progressive Planning* 193:30–34.

Novak, William J. 2008. "The Myth of the 'Weak' American State." *American Historical Review* 113:752–772.

Nunn, Samuel. 1990. "Budgeting for Public Capital: Reinterpreting Traditional Views of Urban Infrastructure Provision." *Journal of Urban Affairs* 12:327–344.

Nussbaum, Martha C. 2006. *Frontiers of Justice: Disability, Nationality, Species Membership.* Cambridge, MA: Belknap Press,

Olshansky, Robert B., and Anderson, Laurie A. 2010. *Clear as Mud: Planning for the Rebuilding of New Orleans.* Chicago, IL: Planners Press.

Olson, Sherry. 1979. "Baltimore Imitates the Spider." *Annals of the Association of American Geographers* 69:557–574.

O'Neill, Karen M. 2010. "Who Sank New Orleans? How Engineering the River Created Environmental Injustice." In *Katrina's Imprint: Race and Vulnerability in America*, edited by K. Wailoo et al., 9–20. New Brunswick, NJ: Rutgers University Press.

Osborne, Thomas. 2004. "On Mediators: Intellectuals and the Ideas Trade in the Knowledge Society." *Economy and Society* 33:430–447.

Osman, Suliman. 2011. *The Invention of Brownstone Brooklyn.* Oxford: Oxford University Press.

Page, Max. 1999. *The Creative Destruction of Manhattan.* Chicago: University of Chicago Press.

Parenti, Christian. 2011. *Tropic of Chaos: Climate Change and the New Geography of Violence.* New York: Nation Books.

Perloff, Harvey. 1957. *Education for Planning: City, State, and Region.* Baltimore: Johns Hopkins University Press.

Pierson, Paul. 2000. "Increasing Returns, Path Dependence, and the Study of Politics." *American Political Science Review* 94:251–267.

Pigden, Charles. 2011. "Hume on <u>Is</u> and <u>Ought</u>." *Philosophy Now* 83. http://philosophynow.org/issues/83/Hume_on_Is_and_Ought, accessed August 14, 2013.

Power, Anne, Jorg Ploger, and Astrid Winkler. 2010. *Phoenix Cities: The Fall and Rise of Great Industrial Cities.* Bristol, UK: Policy Press.

Pressman, Jeffrey, and Aaron Wildavsky. 1973. *Implementation.* Berkeley, CA: University of California Press.

Pristin, Terry. 2011. "In Queens, Neglected Sector Attracts Big Developers." *New York Times*, October 18.

Real Estate Record Association. (1898) 1967. *A History of Real Estate, Building and Architecture in New York City during the Last Quarter of a Century.* New York: Arno Press.

Reckwitz, Andreas. 2002. "Toward a Theory of Social Practices." *European Journal of Social Theory* 5:243–263.

Relph, Edward. 1987. *The Modern Urban Landscape.* Baltimore: Johns Hopkins University Press.

Reynarsson, Bjarni. 1999. "The Planning of Reykjavik, Iceland: Three Ideological Waves—a Historical Overview." *Planning Perspectives* 14:49–67.

Riis, Soren. 2008. "The Symmetry between Bruno Latour and Martin Heidegger." *Social Studies of Science* 38:285–301.

Rittel, Horst W. J., and Melvin M. Webber. 1973. "Dilemmas in a General Theory of Planning." *Policy Sciences* 4:155–169.

Robinson, Andrew. 2005. "Towards an Intellectual Reformation: The Critique of Common Sense and the Forgotten Revolutionary Impact of Gramscian Theory." *Critical Review of International Social and Political Philosophy* 8:469–481.

Rorty, Richard, and Pascal Engel. 2007. *What Is the Use of Truth?* New York: Columbia University Press.

Ross, Andrew. 2011. *Bird on Fire: Lessons from the World's Least Sustainable City.* Oxford: Oxford University Press.

Rotella, Carlo. 2002. "Rocky Marciano's Ghost." In *Good with Their Hands: Boxers, Bluesmen, and Other Characters from the Rustbelt*, 167–230. Berkeley, CA: University of California Press.

Ruben, David. 1989. "Realism in the Social Sciences." In *Dismantling Truth: Reality in the Postmodern World*, edited by H. Lawson and L. Appignannesi, 58–81. New York: St. Martin's Press.

Rudoren, Jodi. 2012. "Israel Defies Allies in Move to Bolster Settlements." *New York Times*, December 20.

———. 2013. "Israeli Move over Housing Poses a Threat to Peace Talks." *New York Times*, November 13.

Rudoren, Jodi, and Mark Landler. 2012. "Israel Advances Settlement Plan Near Jerusalem." *New York Times*, December 1.

Ryan, Alan. 1995. *John Dewey and the High Tide of American Liberalism*. New York: W. W. Norton.

Ryan, Brent. 2012. *Design after Decline*. Philadelphia: University of Pennsylvania Press.

Rydin, Yvonne. 2010. "Actor-Network Theory and Planning Theory." *Planning Theory* 9:265–268.

———. 2012. "Using Actor-Network Theory to Understand Planning Practice." *Planning Theory* 12:23–45.

Sack, Robert D. 1999. "A Sketch of a Geographic Theory of Morality." *Annals of the American Association of Geographers* 89:26–44.

Sacks, Oliver. 2014. "The Mental Life of Plants and Worms, among Others." *New York Review of Books* 61:4–8.

Sagasti, Francisco. 2000. "The Twilight of the Baconian Age and the Future of Humanity." *Futures* 32:595–612.

Sandercock, Leonie. 1995. "Voices from the Borderlands: A Mediation on a Metaphor." *Journal of Planning Education and Research* 14:77–88.

———. 1998. *Towards Cosmopolis*. Chichester, UK: John Wiley.

———. 2003. *Cosmopolis II: Mongrel Cities of the 21st Century*. London: Continuum.

———. 2007. "Spirituality and the Urban Professions: The Paradox at the Heart of Planning." *Planning Theory and Practice* 2:65–67.

Sandercock, Leonie, and Ann Forsyth. 1992. "A Gender Agenda: New Directions for Planning Theory." *Journal of the American Planning Association* 58:49–59.

Sarbib, Jean-Louis. 1983. "The University of Chicago Program in Planning: A Retrospective Look." *Journal of Planning Education and Research* 2:77–81.

Sayer, Andrew. 1982. "Explanation in Economic Geography: Abstraction versus Generalization." *Progress in Human Geography* 6:68–88.

———. 1992. *Method in Social Science: A Realist Approach*. London: Routledge.

———. 2000. *Realism and Social Science*. London: Sage.

———. 2004. "Realisms through Thick and Thin." *Environment and Planning A* 36:1777–1789.

Sayer, Andrew, and Michael Storper. 1997. "Ethics Unbound: For a Normative Turn in Social Theory." *Environment and Planning D* 15:1–17.

Sayes, Edwin. 2014. "Actor-Network Theory and Methodology: Just What Does It Mean to Say That Humans Have Agency?" *Social Studies of Science* 44:134–149.

Schilling, Joseph, and Raksha Vasudevan. 2013. "The Promise of Sustainability Planning for Regenerating Older Industrial Cities." In *The City after Abandonment*, edited by M. Dewar and J. Manning Thomas, 244–267. Philadelphia: University of Pennsylvania Press.

Schleifstein, Mark. 2010. "The Best Defense: The Battle Is on to Save the Marshes." *Planning* 76:30–33.

Schon, Donald. 1982. "Some of What a Planner Knows." *Journal of the American Planning Association* 48:351–364.

Schon, Donald, and Martin Rein. 1994. *Frame Reflection: Toward a Resolution of Intractable Policy.* New York: Basic Books.

Schwartz, Joel. 2007. "Robert Moses and City Planning." In *Robert Moses and the Modern City: The Transformation of New York,* edited by H. Ballon and K. T. Jackson, 130–133. New York: W. W. Norton.

Scobey, David M. 2002. *Empire City: The Making and Meaning of the New York City Landscape.* Philadelphia, PA: Temple University Press.

Scott, James C. 1998. *Seeing Like a State.* New Haven, CT: Yale University Press.

Scott, Mel. 1969. *American City Planning since 1890.* Berkeley: University of California Press.

Selznick, Philip. 1992. *The Moral Commonwealth: Social Theory and the Promise of Community.* Berkeley: University of California Press.

Shaw, Keith. 2012. "'Reframing' Resilience: Challenges to Planning Theory and Practice." *Planning Theory and Practice* 13:308–312.

Shildrick, Margrit. 1996. "Posthumanism and the Monstrous Body." *Body and Society* 2:1–15.

Shorto, Russell. 2005. *The Island at the Center of the World.* New York: Vintage.

Shrum, Wesley. 2014. "What Caused the Flood? Controversy and Closure in the Hurricane Katrina Disaster." *Social Studies of Science* 44:3–33.

Simone, AbdouMaliq. 2001. "On the Worlding of African Cities." *African Studies Review* 44:15–41.

Sloterdijk, Peter. 2008, "Foam City." *Distinktion* 16:47–59.

Smith, Carl. 2006. *The Plan of Chicago: Daniel Burnham and the Remaking of an American City.* Chicago: University of Chicago Press.

Smith, David. 2007. "Moral Aspects of Place." *Planning Theory* 6:7–15.

Söderström, Ola. 1996. "Paper Cities: Visual Thinking in Urban Planning." *Ecumene* 3:249–281.

Sorkin, Michael. 2009. *Twenty Minutes in Manhattan.* London: Reaktion Books.

Spain, Daphne. *Gendered Spaces.* 1992. Chapel Hill: University of North Carolina Press.

———. 2001. *How Women Saved the City.* Minneapolis: University of Minnesota Press.

Staeheli, Lynne A., and Don Mitchell. 2008. *The People's Property? Power, Politics and the Public.* New York: Routledge.

St. Aubyn, Edward. 2012. *The Patrick Melrose Novels.* New York: Picador.

Steffens, Lincoln. (1902) 1957. *The Shame of the Cities.* New York: Hill and Wang.

Stephenson, Janet. 2010. "People and Place." *Planning Theory and Practice* 11:9–21.

Stinchcombe, Arthur C. 1968. *Constructing Social Theories.* Chicago: University of Chicago Press.

Stromberg, Meghan. 2012. "Navigating New Orleans." *Planning* 78:36–38.

Sunstein, Cass. 2014. "How Do We Know What's Moral?" *New York Review of Books* 61:14, 16, 18.

Tait, Malcolm, and Aidan While. 2009. "Ontology and the Conservation of Built Heritage," *Environment and Planning D* 27:721–37.

Teaford, Jon. 1990. *The Rough Road to Renaissance: Urban Revitalization in America, 1940–1985*. Baltimore: Johns Hopkins University Press.

Thomas, Keith. 2014. "The Great Fight over the Enlightenment." *New York Review of Books* 61:68, 70, 72.

Thrift, Nigel. 1996. *Spatial Formations*. London: Sage.

Throgmorton, James. 2000. "On the Virtues of Skillful Meandering." *Journal of the American Planning Association* 66:367–379.

Tilly, Charles. 1998. *Durable Inequality*. Berkeley: University of California Press.

———. 2006. *Why?* Princeton, NJ: Princeton University Press.

Toulmin, Stephen. 1988. "The Recovery of Practical Philosophy." *American Scholar* 57:337–352.

———. 1990. *Cosmopolis: The Hidden Agenda of Modernity*. Chicago: University of Chicago Press.

Tsing, Anna. 2005. *Friction: An Ethnography of Global Connections*. Princeton, NJ: Princeton University Press.

Turner, Stephen. 2001. "What Is the Problem with Experts?" *Social Studies of Science* 31:123–149.

United Nations General Assembly. 2012. "General Assembly Votes Overwhelmingly to Accord Palestine 'Non-member Observer State' Status in United Nations." Press release, Department of Public Information, November 29.

Urban, Florian. 2012. *Tower and Slab: Histories of Global Mass Housing*. London: Routledge.

Van der Tuin, Iris. 2012. *New Materialism: Interviews and Cartographies*. Ann Arbor, MI: Open Humanities Press.

Van Meter, Donald S., and Carl E. Van Horn. 1975. "The Policy Implementation Process: A Conceptual Framework." *Administration and Society* 6:445–488.

Verhage, Roelof. 2003. "The Role of the Public Sector in Urban Development: Lessons from Leidsche Rijn Utrecht." *Planning Theory and Practice* 4:29–44.

Vettoretto, Luciano. 2009. "A Preliminary Critique of the Best and Good Practices Approach in European Spatial Planning and Policy-Making." *European Planning Studies* 17:1067–1083.

Walzer, Michael. 1983. *Spheres of Justice: A Defense of Pluralism and Equality*. New York: Basic Books.

———. 1988. *The Company of Critics: Social Criticism and Political Commitment in the Twentieth Century*. New York: Basic Books.

———. 2004. *Politics and Passions*. New Haven, CT: Yale University Press.

Ward, Stephen V. 2002. *Planning the Twentieth Century City*. Chichester, UK: John Wiley.

Warner, Michael. 2002. *Publics and Counterpublics*. New York: Zone Books.

Watson, Siobhan. 2008. "Sustainability at the Project Level: The Case of Willets Point, Queens." Master's thesis, Department of Urban Studies and Planning, Massachusetts Institute of Technology.

Watson, Vanessa. 2006. "Deep Difference: Diversity, Planning and Ethics." *Planning Theory* 5:31–50.

———. 2008. "Down to Earth: Linking Planning Theory and Practice in the 'Metropole' and Beyond." *International Planning Studies* 13:223–237.

Weizman, Eyal. 2007. *Hollow Land: Israel's Architecture of Occupation*. London: Verso.

Westbrook, Robert B. 2005. *Democratic Hope: Pragmatism and the Politics of Truth*. Ithaca, NY: Cornell University Press.

White, Morton. 1947. *Social Thought in America: The Revolt against Formalism*. Boston: Beacon Press.

Wildavsky, Aaron. 1973. "If Planning Is Everything, Maybe It's Nothing." *Policy Sciences* 4:127–153.

Wilkerson, Isabel. 2010. *The Warmth of Other Suns: The Epic Story of America's Great Migration*. New York: Vintage.

Williams, Raymond. 1973. *The Country and the City*. New York: Oxford University Press.

Williamson, Thad, David Imbroscio, and Gar Alperovitz. 2002. *Making a Place for Community: Local Democracy in a Global Age*. New York: Routledge.

Winkler, Tanya. 2011. "Retracking Johannesburg: Spaces for Participation and Policymaking." *Journal of Planning Education and Research* 31:258–271.

Winner, Langdon. 1980. "Do Artefacts Have Politics?" *Daedalus*, 109:121–136.

Wood, James. 2013. "Why? The Fictions of Life and Death." *New Yorker* 89:34–39.

Wunder, Sue. 2011. "On a Mission to Restore the Louisiana Bayou." *Christian Science Monitor*, March 21.

Yablon, Nick. 2009. *Untimely Ruins: An Archaeology of American Urban Modernity, 1819–1919*. Chicago: University of Chicago Press.

Yaneva, Albena. 2005. "Scaling Up and Down: Extraction Trials in Architectural Design." *Social Studies of Science* 35:867–894.

Yiftachel, Oren. 1989. "Towards a New Typology of Planning Theories." *Environment and Planning B* 16:23–39.

———. 1995. "The Dark Side of Modernism: Planning as Control of an Ethnic Minority." In *Postmodern Cities and Spaces*, edited by S. Watson and K. Gibson, 216–242. Oxford: Blackwell.

———. 1998. "Planning and Social Control: Exploring the Dark Side." *Journal of Planning Literature* 12:395–406.

———. 2002. "The Shrinking State of Citizenship." Middle East Research and Information Project. www.merip.org, accessed May 8, 2013.

———. 2005. "Neither Two States nor One: The Disengagement and 'Creeping Apartheid' in Israel/Palestine." *Arab World Geographer* 8:125–129.

Young, Iris M. 1990. *Justice and the Politics of Difference*. Princeton, NJ: Princeton University Press.

———. 1999. "State, Civil Society, and Social Justice." In *Democracy's Value*, edited by I. Shapiro and C. Hacker-Cordon, 141–162. Cambridge: Cambridge University Press.

———. 2003. "From Guilt to Solidarity: Sweatshops and Political Responsibility." *Dissent* 50:39–44.

———. 2004. "Responsibility and Global Labor Justice." *Journal of Political Philosophy* 12:365–388.

———. 2006. "Katrina: Too Much Blame, Not Enough Responsibility." *Dissent* 53:41–46.

———. 2011. *Responsibility for Justice.* Oxford: Oxford University Press.

Zerubavel, Eviatar. 1991. *The Fine Line: Making Distinctions in Everyday Life.* New York: Free Press.

Zheng, Lingwen, and Mildred Warner. 2010. "Business Incentive Use among US Local Governments: A Story of Accountability and Policy Learning." *Economic Development Quarterly* 24:325–336.

Zitcer, Andrew, and Robert Lake. 2012. "Love as a Planning Method." *Planning Theory and Practice* 13:606–609.

Zizek, Slajov. 2008. *Violence.* New York: Picador.

———. 2009. *First as Tragedy, Then as Farce.* London: Verso.

Index

New York City, 82, 115, 122, 144n14, 162–
67; Brooklyn, 115, 127; Harlem, 116
normativity, and planning, 11, 24, 61

obduracy, 132, 133–34; and planning,
141–47, 172
ontographies, 14–23, 219; defined, 15; lists,
14, 17, 19; litanies, 16; and qualities of
planning, 31–35
orderliness, 27, 28, 219
out-there / in-here, 20, 25, 39, 44, 112,
195, 226

persuasion, 41
Philadelphia, PA, 122–23,164n11
Phoenix, AZ, 123
photographs, 8, 61–64
physical determinism, 2, 3
place, 2, 27, 66–67, 72, 76–78, 85–86, 90–
92; and democracy, 86n12; and people,
90–91; and politics, 88–89; of practice,
39, 76–94; and talk, 85–87; and things,
59, 59n4, 72, 84, 92
planners: actions, 2, 11; basic tasks, 7–8,
9, 10, 12, 15, 30, 32, 38–41, 49, 51, 114;
concerns of, 1, 113, 187; critiques of, 2,
34–35; expertise, 16, 29; politics, 3, 35,
49, 53; prudence, 30; as public intellectuals, 202–10; public presence, 188–90,
204; responsibilities, 2, 37, 48, 131,
206, 210; and texts, 130–31; utopian visions, 27n13, 30; value-neutrality, 23
Planners Network, 207–8
planning: city and regional, 10, 25–27; consequences, 30, 36, 38, 59, 114; control,
25–26; definition of, 10–11, 13, 31–33,
34; democratic, 78, 82, 134–35, 143, 146;
departments, 52; doctorates, 194; ethical
planning, 98–102, 111; events, 18, 60–
61, 65, 83, 88; heroic model of, 23–24;
and humanism, 24–26, 33; modernist,
213–24; narratives, 117–18; nondemocratic, 134n3, 177–78; normativity of,
9, 11–12; for people, 2, 56; principles
of practice, 40, 114, 122–25, 131–32;
process, 7, 79, 88; profession, 24, 27, 33,
38n2, 202, 221, 225; purpose, 71; qualities of, 16, 23–30, 33–34; reports, 38,
40; scholarship, 193, 202, 205, 210, 214,
226; social, 25; and social reform, 1, 23,
29–30, 125, 132; and the state, 176, 186–

87; technocratic, 3, 215–16; and things,
1, 14–15, 24, 32, 41, 57, 74–75; tools, 62
planning, state-level, 182–84
planning in: Aalborg, Denmark, 40–41,
113n1; Chicago, 1; Linn County, IA,
79–82; Minneapolis–St. Paul, MN, 38–
40; New York City, 51, 137–41, 144n14,
145, 162–67
planning history, 157. See also city planning, history, New York City
planning theory, 10, 12, 34, 59–60, 70, 75,
192–95; theorists, 34, 57n1, 57–60, 98,
101, 173, 195–202, 209, 212, 225
Plan of Chicago (1909), 1, 221
plans, 1–2, 37, 155, 189; comprehensive,
38, 53, 153–54, 218; strategic, 80
policy transfer, 85n10
politics, 6, 12, 35, 55, 87, 134–35,
141–42, 150; and things, 6. See also
micropolitics
possibilism, 56, 120, 122, 167–71, 187. See
also truth
post–World War II era, 7, 16, 57, 174–75,
214–15, 222
practice, of planning, 37n1, 41, 58–59, 66–
69, 113, 194; progressive or radical, 54–
56, 113, 187. See also place: of practice
pragmatism, 10, 119, 203
predictability, 26. See also uncertainty
Program for Education and Research in
Planning, 194
progress, 157
Progressive Era, 1, 27; and planning, 29–
30, 124
promise of planning, 172–73, 186, 188,
191, 226
public good, 23, 28
publics, 9, 29, 56, 85–87, 88, 134–35, 145,
172, 190–91, 195, 204–5

rationality, 23–24, 26; and modernity, 212;
and planning, 176
Rawls, John, 99n3, 200
reality, 8, 11, 63, 115, 119–21, 124, 133,
144, 159, 196
reasons, 43, 48, 219
repleteness, and ontographies, 22, 31
representation, 4, 7, 14
responsibility, 2, 53, 94, 98, 102–4, 105,
111–12; and action, 48; delegation of, 9.
See also moralism